Debating Catholicism

Karl Keating

RASSELAS
HOUSE

Published by Rasselas House
El Cajon, California
RasselasHouse.com

Cover design by EbookLaunch.com
Formatting by PolgarusStudio.com

ISBN 978-1-942596-27-1 Paperback
ISBN 978-1-942596-26-4 Ebook

Contents

Preface

This omnibus volume contains the complete text of four books: *The Bible Battle*, *High Desert Showdown*, *Tracking Down the True Church*, and *Face Off with an Ex-Priest*. They are edited transcripts of public debates I had with prominent anti-Catholics, men who devoted all or large parts of their careers to opposing the Church of Rome and its distinctive teachings.

The topics discussed and the arguments used, on both sides, are perennial. So, unfortunately, are the misconceptions and imprecisions exhibited by my opponents. I tried to correct those misconceptions and adjust those imprecisions in the heat of public exchanges. I hope my limitations as a debater did not obscure the unity and sensibleness of the Catholic position, and I hope the reader will find these pages instructive, consoling, and even amusing.

Notes on the Text

The following transcripts have been edited for clarity and concision. I have taken the liberty of correcting grammatical errors and obvious misstatements, and I have removed those seemingly unavoidable hesitations and starts (ah's and um's and their cousins) that may not be particularly off-putting when spoken but seem to gouge the eyes when in print. The four debates in the series have been made roughly uniform in length. When given publicly, they ranged from two hours to an almost unendurable four hours, counting question-and-answer sessions. Each is now short enough to be read at a single sitting.

I have attempted to retain each speaker's best arguments, feeling no temptation to omit my opponents' most persuasive comments. (I think the Catholic position, however inadequately expressed by me, is match enough for any charge leveled against it.) I have omitted or truncated exchanges that were redundant or seemed unhelpful to the audiences. Also omitted have been audience questions that strayed too far from the topics of the debates or that were not true questions but attempted preaching sessions.

Looking back at my own arguments, particularly those made when on defense, I find places where I could have made a better reply. I have not gussied up my remarks. A reader may say, "But you could have said *this*!" My excuse must be that *this* didn't occur to me at that moment. Perhaps I was taken off guard. Perhaps my mind went blank. Perhaps I just didn't yet know the best answer and could offer only the second-best answer. What is presented here is verisimilitude. I can use a phrase from nineteenth-century German historian Leopold von Ranke. I have attempted to give the story *"wie es eigentlich gewesen"*—"how it really was."

And how it really is today. There is not a single anti-Catholic claim in this book that has fallen out of circulation. The claims have been around for lifetimes, and there is no likelihood that they ever will disappear completely, human nature and human obstinacy being what they are. I have tried to respond to the claims with candor and fairness. Whether I have succeeded is for readers to judge. Throughout the debates I kept in mind that "the truth shall set you free." I always have found searching for truth—and debating what is true—to be exhilarating. I hope you will too, as you read what follows, and I hope these pages bring solace and confidence to Catholics and intrigue and light to non-Catholics.

BOOK 1

The Bible Battle

Karl Keating vs. Peter S. Ruckman

Introduction

If any of my debate opponents could be called a "character," it was Peter S. Ruckman. He styled himself a Fundamentalist, but most Fundamentalist writers disavowed him, partly for his singular beliefs but mostly for his acerbic personality. Even when other Fundamentalists thought Ruckman was right in his ideas, they usually thought he was wrong in his attitudes and approach, doing their cause more harm than good.

I was invited to debate Ruckman as the final event in a weeklong Bible conference. The topic was whether the Catholic religion is true. The venue was the First Baptist Church of Long Beach, California, the city in which I grew up. More than 400 people attended, the large majority of them conference attendees or other Fundamentalists, but there were some Catholics present.

All I knew about Ruckman was that he was the pastor of a church in Pensacola, Florida. I had tried locating his books—I had been told he had written several—but was unsuccessful. By a happy chance, the day before the debate someone sent me two copies of his monthly, the *Bible Believers' Bulletin*. From the letters column, which included pleas to remove the correspondents' names from the mailing list, I took it that Ruckman's publication was distributed to many people who preferred not to get it. These were not Catholics but other Fundamentalists.

Fundamentalism is by no means monolithic. Ruckman dismissed most fellow Fundamentalists not just as compromisers but as non-Christians, apparently little better than Catholics. He faulted them for using what he regarded as faulty Bibles, anything other than the original, 1611 edition of the King James Version. Indeed, he wrote that "modern Fundamentalists are cockeyed with apostasy." Ruckman, it turned out, was one of the chief proponents of the so-called King James Only school. He maintained that that translation not only was far superior to any other but provided "advanced revelation," a term I never found a good definition of.

I got to the church early and introduced myself to the hosting pastor. Later, in the hallway, he was walking with Ruckman. The pastor introduced us, I said I was pleased to meet Ruckman, and Ruckman gave a harumph. He shook hands but wasted no time in small talk. It was as though he was afraid of catching something from me. This impression was reinforced at the end of the debate—actually, before what was supposed to be the end of the debate— when he went to the podium and said these would be his last remarks. As soon as he finished making his comments, he walked out of the room, leaving me to give my final talk. No handshake, no goodbye.

I wasn't surprised. His attitude during the debate said a lot. Like every professional anti-Catholic, he claimed to like and respect Catholics, but actions do speak louder. Whenever I made a point he found discomfiting, he gave a large, theatrical yawn or held up a placard for the crowd to read. I don't recall what the placard said, but it wasn't in praise of the Catholic position. In this Ruckman was mimicked by a fan of his in the front row. This man had two signs. One, in red lettering, said, "Amen, Brother Ruckman." The other, in black, said "Repent Catholic." The signs alternated, depending on who was at the microphone.

One could spot the Fundamentalists at the debate easily, and not just from the signs. Each came armed with a Bible. Many Catholics had them, too, but the Fundamentalists seemed to wield the Good Book aggressively. Many questions directed to me were of the "How do you square this verse with Catholicism?" type. Clearly, some people had taken pains to prepare themselves to ask just the right question, the one that would throw the Papist for a loop.

Ruckman, like most Fundamentalist speakers, did not debate so much as preach. He flipped through the Bible, instructing the audience to turn first to this verse, then to that one. (Most of his tedious page-turning instructions have been edited out of the transcript.) He asked listeners to read aloud with him. He pumped them for shouted "amens" as though he were a cheerleader at a football game.

It was hard to keep a straight face when he was doing this kind of thing because the tactic worked against him. His rudeness backfired. Dozens of people, Catholics and Fundamentalists alike, came up to me during the breaks and apologized for Ruckman's behavior. I may have made few converts, but it was clear he made none. One woman said to me something like, "Your composure in the face of this hostility speaks well of your religion." I like to think that's how it came across, but no doubt a portion of that "composure" was simple bewilderment at Ruckman's antics.

As I said, Ruckman preached from the Bible—yes, he did thump it a few times—and most adults in the audience had Bibles in their laps. (There were many children present, too, perhaps brought by their parents so they could see that strangest of animals, a believing Catholic.) During a question period, one fellow asked me, "Why didn't you bring a Bible?" I explained that speaking styles differ. I prefer to speak either from memory or from detailed notes that include scriptural quotations. Using notes is more convenient than noisily flipping through the pages of the Bible. As a spectator, I've never liked watching a speaker read from (and get lost in) a book. I think I should know my material well enough that I don't have to impose that annoyance on the crowd.

What's more, I don't like citation-dropping. Sometimes a speaker may need to give chapter and verse, but usually not. If the quotation is "Thou art Peter, and upon this rock I will build my church," a mention of "Matthew 16:18" is nearly useless: if you already know the verse, a citation is unnecessary; if you don't know it, a citation is almost pointless, since it would take you a while to locate the quotation, and by that time the discussion would have turned to a different verse.

However true all this may have be, I took the questioner's complaint into account. Next time I debated I took along a Bible plus my notes. I spoke extemporaneously with some reference to the notes. I placed the opened Bible before me, occasionally and randomly turning the pages, thus pacifying those who looked at Scripture as a talisman, thinking that if you don't touch the sacred pages, you can't say anything intelligent about Christianity.

So that was one lesson I learned. Another and more important one was this: keep calm, don't let the antics of the other speaker or of the audience throw you off. Let's face it. Few people are converted by arguments aired at a single debate. What the Catholic debater wants to do is leave a certain impression. That is usually the most he can hope for. With Fundamentalists, so suspicious of things Catholic, so confused about the Catholic religion, the goal is to leave them with the notions that (a) Catholics do not have fangs, (b) something intelligent, even if not entirely convincing, can be said in favor of the Catholic position, and (c) the Bible has more to say in favor of Catholic beliefs than they imagined.

Another lesson: keep an eye on the literature table. I put several hundred copies of one of my tracts in the foyer. By the lunch break they were all gone, yet I knew few people had picked up copies, since it wasn't until after lunch that I had a chance to mention their availability. Clearly, someone had "liberated" the tracts. But I had come prepared, went to the car, brought in plenty more, and posted a friend at the table.

Given annoyances like these, are debates worthwhile? I think they're absolutely necessary, for three reasons. First, anti-Catholics need to know they'll be called to account in front of their Fundamentalist admirers. In the long run, this can do wonders for their honesty. Second, Fundamentalists need to see Catholics defend their faith. If it isn't worth defending, why should anyone believe in it? Third, Catholics need to learn there are sensible replies to the standard charges. They should rest comfortably knowing the slanders are groundless.

Whether I succeeded in any of that must be left to the reader of these pages.

Debate Transcript
Karl Keating vs. Peter S. Ruckman

MODERATOR: The format that we have decided upon has been agreed upon by the principals. These gentlemen will be exchanging comments at ten-minute intervals. If they go over the ten minutes, it's my job to step up here and say, "Shut up, you're done."

They're going to swap comments and rebuttals for somewhere between 40 and 60 minutes, and then we are going to open it to questions from the floor. I will field the questions. If your question is irrelevant, I will tell you so. You are not a participant in the debate. These two gentlemen are. You are not debating anyone. You will be given the option to ask questions. There is a difference. If you stand up and try to preach a sermon and straighten these gentlemen out, I'll tell you you're out of place, sit down, and be quiet. I've become reasonably proficient at that.

All right, we're giving Mr. Keating the option to open his comments, and whatever introductory comments he has is fine. Whatever subject he'd like to pursue, initially, is fine, and then Dr. Ruckman has said that he would be glad to respond to whatever he has to say. Mr. Keating, the floor is yours, fire away.

KEATING: I'd like to begin with the inspiration of Scripture. As most of you realize, today's event is the culmination of a week-long Bible conference, so it seemed to me I ought to begin with this topic. The question really is, why should the Bible be taken as a rule of faith? Well, because it's inspired, one might say. But how do we know it is inspired? Now there are some inadequate reasons for thinking so.

First is the cultural reason. In our country, we come from a Judeo-Christian heritage. No matter how lax our faith might be, we think that the Bible has a certain official status, and we would not speak about it the way we might speak about the Koran or the works of Confucius. Unfortunately the cultural view of the Bible is not enough to show its inspiration. After all, if you lived in a Muslim country and were brought up there, that kind of argument would demonstrate to you the truth and the inspiration of the Koran, which we know is not inspired.

The second reason one might think the Bible is inspired is family tradition. "I was brought up with it. It was good enough for my ancestors, so it's good enough for me." There is a certain logic to that, but it doesn't prove the inspiration of Scripture.

As a third reason, some people say, "Scripture is so inspirational. I can tell from reading it, it moves me so." "Inspirational" is a word with a double meaning. We use it, in the wider sense, to refer to many different kinds of writing. The problem is that some parts of the Bible are not at all emotionally moving. Some are as dry as military statistics because they are military statistics, such as much of the Book of Numbers. On the other hand, some non-inspired books, such as *The Imitation of Christ* by Thomas à Kempis, are more moving than many whole books of the Bible, yet the *Imitation* is not inspired.

Now we come to a fourth, better argument, the Bible's own claim to inspiration. It's infrequent. In the New Testament, the only writer who seems to have been aware that he was operating under the inspiration of the Holy Spirit was the writer of Revelation. In the Old Testament, several books say that what follows in them is inspired, but most of the books don't. Even if each book of the Bible claimed inspiration, that would not prove the matter because the Koran, the Book of Mormon, and the writings of Mary Baker Eddy, the founder of Christian Science, claim the same thing. That the Bible says it's inspired, at least with respect to some of its books, is not sufficient.

The fifth inadequate reason is the claim that "the Holy Spirit tells me so. I read the Bible, and I receive a conviction that the Bible is inspired, so it must be inspired." Here we fall into subjectivism. The good Muslim is going to say the same thing about the Koran. And someone who is neither a Muslim nor a Christian would have no rational basis for distinguishing from the other.

In the long run, it's only the Catholic position on inspiration that can prove the inspiration of the Bible. This is how the argument works. First we consider the Bible as a non-inspired book, just another ancient manuscript. The first thing we discover is that we have a very reliable manuscript, compared to all the other ancient manuscripts. We have manuscripts going back even to the first and second centuries, many of them. For many ancient writers, the oldest manuscripts we have are ones that were written long after they died. For Livy it's 500 years; for Horace, 900; for Plato, 1,300; for Euripides, 1,600. Nobody argues that we don't have authentic manuscripts from those writers. Thus, from textual criticism we are able to determine that the Bible, as we have it, is accurate as a manuscript.

Then we argue from the historical reliability of the Bible. From what we find in other ancient Christian writings, and from what we know of human nature, we say there is only one solution to the empty tomb, which is that Christ was what he said he was, namely God, and that he rose from the dead. We then find that he said he would do something, which is to found a Church that would continue throughout the ages. That Church must have as one of its notes the note of infallibility. It must be able to teach its doctrines correctly and not defect from them. Seeing that the Church is infallible in its official teaching, we know that when it tells us that the Bible is inspired, we can accept its word.

Note, this is not a circular argument. A circular argument would say, "The Bible says the Church is infallible, and the Church says the Bible is inspired." That's a circular argument. This instead is a spiral argument. The circular argument presupposed inspiration of the Bible. In the Catholic argument, we don't make that presupposition. We begin with the Bible as a regular historical text and then we argue from it to the infallibility of the Church. Once we have that, we listen to the Church that tells us the Bible is, indeed, inspired.

RUCKMAN: In regards to proof for the inspiration of the Bible, we don't assume anything, least of all that something as obtuse as reaching back in the Church Fathers to prove that a church would be the authority. Nothing that obtuse. Our reason for believing the King James Bible is the Word of God and that the Bible was originally given as inspired is not a historical argument or a comparative argument. It's a scientific argument. We think of the Bible as inspired because of mathematical computers. We don't rest by any assumptions at all.

You say what's the proof of this? The Bible says, "Prove all things; hold fast to that which is good." And reading from Isaiah, the Holy Spirit told you how to tell whether or not he was doing the writing or somebody else was. I'm in Isaiah 44:7: "The proof of inspiration is prophecy." He doesn't rest on anything as obtuse as what somebody thinks about their religion. That's immaterial. We're talking about mathematics here.

We know the Bible is inspired because of its mathematical statistics. I have here a book that gives 48 prophecies about a man before he is born, anywhere within 400 to 1,000 years before he was born. All of them come true on the money. We're not dealing with religion at all. We believe the Bible is inspired because of scientific, mathematical, computerized, statistical probability. There isn't any question about it.

Now, if you want to get a computer to work this thing out, you work it out like this. In the Bible, you are told more than 400 years before Christ was born that he would be born in Bethlehem of Judea. You got to figure one chance out of twelve, with twelve tribes, Judah is only one of them. You've got to figure a chance one out of 27. There are 27 towns in Judah. Now you take 48 prophecies and one man and figure what the chances are of 48 prophecies coming to pass, one individual, 400 years before he was born. And those chances, and I'll leave you to your own computer to figure it out, are ten to the hundred and fifty-seventh power. That's ten with a hundred and fifty seven zeros after it. You say how do we know the Bible is inspired? By mathematical, scientific, statistical evidence that can be proved in court. Figure out the probability.

For example, suppose I got up this morning and I said, "In the year 2154 a man is going to be born, in Dothan, Alabama, who lives to be 28 years old and is killed in a traffic accident in downtown Chicago, between Newberry and 12th street, at 1:30 in the afternoon. His funeral will cost $2,154.25. He'll be buried in West Long Cemetery in St. Louis after the body is shipped, and the presiding preacher at the funeral will be Reverend So-and-So." You'd say you're crazy. The computer couldn't handle it. Somebody said it can store up one hundred fifty million facts a second. That won't do at all. This book is 48 prophecies of a man before he was born and all of them came through, on the money.

Finally, I'll say this: we know the Bible is inspired, not because any Catholic said anything. The word "Catholic" doesn't appear in history until 113 A.D. It was invented by a man named Ignatius, a Church Father, not an early Christian of the Bible. No early Christian of the Bible ever referred to any church as the Catholic Church. That's a Greek term. Comes from Ignatius. It's borrowed from Greek philosophy. We wouldn't have to ask any Catholic if that book is inspired. If it wasn't inspired, we wouldn't take his opinion on it if he thought it was.

I'm not accepting the Bible to be inspired because any church told me. I'm accepting it inspired because it proved itself to be so mathematically, and two other things. The Bible says, "He that is of God heareth God's word. If any man will do his will, he shall know the doctrine, whether I speak of myself or whether it be of God."

The brother said it was only in Revelation they talked about inspiration. That's incorrect. In 2 Peter 3, Simon Peter, the prince of apostles, said that Paul wrote Scripture. In 2 Timothy 3:16, Paul said, "All Scripture is given by inspiration of God." Simon Peter said the Pauline epistles were Scripture before the Catholic Church ever showed up.

KEATING: I confess I am somewhat taken aback by the mathematical argument. I never thought I would hear a Christian use an argument that might be used by Carl Sagan, the astronomer, an agnostic.

His argument is that, mathematically, the odds are such that there must be other inhabited planets in the universe. He calculates the number of galaxies, the odds that one star might have planets, the odds that a planet might have an atmosphere, the odds that the atmosphere might have oxygen. He comes to the conclusion that it's a mathematical certainty that there are zillions of other worlds like ours, with human beings on them. I don't put much stock in Carl Sagan's calculations because they don't really prove the matter. In fact, I could mention to you astronomers who have shown that, mathematically, he's just wrong.

I've never had anybody argue the inspiration of the Bible on mathematics. I don't believe that it's a good proof. No matter what statistic you may come up with, it is not 100 percent. You always have a probability—that was Dr. Ruckman's word. There is no disagreement between us as to whether the book of Isaiah is inspired. I accept it. I accept its true prophecy. That's not a problem. But did you notice that the most that can be proved from that argument—let us presume that the argument, in fact, can prove inspiration based on mathematics—the most that can be proved is that the book of Isaiah is inspired because it is a prophetical book? What about the Song of Songs? What about one of the shorter epistles? What about some of the other Old Testament books that don't have any explicit prophecy in them?

You might say, well, if I could prove one book's inspired, the whole Bible is inspired. That doesn't follow because you first have to prove what constitutes the Bible. What books belong to the canon of Scripture? That's the key. The Catholic Church has identified a list of 73 books that it says are inspired and belong in the canon.

Another point you brought up was that the word "Catholic," which means universal, was not used until Ignatius of Antioch used it. Quite true. It's not used for the name of the Church in the Bible. On the other hand, the word "Trinity" is not found in the Bible. We believe in the Trinity. The word "Incarnation" is not found in the Bible. We believe in the Incarnation. We believe in those because they are described in other words in the Bible. The Catholic position is that the existence of the Catholic Church is taught in the Bible, even though the word Catholic Church is not there.

MODERATOR: All right, we'll allow Dr. Ruckman his next time period.

RUCKMAN: I was talking about mathematical possibility that was fulfilled. Past tense. I'm dealing with a case, not where a fellow is going to guess out there, I'm talking about a guess where he found them out there.

Now, the statement was, what about books like the Song of Solomon that don't contain prophecy? I would like sometime, before this meeting is over, and this discussion is over, I would like to see our brother find me one book in the Old Testament that doesn't have any prophecy in it. One will be just fine. He can take Obadiah if he wants to; it only has one chapter. I'll show him, at least, three items in it that are future. There are 39 books in the Old Testament.

I don't know of a single book in the Old Testament that doesn't have a prophetic subject in it. If you ever find one, let me know. I'm not too bright. I've only read the Bible though about 106 times. I may have missed something. But if I've missed it, I certainly missed it somewhere. I can take you to the Song of Solomon and show you the rapture, and the advent, and the Antichrist of the Church, and a dozen other things in there.

Now, in regard to this authentic interpreter, infallible interpreter, fortunately, we have a self-interpreting book. Simon Peter, the prince of apostles says, "No prophecy of the Scripture is of any private interpretation. Holy men of God spaketh and were moved by the Holy Ghost." The interpreter is the Holy Ghost, not some body of people who profess to be the one true Church that Christ founded, which might be true and then again it might not be true.

Luke 24:44: "These the words which I spake unto you while I was yet with you. All things must be fulfilled which were written in the law of Moses and in the prophets and in the psalms concerning me." Watch it, verse 45: "Then opened he their understanding that they might understand the Scripture." The infallible, divine interpreter is the Lord himself. He opened their eyes. No church had any part in that thing at all.

1 Corinthians 2:9: "But as it is written, eye hath not seen nor ear heard neither have entered into the heart of man the things which God hath prepared for them that love him." Watch it, verse 10: "But God hath revealed them unto us by his church." Right? No, that isn't right. Some fellow made that up. God hath revealed them to us by his what?

PEOPLE: Spirit.

RUCKMAN: By his what?

PEOPLE: Spirit.

RUCKMAN: By his what?

PEOPLE: Spirit.

RUCKMAN: One more time.

PEOPLE: Spirit.

RUCKMAN: Louder.

PEOPLE: Spirit!

RUCKMAN: Okay.

KEATING: Maybe I should have brought a cheering section of my own.

You know it's very difficult for anybody who's on the defensive to be able to respond to every potshot. It's much easier to make an accusation than a reply, particularly if the accusation is partly true and partly false. First, you've got to distinguish which is which. Then you've got to explain why the false part is false.

Dr. Ruckman says he's read the Bible 106 times. Well, he's read it more often than I, but it's evident to me, through my lesser number of readings, that the Bible is not self-interpreting. A book cannot interpret itself. It's a mind that interprets, either the mind of the reader or the mind of an authority, like God himself, or the mind of a living Church. A book, by itself, cannot interpret. We need an interpreter.

When we sit down and read the Bible, how do we get the proper interpretation? What it comes down to in most cases is either what we've been brought up with as an interpretation or what our minister or pastor says.

What constitutes the New Testament? Our Lord didn't say. None of the writers said these are the 27 books that make up the New Testament. You do not find anything like that in the Bible. You find no listing of the New Testament books within the books themselves, so how do we know which ones belong?

Now we know that Paul wrote books other than those that appear in the Bible, books that were lost. Presumably other writers wrote other things. Peter must have written other letters during his life but we presume that those lost books were not inspired. How did the early Christians know which were inspired, which were not? The New Testament does not tell us. We need an infallible authority to inform us what constitutes the canon. Without that authority, we can't know what comprises the Bible.

I want to point out that when we say, "the Holy Spirit tells me," what we're really saying is these books move me, that I see religious truth in them. Luther said the proof of inspiration is what? It's the power to convict us of the truth of the Christian message. The problem with Luther's standard is that he could have written a book that could convey the Christian message, but that book would not have been inspired. You could write one sentence that would be true and moving, but it would not be inspired. So we have to find out some other basis for deciding that our four Gospels and the epistles belong to the canon of Scripture.

RUCKMAN: How many of you people here were Catholic before you were born-again, you received Christ and left the Catholic Church? Would you stand. Would you stand. I'll stand with you. All right, thank you. Be seated. I have here *A Catechism for Adults* by Rev. William J. Clogan. Nothing objectionable. Imprimatur by the archbishop of Chicago. There it is. This is since Vatican II. Vatican II won't cover up this work. This is 1972, a catechism for adults. I'm an adult. I want to know what Catholics believe.

When I went to school, they taught reading, writing, and arithmetic, and we learned how to read. So I read on page 54, "Has the Catholic Church ever changed its teaching? Answer, no. For 2,000 years the Church has taught the same things which Jesus Christ taught." What I think a Catholic teaches is immaterial. I want it from the horse's mouth.

Now regard to the Holy Spirit leading people. I want to call your attention, very quickly, to about three items. In Acts 11:24, Barnabas is said to be a good man filled with the Holy Ghost. Acts 11:24. And that fellow, good man, filled with the Holy Ghost, who was around before Ignatius, knew what the word "Catholic" meant. That fellow got into an argument with Paul, who was the most Spirit-filled apostle in the New Testament. In Acts 15:39 there are two Spirit-filled, born-again men that don't agree, and the Holy Spirit is leading both of them. The contention was so sharp between them, they departed asunder, and Barnabas took Mark one way and Paul took Silas the other. You see that? Both those men were filled with the Holy Ghost. The Lord leads one bunch this way, other bunch that way, and they're both filled with the Holy Ghost.

Our brother says how are you going to know what's right? How are you going to prove all things? John 16:13: "when the Holy Spirit is come, he will guide you and lead you into all truth." Now, he didn't say you'd accept it, but he said he'd guide you. He didn't say you'd believe it, but he said he'd teach it to you. The fact that some Christians reject what the Holy Spirit revealed—that's between them and the Lord.

I was in the spa the other day. I go to the spa once in a while and pump a little iron. Of course, real little, you know. At my age, it isn't body building. It's care and maintenance. And I was in the spa, in the steam room one time, with a fellow, talking about Christ, witnessing to him. Finally he said, "Well, how do I know what to believe? The Catholics say they're right, and the Baptists say they're right, and this Methodist quotes Scripture, and the Charismatics showed me that so-and-so says this. How do I know which one is right?" I said, "How old are you?" He said, "I'm 22." I said, "You got a college education?" He said, "Yes." I said, "You have a college education." "That's right." I said, "You mean to tell me you're 22 years old and don't know when a man is perverting the Scripture or not?" I said, "You ought to be ashamed of yourself."

"Are you an American with an eighth-grade education? You mean to tell me you can't tell when a man is lying to you, from the pulpit, from the Scripture, and you can't tell? You ought to go soak your head in a bucket three times and pull it out twice. You say, how do you know whether they're teaching the right things or not? You've got the commandment in 1 Thessalonians: 'Prove all things.' Well, I could tell in a half minute if he was misusing the Scripture. You say, 'How?' Open the Scripture and check him out. What do you mean, you can't tell who's right? You ought to be ashamed of yourself.

"If you can read and write, you can buy you a Bible to open it up and see if he is telling you the truth. Maybe he says you ought to pray to blessed Mary, blessed John the Baptist, blessed Joe, that kind of stuff. You ought to be able to turn right to it. There is one mediator between God and man, the man Christ Jesus. There is no problem. Check him out. Check him out. Check him out. If tradition says one thing, and the Bible says another, you should know where they conflict. And you should know where they're correct. Sometimes tradition will line up with the book, sometimes it won't line up with the book. You say I don't know. Hey, Sonny, buy you a book and read it. Can you read? You better get one and read it while you can."

I took my convert course under Father Sullivan, of St. Michael's Church in Pensacola, Florida, who was a Ph.D. from Loyola University. We had quite a time of it. Now, after a while, I finally left and went my way and he went his. And later on, he asked me, "Why did you leave?" I said, "Because I got to the place where I could either believe what the book said or what tradition said." He said, "Yes, but they agree." I said, "I'll show you ten places where they don't." When I showed him the ten places, he said, "Well, where the two conflict, you need the Church. You need an infallible interpreter, an authentic interpreter to show you what it means." I said to myself, "Hey babe, if this is one authority, the Word, and that's the other authority, tradition, and I've got to have a third authority to tell which one's right, I know who the final authority is: it's the third one."

MODERATOR: What we're going to do now is open this thing up for questions. Now, the first thing I'd like to do is ask you to try to make your questions relevant to the subject that has been discussed this morning. The subject has been the inspiration of Scripture. Let's try to gear our questions to that direction. Again, I remind you, your position is to ask a question.

SPEAKER: Mr. Keating, I'm a pastor at a Baptist church. Why are so many Catholics becoming Fundamentalists? What is your feeling on that? Is it the Bible or what?

KEATING: In the last few decades, tens of thousands of Catholics have left the Church and have joined Fundamentalist congregations. That statistic is what prompted me to establish Catholic Answers. This problem—and a Catholic would view it as a problem—is particularly acute among Hispanics in America. As many as one out of six now are Fundamentalists, whereas a few decades years ago you could not find any, almost. To what is this to be attributed? Some Catholics might think the attraction to Fundamentalism is not a matter of theology but of pathology, that a person who leaves the Church for Fundamentalism does so because he's lonely, or he got the brush-off from a priest, or people from the Fundamentalist church came over and shook his hand and patted him on the back. That's a misunderstanding.

I know people who became Fundamentalists, having been Catholics, and who have come back. Some are here tonight. Universally, they say that the first attraction to Fundamentalism was the sincerity, the charity, and, very often the excellent speaking ability of the pastor. Those make a difference, but those are quasi-emotional things. That is not why they became or stayed Fundamentalist. They became and stayed Fundamentalist for doctrinal reasons. Those are the same reasons they cite when they explain why they came back to the Catholic Church.

I have to say that in the last several decades catechesis, instruction in the faith, has been lousy within the Catholic Church. Many people who find a real love for Jesus within the Fundamentalist churches go on to study further. As they continue their journey, they come back to the Catholic Church. Thus the fault is largely among Catholics. For decades, we didn't pay much attention. We figured things would just go on. Now we are paying the piper.

MODERATOR: Is there someone who has a question to direct to Dr. Ruckman? All right, yes sir. Stand up and state it clearly.

SPEAKER: How do we know that we have, in the New Testaments, all the canonical books, that there aren't any extras, there aren't any missing?

RUCKMAN: My answer to that is two-fold. The first answer to that is this: if you are going to trust the Catholic Church at the Council of Carthage, that tells you that the 27 books constitute the New Testament canon, you are going to make a bad mistake because they misled you on the 39 in the Old. If that's the only thing for believing the 27 were inspired in the New Testament, I would say, surely there must have been only 20. Because they just told me there were 46 in the inspired Old Testament books and there wasn't, there were 39. A church that messed up the Old Testament cannot be trusted with the New Testament.

Well, the answer to your question is this, which is very difficult for people to get a hold of. In the New Testament, there is no priest class that needs to determine anything. In the Old Testament, the Levites are in charge of the Scriptures. Therefore, a priesthood, a select chosen priesthood tribe, was in charge of determining what was canonical and what was not. In the New Testament, according to the principal apostle, Simon Peter, all Christians make up a holy priesthood. Therefore, it is left up to the body of believers to determine what books are canonical and which ones aren't. It is not left up to a priest class of scribes meeting in a council to tell you anything. It's left up to the body of believers.

MODERATOR: All right, someone has a question for Mr. Keating. Yes, sir.

SPEAKER: Mr. Keating, I don't know if you have access to a Bible or not. But if you do, I'd like, if you would, please, to interpret one word of Scripture. In 1 Timothy 2:5, the Bible says, "For there is one God and one mediator, between God and men, the man Christ Jesus." Can you explain to us the word "mediator" and the fact that the Bible says there is only one?

KEATING: The word "mediator" means a go-between, but I presume you want a fuller explication than that.

SPEAKER: Yes, sir.

KEATING: The standard objection to the Catholic position on, for example, the veneration of saints is that the Bible says there is one mediator, which is Christ. Quite true, and the Catholic Church acknowledges that. The Catholic Church also says that Christ was free to arrange his mediation in any way he might choose. Now one way is that he told us to pray for one another. I'm sure everyone here at some time, probably daily, prays for the spiritual or physical health of family members and others. What do we do when we do that? We are acting as mediators. When I ask God to protect you, to make you healthy, I am being a mediator. That's what it means.

The Catholic position is that Christ is perfectly at liberty to allow the saints in heaven also to act as mediators. There is no contradiction here. Just as Christ told us to pray for one another here below, we can pray for one another in the hereafter. So there's no contradiction between the two, because the mediation of the saints, any prayer a saint might give, on your behalf is only efficacious because of Christ.

MODERATOR: Mr. Keating was gracious to answer that question. I don't know that he was obligated to because the question at hand is inspiration. Now, we can broaden this thing if these gentlemen are agreeable. But what we have been discussing is inspiration of Scripture. I think it would behoove us well to at least try to conclude any questions that are directed to that subject. I believe there are several that still want to address the subject of inspiration, based on what they've heard. So, if possible, let's try to confine our remarks or questions to that.

SPEAKER: Dr. Ruckman, the question I have, as it regards to the Bible, and we talked about the Bible being the one source of information we can go to, knowing Christ. Before the printing press, all the thousands and millions of souls that were before us, from the time of Christ, up until the fifteenth century—were those people saved through the teaching Church or through the Bible?

RUCKMAN: The idea is until this book came out, how did the people get the truth? How did they get the teaching for four hundred years when there wasn't any New Testament written at all? The answer to your question is found in Romans 2. In Romans 2 you are told that a man is judged by his conscience until his conscience leads him to Christ. After that, he is judged for rejecting or accepting Christ, whether there was any church present or any Scripture present or not. Romans 2:12: "For as many as have sinned without law"—don't have any Bible, don't have any Ten Commandments—"shalt perish without law." They're lost.

The answer to that question is, when Scripture is not available for a fellow, God deals with that fellow and his conscience and will judge that fellow according to his conscience. The prime example is in the Old Testament, where in a dream the Lord says to Abimelech, "You're a dead man. The woman you've got is another man's wife." Right away that bird starts stumbling all over himself and says, "I haven't done a thing wrong." Why does that fellow start stumbling all over himself, if he didn't know "thou shalt not commit adultery"? When God said, "You're a dead man, you've got another fellows wife," you start arguing with God about being innocent. Abimelech didn't know the commandment, he didn't have an Old Testament. So the answer to that is the heathen, without light, are judged by their conscience until they have a chance to receive Christ. After that they are judged for receiving or rejecting Christ. I'm sorry, that goes fast.

SPEAKER: I wish Mr. Keating would comment on a book proving archeologically that the bones of St. Peter were found beneath the Vatican. If you could comment on this book.

KEATING: The book you're referring to is John Evangelist Walsh's *The Bones of St. Peter*. It's a popular account rather than a technical archeological account. It examines the archeological and historical evidence for Peter being in Rome and his bones being found in the necropolis, which is the "city of the dead" underneath St. Peter's Basilica.

What was discovered, in archeological excavations beginning mainly in the 1940s, was that there is indeed a first-century graveyard directly beneath the high altar of St. Peter's Basilica. There are inscriptions on the walls of various tombs saying, "Peter is here" or "Peter is nearby." There was discovered a little tomb in the shape of a niche, identifying itself as the place where Peter was buried. This corresponded to various writings from the early centuries which had said the same thing. The tradition had always been that the first church on that site—not the present Church, of course—the first cathedral there had been built right above Peter's tomb. It turns out, archaeologically, that's a fact.

You have some professional anti-Catholics, such as Loraine Boettner, author of *Roman Catholicism*, which is the main handbook for anti-Catholics, who says there is not one shred of historical evidence that Peter was ever in Rome. Boettner says there's no archeological evidence, but there is a wealth of archeological evidence. We have more evidence to that effect than we have for the location of many other Roman and Greek personages and sites. Archaeologically, there is no doubt that Peter was buried there.

MODERATOR: We are not going to deal with any questions for a while. So we go back to our ten-minute, alternating schedule. Mr. Keating will be first.

KEATING: What I'd like to do, at this point, is discuss Peter and the papacy and papal infallibility. First, Peter's status. We know, from the New Testament, that he had a primacy among the apostles. He always heads the list when they're named. Sometimes, it's just Peter and his companions. He's always in on the most dramatic scenes. He was the first to preach at Pentecost, work the first healing, had the revelation that baptism was for the Gentiles also. Something very special is that, when Christ first saw him, he gave Simon a new name. Most of us don't realize that he gave Simon a non-name. Up to that time, "Peter" was not actually a name. People didn't have the name of Peter. Christ came up to him and said, "Simon, you are now going to be known as Peter." Whenever we have a name change in the Bible, there is a change in status of the person whose name is changed. Abram was changed to Abraham and Jacob to Israel. You know of others. Every time that happens, it indicates that person's status has been changed in some way. Now, consider where Peter's name change came. Caesarea Philippi, which no longer exists. Today there's a small Arab town of Banias.

One of the headwaters of the Jordan is there. The interesting thing, geologically, is that there's a gigantic wall of rock, 200 feet high, and 500 feet long. Out of it, at the time, came the waters of the Jordan, although it's no longer coming out there. Here it was that Christ said to Simon, "Thou art Peter, and upon this rock I will build my church." He gave him authority when he said, "Whatever you bind on Earth will be bound in heaven. Whatever you loose on Earth will be loosed in heaven." Later the other apostles were given a similar authority, but here Peter is given it in a special way.

I had mentioned, a moment ago, his non-name. If I came up to you and said, "Your name is Sally, or Jack, but hereafter you will be known as Asparagus," you would ask me, "What does that mean? What's the purpose of renaming me?" Why name Simon the Rock? It must signify something. In the Old Testament, only God was called a rock. Here Peter, in some way, is having a participation in God's authority, by Christ's naming him a rock. This isn't to say he's a rock to the exclusion of Christ. Obviously, it must be some secondary foundation that he is being made. Christ also said to him, "I will give to thee—singular—the keys to the kingdom of heaven." Keys, in ancient times, were hallmarks of authority. A walled city would have one gate, opened by one lock, with one key. Peter was given authority over the Kingdom of heaven, which meant the Church here on Earth.

Much mention is made of the Greek, in Matthew 16:18: "Thou art *petros* and upon this *petra* I will build my church." The argument is made, "Well, *petros* and *petra* are different words. *Petra* means a large rock. *Petros* is a stone or a pebble," something, by comparison, insecure. So the argument is *petros*—Peter—cannot be the rock. The rock must be something else, either Christ himself or Peter's affirmation, which appeared in a previous verse. But this obscures something. Christ was not speaking in Greek. The common language of Palestine was Aramaic, and the word in Aramaic is *kepha*.

If we were to put that word into our English sentence, it would read, "Thou art *kepha*, and upon this *kepha* I will build my church." Nobody could mistake that play on words. When Matthew's Gospel was translated into Greek, the word *petra* could be used for *kepha*, large rock, but it could not be used for the name of Simon. In Greek nouns have endings according to gender. *Petra* is feminine. You cannot use it as a man's name. But if you give it a masculine ending, you have *petros*, a pre-existing word that means stone. You lose something of the play on words.

RUCKMAN: The term *pope* doesn't occur anywhere in history until 366 A.D. That's in the *Catholic Encyclopedia*, volume 12, page 270. The idea of the primacy of Peter is an interesting thing, but let's, for fun, turn to the passage we were discussing, Matthew 16. Nothing like a Bible to clear up a Bible conference. The gentleman removed two verses from the entire context. He didn't give you the context. The context is very interesting. Now we Bible-believing Protestants say the rock is Jesus Christ. He says it's Simon Peter. Obviously we have two different rocks. Let's see what this rock here is. Verse 22, which he did not read: "Then Peter took him and began to rebuke him saying, be it far from me Lord, they should not be unto thee; but he turned and said to Peter, Get thee behind Me," who?

PEOPLE: Satan.

RUCKMAN: Who?

PEOPLE: Satan.

RUCKMAN: Oh, you're interpreting. No, you're not interpreting, you're reading. You know who Jesus said that to? He said that to Simon Peter. He called him the Devil. If your church is built on Simon Peter, you have a rough foundation. Now take your Bible and turn to 1 Corinthians 10 and let's look at the difference here. This is Paul writing: "And yet all drank that spiritual drink, and they drank of that spiritual rock that followed them. And that rock was Christ."

You know what "Simon" means? Shifting sand. Look it up in a Greek dictionary. Simon's first name is shifting sand, his new name had to do with the rock, but not the rock our church is built upon. The rock his church is built upon. He and I can both come to one agreement. We can both come to the agreement we have different rocks. We have two different kinds of wine we drink of, as well as two rocks. This gentleman drinks fermented liquor at the Mass. We drink grape juice, at the Lord's Supper. So our vine's not the same, and our rock's not the same. Aren't we going to have a time getting together ecumenically?

If Peter was at Rome, here's the question. In Romans 16, the last chapter in the book of Romans, Paul gives sends his greetings to 25 Christians at Rome and doesn't mention the pastor. If Peter is the Vicar of Christ and head of the first Church at Rome, why is it when Paul, the apostle of the Gentiles, writes to the Romans, he won't mention the head of the Church? I never saw such a breach of etiquette in all my life. What an unethical thing to do, to greet all these fellows in Rome and then forget to say hello to the bishop of Rome.

KEATING: Presumably Peter was out of town at the time, and Paul knew it. We know Peter went to the Council of Jerusalem around A.D. 49, for example. There is no reason to think he was always in Rome, and the Catholic Church has never claimed that. To note his name not being not mentioned doesn't prove much. Another thing that doesn't prove much is the fact that the word "pope" was not used until 366 or whatever year. Does that prove that the papacy does not exist? If so, then you would have to say the Trinity does not exist because that word was not used before 181.

The word "pope" comes from the Greek *papa*, which means father. It's merely an honorific. The office can exist without that particular title. In fact Dr. Ruckman didn't bring this up but he could have—at first it wasn't even restricted to the bishop of Rome. All the major bishops, for a few centuries, were using the title. The Coptic patriarch, in Alexandria, is still known as the pope. He's not a Catholic, but he is known as the pope today. So the use of a word, whether "pope" or "Trinity" or "Transubstantiation"—the use of the technical term doesn't prove anything as to when the doctrine was first believed.

I want to start talking about papal infallibility, and I want to begin with what it is not. It is not what many Fundamentalists believe. It is not impeccability. The Catholic position is not that a pope cannot sin. So, please, in your questions do not say, "But didn't pope so-and-so commit this sin?" He may very well have, but that has nothing to do with the question of infallibility. Infallibility means the inability, when teaching officially, to teach an error in faith or in morals. It's limited to faith and morals. If the pope tries to predict the World Series winner, his guess is no better than yours or mine. If he teaches officially that Christ rose from the dead and that the Resurrection is not symbolic but historical, he teaches infallibly. His infallible teaching extends to doctrine about faith and morals, and he must be teaching officially, not in private, not over the dinner table to his neighbor.

I mentioned earlier Loraine Boettner's book *Roman Catholicism*. I know quite a few of you have read it. You might remember that passage where he talks about papal infallibility. He quotes Vatican I, in 1870. Boettner says, "Well, the Catholic Church position is that the pope is infallible only when he speaks *ex cathedra*, Latin for 'from the throne,' 'from the chair.' Therefore, he's infallible only when he is seated in Peter's chair. We know that what is venerated as Peter's chair, at St. Peter's Basilica, is probably only from the ninth century and of French origin. Therefore, even if the pope theoretically has the power, he could issue no infallible opinion because he can't sit in the real chair that Peter used."

That's not what *ex cathedra* means. When a judge issues a judgment, we say he rules from the bench. He doesn't have to be sitting on the bench. He can be in the courthouse hallway, and his judgment is still official. When Catholics say that Peter speaks *ex cathedra*, that just means he speaks officially, with the intent that what he's saying is to be held as true. He doesn't often exercise that power, and when he does, it's clear that he is doing it.

"He who listens to you, listens to me," Christ said. "All that you bind on Earth shall be bound in heaven." Infallibility belongs to all the bishops when teaching in union with the pope. This is a doctrine that hasn't changed, and it was repeated by Vatican II. The pope has the ability to teach infallibly by himself. The bishops of the world gathered together in ecumenical council can teach infallibly too, so long as their teaching is ratified by the pope.

"I've prayed for thee that thy faith may not fail." "Feed my sheep." "Thou art Peter." Those are the three main verses on which papal infallibility rests. I'll discuss a little more about it next time.

RUCKMAN: The Trinity turns out to be a biblical doctrine. If the papacy turns out to be a biblical doctrine then we'll accept it. If it doesn't, we'll throw it out. He quoted Eusebius. When a Catholic wants to prove something contrary to Scripture, he goes to the Church Fathers. Those are Ignatius, Polycarp, Tertullian, Justin Martyr, and the like. Martin Luther used to say some of the Church Fathers ought to be called the Church babies. That's our sentiments, exactly.

In regarding the pope speaking infallibly, he doesn't do it often—that's a masterpiece of understatement. He's only done it twice. He made one statement about Mary's Immaculate Conception, being born sinless, and one time about Mary being assumed into heaven, the Assumption of Mary.

In regards to Peter's power, and the loosing in heaven and Earth that he's quoted, I don't think you realize what that means. So I'll read you from *A Catechism for Adults*. "Question: when did Jesus promise to make Peter the pope? Answer: several months before he died. Question: when did Jesus actually make Peter the first pope? Answer: shortly before he ascended into heaven. Question: who will go to hell? Answer: only those who die with mortal sin on their souls. Question: who has power to forgive sin today? Answer: all bishops and priests of the Catholic Church can forgive sin."

Will you pardon a personal interjection? Bologna. I'm not worried about some Catholic priest or bishop forgiving my sins. Let him go play with his little push cart. Nothing to me one way or another. I received forgiveness for my sins the fourteenth of March, 1949, at 10:30 in the morning in downtown Pensacola, Florida.

KEATING: Some small corrections first. Tertullian was not a Church Father. He was a Montanist heretic at this death. He's never been considered, by Catholics, to be a Father of the Church. Fathers of the Church were those whose writings were not heretical. Second, in the last century-and-a-half, there have been more than two times when the pope has exercised what's known as his extraordinary magisterium to define a doctrine. But it happens fairly commonly, in every canonization. The Church is saying that this person's life is worthy of emulation and he is now in heaven. The Church has to be able to say that accurately. You can't very well set up for emulation somebody who's now in hell. In ages gone by there were other instances of the papacy teaching infallibly.

Let me turn to the forgiveness of sins. Christ himself forgave sins. It's mentioned several times in the Gospels. He did this as man, in and through his human nature. He said, "This is done to convince you that the Son of Man has the authority to forgive while he is on Earth." Now since he wouldn't always be on Earth, he gave this power to the apostles. And since they also would not always be on Earth, the power must be communicable. It's passed down through the bishops. We read that Christ breathed on the apostles and said to them, "Receive the Holy Spirit. When you forgive men's sins, they are forgiven. When you hold them bound, they are held bound." This is one of only two times in the whole Bible that God breathed on man, the other being Genesis 2:7, when he made man a living soul. Something key is going on here. He told the apostles to go out and gave them authority. "As the Father sent me, so am I sending you." What he did, they were to do.

The power to forgive sins definitely was not from themselves. "This, as always, is God's doing. It is he who, through Christ, has reconciled us to himself, and allowed us to minister his reconciliation to others." People try to say, look, when it said, "Whose sins you shall forgive, they are forgiven, whose sins you shall retain, they are retained"—that just meant the power to declare sins already forgiven. That doesn't wash. It doesn't say anything about telling people their sins already are forgiven if they accept Jesus. It doesn't say that. You have to do violence to the text to get that out of it. It's very clearly giving the apostles the power to forgive.

If this power didn't exist in New Testament times, one thing we should expect to see is a big uproar in early Christian literature. We should be able to find records of protest about this usurpation. There are none. We do not find any Christian writers of the early centuries saying, "Christ did not give the apostles the power to forgive sins."

We have records from the early centuries that say that a Christian is to confess his sins to a priest. Origen? Not a Father of the Church, but an early Christian writer testifying to this. Cyprian in the year 251, Methodius a century later. The power to forgive sins, or to hold them bound, necessarily implies that the priest has to be told the sins. He can't forgive what he doesn't know about. Therefore, you have, ultimately, auricular confession. "Auricular" means "to the ear." In the early Church, confession was public. You confessed your sins in front of the whole congregation. In a few centuries that practice was discontinued. There were obvious psychological difficulties with that. Many people would not confess at all or would stay away from church.

In the Catholic doctrine of the priestly power to forgive, there is no contradiction with the notion of Christ being the one mediator. Every Catholic theology manual acknowledges that. It points out that there's no contradiction because Christ could arrange things however he wished. He didn't have to become man for us—he could have just willed our salvation—but he became incarnated and took flesh. He wasn't forced to do it that way. He could have just decided that we just pray to him and that's it, and our sins are forgiven.

The Catholic position is that sins indeed can be forgiven if you pray and are sincerely contrite, sincerely repentant. But the reason confession was instituted is that we can't usually tell whether we're sufficiently contrite or are fooling ourselves. It's a common human failing. We're all subject to it. We tend to have favorite sins that we do over and over, and we can fool ourselves into thinking that we're sorry for them when we're not really.

It's often said that confession makes it too easy for Catholics. You sin on Friday, you go to confession on Saturday, and you're ready to sin the next week. Actually it's easier from the Fundamentalist's point of view because all you have to do is go to your bedroom and pray. You don't have to tell a priest. And then you too go out and sin again. So if that's an argument of convenience against the Catholic position, there is more of an argument against the Fundamentalist position.

When Christ said that the apostles had been given the power to forgive, he wasn't saying they had the power to declare somebody forgiven. It's not what those words are saying. He said, "Whose sins you shall forgive, they are forgiven." I don't see what could be any plainer than that. All the Christians understood that's what he meant. The notion that there was no priestly power to forgive came about fifteen centuries later.

MODERATOR: Let's take questions again.

SPEAKER: This is directed toward Mr. Keating. If you say that the Bible is the inspired word of God, where is your Bible? Why is it that I can walk into the Catholic church, in my hometown today, and not find one Bible but instead a missalette?

KEATING: People have different ways of speaking, different styles. If you were to see my notes, you'd see that everything I've quoted from the Bible has a reference. I don't believe in giving chapter and verse, because it's a waste of time. I presume that most of you know the verses. Second, I didn't bring my Bible because I don't like to flip through pages and read from it to the audience. I prefer to use notes. I don't think I need to use the Bible as a prop.

Regarding your other question, the missalette gives the words that are used in the Mass. If you look through the missalette, you'll find it's mainly made up of selections from the Bible. It has the Bible readings that are pertinent to the Mass of the day.

SPEAKER: What about "Call no man your father"?

KEATING: Paul wrote telling some people that they were his children in faith, that he was their father. When we call a priest "Father," what we mean, and the reason he's given the title, is because at baptism he regenerates us. The notion of fatherhood deals with generation, the giving of life. The priest, by administering baptism, effects a spiritual regeneration. We believe that baptism confers grace. It actually does something to us. If you are going to use a terribly literalistic sense of "Call no man your father," then you are going to have a problem regarding your mother's husband.

SPEAKER: You made a statement, "Why should the Bible be taken as a rule of faith"? Do you believe there is more than one rule of faith?

KEATING: The Catholic position is that the Bible alone was never meant to be the rule of faith, that the notion of sola scriptura is improper. The true rule of faith is Scripture plus Tradition. By Tradition, I don't mean customs, I don't mean habits, I don't mean styles of dress. It's unfortunate that we have one word having several meanings. That's not what Tradition means. Tradition, in the Catholic theological sense, is the continuation of the oral teachings of the apostles through the living Church, the living magisterium, which means teaching authority. Fundamentalists would not acknowledge the existence of that teaching authority, since Fundamentalists do not acknowledge a visible, hierarchical Church. When I was asking whether we should take the Bible as the rule of faith, I was referring, of course, to the Fundamentalist position, which is that the Bible is the sole rule of faith.

MODERATOR: Does someone have a question for Dr. Ruckman? Yes sir, in the checkered shirt.

SPEAKER: Dr. Ruckman, before I got saved, I was raised Catholic. When I went through parochial school, in catechism classes they taught us the Ten Commandments. After I got saved, I discovered that the Ten Commandments that I was taught were not the same Ten Commandments that the Bible speaks about. Namely, the second Commandment is omitted in the catechism, and the Tenth Commandment is split up into two commandments. Could you comment on that, please?

RUCKMAN: The official teaching of the Roman Catholic Church is there is no commandment forbidding you to have graven images. There is no second commandment in the Catholic Church. You say, how did they get ten? They take the last one and bust it down into two. Nice piece of work, baby. Ninth commandment, "Thou shall not covet thy neighbor's wife." Tenth commandment, "Thou shall not covet thy neighbor's goods." So you make two out of one and that way you get rid of the commandment to prevent you from having graven images. That means somebody wants you to have graven images. If they don't, what did they take it out for?

MODERATOR: We will again begin a debate format.

KEATING: I ought to say something, I suppose, about the Mass, because those of you who never have been Catholics may not know what happens at the Mass. I debated, a while back, another Fundamentalist minister, and someone from the audience said, "You people never hear anything about the Bible at Mass." I explained to her that the Mass is divided into two parts. The first part is called the Liturgy of the Word, where we have readings from the Bible. At Sunday Mass there are four of them. The first is a reading from the Old Testament. Then, one of the psalms is read, often sung. Then comes a reading from the New Testament, other than Gospels. The fourth selection comes from one of the Gospels.

Each day during the year, a different set of readings is given. There is a three-year cycle of readings, so that, in a Catholic church, if you were to attend daily Mass, in three years you would hear read out to you virtually all of the New Testament and a very large portion of the Old.

I submit to you that if you belong to a Fundamentalist congregation, you don't hear nearly that much of the Bible read out. Different Fundamentalist congregations are different. Some will concentrate on the rapture or eternal security or some other doctrine and will go over and over such points but leave out large parts of the Bible otherwise—not that you're discouraged from reading it, but those other parts are not part of the service. I would dispute anybody who says that the average Catholic hears less of the Bible than the average Fundamentalist. If he goes to daily Mass, he hears quite more.

Now let me go on to another topic to which Dr. Ruckman alluded, namely salvation and our assurance. Several people, during the break, asked me about it. The Fundamentalist notion is that, after accepting Christ, one's salvation is guaranteed. No sin can undo it. It doesn't matter what sin you may commit later, you will not be condemned to hell for it. The Catholic idea, obviously, is different. The Catholic idea is that your salvation, which is to say, getting into heaven, is dependent upon the state of your soul when you die.

If we were to be transported now to the Moon, we would die. We are not equipped to live on the Moon, where there is no air. We need special equipment to live there—equipment that is above out nature: supernatural, so to speak. Same for heaven. We are not naturally equipped for heaven. We must be filled with supernatural grace. The Catholic Church says that only a soul in the state of grace is able to enjoy heaven. If you are not grace filled— if you have a dead soul, from which grace is absent—you go to hell. This means that it's possible for anyone to be saved, possible for anyone to go to hell. It does depend how you die, what the state of your soul is at death.

A Fundamentalist will say, not so. The soul remains depraved. Your sinful condition stays but is covered, as by a cloak. The righteousness of Christ is imputed to you. Your soul, though, does not become itself holy. The Catholic position is that through grace your soul becomes holy and good.

I was talking some months ago with Bart Brewer of Mission To Catholics. You may know of Bart, an ex-priest who tries to convert people to Fundamentalism. He was pointing out priestly sins. I said to him, Bart, what about pastor so-and-so, who had been an institutional supporter of your group? He was arrested for child molestation, a serious sin. Are you telling me that, under your own theory, this man is just as saved as the fellow in your congregation who "gets saved" and then immediately dies, never having a chance to sin? Bart had to say, sure, that's our position, which, I think, is a repugnant position because it leads to antinomianism, which is lawlessness.

If there is nothing you can do after being saved that will affect your salvation, why not have fun, here below, while the having's good? There is nothing you can do, no matter how perverse, that could condemn you, on Bart's theory. That's not the Catholic theory. The Catholic theory is that you must remain grace-filled.

When I moved to my present home, a few days later, the minister of the Fundamentalist church across the way came to the door. I invited him in. We had a nice talk. The first question he asked is: "Do you have an assurance of salvation?" I said "No, because it's not biblical." He had never heard anybody say that before. We had a nice discussion.

RUCKMAN: Now, what happens when a Christian sins? Talk about preachers in jail for child molestation. Yes, we had a case of a Catholic priest, down in Louisiana, last year. All over the newspapers for about four or five months. Parents wanted to sue him, and the Catholic Church tried to buy the parents off so it wouldn't become a public scandal. Common news in the *Picayune*. You don't believe it, go read it. I'll show you what happens when a Christian sins. I'll show you what happens when you become a child of God and don't live right.

1 Corinthians 11:30: "For this cause many are weak and sickly among you"—sick Christians—"and many sleep"—dead Christians. Verse 31: "For if we would judge ourselves, we should not be judged." But when we are judged, we don't go to hell. When we're judged, we're chastened of the Lord. You know what God does with the sin, in the Christian? He whips him. He takes out the belt. Whom the Lord loveth, he chasteneth. If you endure chastening, God deals with you as a son, for what son is he whom the Father chasteneth not?

This ridiculous idea that you have to be born again and again and again is nonsense. You are born again or you're not born again. I've got three sons, Peter, Michael, and David. They are born of my seed. You know when they cease to be my sons? Never. You know why? They can't be born again, out of their mother's womb. Those boys will be Ruckmans when they're dead, Ruckmans on their tombstone. If they change their names, they'd still be Ruckmans, because they're born of my seed. How many of you have been born of incorruptible seed, by the word of God? Let me see your hands. All right then, be careful how you live. But you ain't going to change your family, no matter what happens. Even if God has to kill you.

KEATING: Let's look at a few verses that he forgot to mention, such as 1 Corinthians 9:27: "I buffet my own body and make it my slave, for I, who have preached to others, may myself be rejected as worthless." I use the Ronald Knox translation; yours is similar. I can talk later about the question of the King James, if you wish, but I prefer an accurate translation. But the essence of the passage under either is the same.

What Paul is saying here is that he might be lost. "You must work to earn your salvation in anxious fear." Now what did he mean by that? That's not the language of self-confident assurance. He's had the Damascus road experience already, so if anyone was ever born again, surely it was he. "All of us have a scrutiny to undergo before Christ's judgment seat"—this is 2 Corinthians 5:10—"for each to reap what his mortal life has earned, good or ill, according to his deeds." And Romans 2:6: "God will award to every man what his acts have deserved." Under the Fundamentalist notion, that doesn't have anything to do with salvation.

Luther, as you well know, or as you should know, mistranslated when he said that "salvation is by faith alone." He took the Latin Vulgate and added the word "alone" in the margin. The word "alone" doesn't appear in the original Greek, but he had to put that in because the text, he realized, didn't otherwise support the salvation-by-faith-alone theory. At Romans 5:2, Paul says, "We are confident in the hope of attaining glory as the sons of God." Now saints in heaven do not exercise the virtues of hope or faith. A saint has no need of hope because he already is in heaven. A saint in heaven has no need of faith because he sees God. He has charity in perfect abundance. Of the three theological virtues, that's the only one you find in heaven.

"Our salvation is founded on the hope of something"—Romans 8:28—"Hope would not be hope at all if its object were in view." How could a man still hope for something he sees? How could a man still hope for something he has absolute assurance of? That's contradictory. There is no need to hope for something you have absolute assurance of getting. If salvation were as assured as the Fundamentalist might think, then this hope that Paul talks about is meaningless. There would be no purpose to it. When Paul says that he might be lost, that doesn't fit in either. You can have a moral certainty of salvation, but you can't really have absolute assurance, and the reason you can't is because it doesn't mesh with other verses in the New Testament.

MODERATOR: We are going to open it up for questions again. This gentleman down here.

SPEAKER: My question is for both of the men. What is their definition of Fundamentalism?

KEATING: This may be something I should have brought up initially. Many people use the term "Fundamentalist" in a purely pejorative sense. I do not. The trouble with terminology is that often we can't find a precise enough word. I think it's easy enough, if I say "Catholic," that you understand what I'm talking about. What word am I to choose, otherwise? Some people would say well, "I prefer Evangelical." Well that's a wide word, and it goes from liberal Protestantism and overlaps Fundamentalism. Most of those are not people I'm talking about. Others say, "Well we're just Bible Christians." Again, that's imprecise; besides, I believe that Catholics are as much Bible Christians as you are. So, that's not a precise term.

Unfortunately, there really isn't a perfectly precise term. I use "Fundamentalism" in a narrow sense but not in a pejorative sense. If you are familiar with the books called *The Fundamentals* written about 1915-1919. The principles enunciated in those, that kind of faith is what I'm talking about when I mean Fundamentalism. Some people that I would call Fundamentalists don't like to use the term. Others welcome it. There is considerable variety. I just don't know of any other word that is more accurate.

MODERATOR: All right. The gentleman in the green.

SPEAKER: My question is to Mr. Keating. In Psalms, God said that he holds his word above his name. Also in Psalms he says his word will endure forever. I can't quote the verse verbatim right now. If that's so, how come you made that statement that you believe the Bible is not a rule of faith?

KEATING: What I believe is not that the Bible is not a rule of faith but that it is not the sole rule of faith. The Catholic position is that the Bible plus Tradition make the rule of faith. We don't throw the Bible out and replace it with something else. There are two founts, as Vatican II put it, two sources of faith, which must be taken together.

SPEAKER: Dr. Ruckman, could you give us some Bible verses on tradition as opposed to Scripture?

RUCKMAN: Yes, there are many of them. I'll show you the main one. So far you've been given tradition as an equal authority with the Word of God, without any regard for the particular nature of that tradition. And the nature of that tradition has been citations from the Church Fathers. Mark 7 was written before there were any Church Fathers.

Mark 7:5: "Then the Pharisees and scribes asked him why walk not thy disciples according to the tradition of the elders?" Verse 6: "Well did Isaiah prophesy of you hypocrites. It is written, this people honors me with their lips but their heart is far from me. How be it in vain do they worship me, teaching for doctrine the commandments of men?" Verse 9: "And he said of them full well you reject the commandment of God, that you may keep your own tradition."

MODERATOR: All right. I think we'll just take one or two more. Gentleman back there on the aisle.

SPEAKER: Being a non-Fundamentalist and a non-Catholic, I'd like to ask both of you a question. The question is on the assurance of salvation. Does the Baptist believe that one who is a practicing Catholic and a member of the

Catholic Church will have any problem on judgment day, and vise-versa for the Catholic?

MODERATOR: All right. As I understand it, the question is do both groups believe that the other one will have problems on judgment day. Mr. Keating, you're first.

KEATING: I think the real question is, to narrow it down, do they have any hope on judgment day? The Catholic position is that non-Catholics can be saved. The Bible says that we must be born again through water and the Holy Spirit. The Catholic Church understands that to be baptism and that there are really three forms of baptism. One is sacramental, water baptism. Another is the martyr's death, baptism of blood. The third is baptism of desire, which is not a sacrament; it's where a person, in what the Church calls invincible ignorance, tries to do good and lives a life according to the lights given him.

So the Catholic position is that a Jew, a Muslim, a non-believer, or a Protestant can be saved but not necessarily that they would have the same likelihood as a Catholic, all things else being equal. The Catholic has the advantage of recourse to the sacraments, which most non-Catholics don't, and to the full teaching of Christian truth. So there are great advantages to being a Catholic. But, is it possible that a non-Catholic can be saved? Yes.

MODERATOR: All right. Dr. Ruckman?

RUCKMAN: My answer, very quickly, is I believe many Catholics are saved, in spite of what some of the brethren think or how anti-Catholic you may think I am. I've talked to hundreds of Catholics in America who I think were truly born-again Christians and children of God, in spite of their Church's teachings. I say that because I'm about to quote the Church's teachings from the most important council they ever had. What I'm quoting you is not what Mr. Keating just said. What I'm quoting you is from the largest official, most important council the Catholic Church ever held. The Council of Trent takes the first place, not only because of its restatement of Catholic doctrine but because of its extraordinary influence both within and without the Church.

No Baptist believes that Roman Catholic water baptism saves anybody. There isn't a Baptist in this church that believes that. So according to the Catholics, he's an anathema. Not according to Mr. Keating but according to the Council of Trent. "If anyone say that baptism is optional, that it is not necessary for salvation, let him be anathema." Whoever heard of a Baptist saying if you don't believe what I believe, you're anathema? Whoever heard of such intolerant bigoted, narrow-minded, prejudiced dogmatism?

I didn't write that. That's official Catholic literature, of the most important council they ever held. According to that, there isn't a saved Baptist in this room. I would say this: any Catholic can be saved by simply believing in the Lord Jesus Christ and receiving him as his Savior. I'll go even further than that. Show you how much grace I've got. A great deal more grace than some of you narrow-minded bigots.

I might even suggest that perhaps Mr. Keating is saved. I don't know already what he is trusting. He may not have told the whole truth about exactly what he's trusting, but I'm sure he believes Christ is Virgin born. I'm sure he believes he died on the Cross. I'm sure he believed he rose from the dead. I'm sure Mr. Keating, in his heart, wants to please the Lord. I don't know whether Mr. Keating has personally received Christ himself, not as a wafer but as a Savior. If he has, he is just as saved as I am. He just isn't enjoying it.

KEATING: I'm going to take a few seconds to reply to that because the impression you have been left with is that anybody who is anathematized is condemned to hell. Is that what you understood it to mean? That's not what it means. In a Catholic ecumenical council, the anathema means you are excommunicated. That is, you are no longer a member of the Catholic Church. You're no longer a Catholic because you don't believe what the Catholic Church believes. Truth in advertising.

The Catholic Church has never condemned people to hell. As a matter of fact, it is not even a doctrine that Judas is in hell. There is no official infallible statement that any particular individual is in hell. When you read something that says you're anathematized, it means you're no longer a member of this club. Don't read into it what isn't there.

Another point is that the council Fathers were addressing Catholics. None of that applies to non-Catholics. You can't be a heretic if you are not a Catholic to begin with. A heretic is a Catholic who understands the truth of the Catholic faith or a doctrine and then rejects it. That's the only way you can be a heretic.

RUCKMAN: I'll give Mr. Keating grounds on this: there are some verses in the New Testament that would seem to teach Christians can lose salvation. Turn back to 1 Corinthians 9 that he quoted you before the break and show how he took the verse clean out of the whole chapter. In the legal practice where he practices law, a text without a context is a pretext, and he took 1 Corinthians 9:27 clean out of the chapter. Notice the chapter had nothing to do with salvation at all. First of all look at verse 5, and notice that Cephas, Simon Peter, was a married pope. Look at 9:5. Simon Peter was married. He had a mother-in-law who was sick in Matthew 8. The entire chapter is talking about a ministry, and there's no discussion in this chapter about an individual being lost at all. He was talking about the salvation of a ministry when he said, "When I have preached to others, I, myself, should be cast away."

Now come to 1 Timothy and watch the same thing again. In 1 Timothy 4:16 notice how even the word "saved" sometimes does not refer to the salvation of a man's soul at all but the salvation of his ministry. "Take ye to thyself and to the doctrine, continue in them, for enduring this, thou shalt save thyself." Look at the context. Verse 12, ministry; verse 13, ministry; verse 14, ministry; verse 15, ministry. He's talking about the salvation of the ministry.

One more time, Romans 8. Mr. Keating went to some degree talking about hope and faith, and again he forgot to show you the context. I'll show you what he was quoting. He was quoting Romans 8:24 and forgot to read to you verse 22 and verse 23, and the context of Roman 8 had nothing to do with you getting to heaven at all. Look at the passage, Romans 8:22. "For we know the whole creation groaneth and travaileth in pain together until now. And not only they but ourselves also, which have the first fruits of the Spirit, even we ourselves groan within ourselves, waiting for the adoption, to wit, the redemption of our"—what?

PEOPLE: Bodies.

RUCKMAN: What?

PEOPLE: Bodies.

RUCKMAN: Again.

PEOPLE: Bodies.

RUCKMAN: Again.

PEOPLE: Bodies.

RUCKMAN: Again.

PEOPLE: Bodies.

RUCKMAN: No salvation of the soul in the passage. No reference of salvation of the soul in all of that passage. It's talking about the salvation of your body at the second advent. He left out the first verse. That made you think you were waiting to see whether or not you're gonna get to heaven.

KEATING: Dr. Ruckman made a reference to Peter being married. A lot of Fundamentalists bring that up to Catholics as though Catholics were to be surprised by it, when, in fact, it's something well-known to Catholics, and Catholics, at least I, respond by saying yes, and did you know even today many priests in the Eastern Rite Catholic Churches are married, and some of the early popes were married? Sort of an immaterial point. This brings to mind a Fundamentalist perception of the origin of Catholicism. I mean the notion that Catholicism is real Christianity but with the addition of non-scriptural or non-Christian pagan influences. There seem to be two basic versions of its history, what I call the pagan convert theory and the Babylonian cult theory.

The pagan convert theory—something Loraine Boettner, for example, pushes, as do many other professional anti-Catholics—says, "Look, here are many Catholic inventions," as they're termed, things that were not mentioned directly in the Bible and were brought up some centuries later. The anti-Catholics' lists always start in the fourth century. They say what really happened is that when Constantine in 313 legalized Christianity—he didn't make it the official religion; that was a lifetime later—when he legalized Christianity, pagans entered the Christian Church in hopes of secular and political preferment. There were so many newcomers that there wasn't time to catechize them properly, so they brought in their customs, and the Catholic Church developed out of the original Christian Church taking on these foreign things.

That particular theory breaks down because of the dating. Everything depends on the legalization of Christianity in 313. You can look at early Christian writers and may disagree with their beliefs, but in the second and third centuries, long before this legalization, they're mentioning prayers for the dead, the veneration of saints, the Eucharist as the real body and blood of Christ—the kinds of things we say are peculiarly Catholic beliefs.

Some Fundamentalists point out that, according to Cardinal John Henry Newman, such things as incense, lamps, candles, votive offerings, and sacerdotal vestments are all of pagan origin. Quite true. Also quite irrelevant. Most of you who are Fundamentalists and who are married I presume were married in a church ceremony. Probably the bride wore white, carried a bouquet, maybe had on a veil. After the vows, rings were exchanged. Are you aware that the exchanging of rings, the wearing of a veil, the wearing of a white dress, the holding of a bouquet are all of pagan origin? They are. Does that mean Fundamentalism came from paganism? Of course not. Similarity does not imply descent.

What I mentioned is the standard anti-Catholic history. There is a more exotic history, the idea that Catholicism arose from Babylonian cult worship.

The chief writers for that are two. One was Alexander Hislop who wrote in 1853 *The Two Babylons*. More recently, Ralph Woodrow wrote *Babylon Mystery Religion*. They don't understand the nature of the non-Christian religions of ancient times, and their proofs are laughable. In Woodrow's case, most of his "facts" about what the Babylonian religion was are wrong, even before he gets to the point of comparing it to Catholicism. He doesn't identify what the Babylonians believed or the Egyptians or others.

So the first theory, what I call the pagan convert theory, falls apart because of the dating. You can look back at the Fathers of the Church and other Christian writers that Catholics would not consider Fathers. You can read even those considered heretics by Catholic standards. They all refer to Catholic practices—confession, the Eucharist, the Mass—as existing prior to Constantine. On the other hand, the more exotic theory, of the Babylonian origin—again, there's no basis to that.

What both Catholics and Protestants need to do is to go back and to read a good history. There are good histories by Protestants as well as Catholics. A particularly good history by a Catholic is Philip Hughes' three-volume *History of the Church*. He was a Catholic priest. You would find nothing, I think, objectionable in his explication of the facts, though you perhaps would differ in some interpretations. Don't worry. You won't automatically be converted just by reading a Catholic-written book. I hope that you read such books because you'd find out the history that professional anti-Catholics give about where Catholicism came from is bunk, and you should know it.

RUCKMAN: Now I'm going to close my session here with Romans 4, and I won't have any more to say this afternoon. I'm about through for a while. I'm going to close with Romans 4:5–8, and before I sit down, I'd like to illustrate what a Bible-believing Baptist means when he talks about eternal spirit. Romans 4:5: "But to him that worketh not, that believeth on him that justifies the ungodly, his faith is counted for righteousness even as David also describeth the blessedness of the man unto whom God inputeth righteousness without works, saying blessed are they whose iniquities are forgiven, and whose sins are covered." Hear the verse: "Blessed is the man to whom the

Lord will not impute sin." Here's a fellow that's sinned, and God won't charge him with it. "Blessed is the man to whom the Lord will not impute sin." We call that imputation. I'll show you what that means.

Here's a diary, life of Peter S. Ruckman, filled with sins. There are mistakes, godless depravity, every kind of sin. You name it, it's there. Here's the life of Jesus Christ, spotless, perfect, sinless, Holy Son of God. I've come to Christ and taken him as my Savior. God takes this book here, and writes across it, "This is the life of my Son, Jesus Christ," and God imputes my sins to him. Behold the Lamb of God. Christ became sin for us, he who knew no sin, who bore on his body my sins on the cross. He takes my filth and my dirt and with his stripes I'm healed, and my crime is just laid on him. My dirty rotten life is imputed to Jesus Christ. This is the life of Peter S. Ruckman.

I get God's imputed righteousness when I trust Christ. When I trust Christ, God gives me his righteousness. Romans 10:1-10: "Brethren, my heart's desire and prayer for Israel is that they might be saved, for I bear them record that they have a zeal of God, but not according to knowledge, for they being ignorant of God's righteousness and going about to establish their own righteousness have not submitted themselves unto the righteousness of God, for Christ is the end of the law for righteousness for everyone that believeth."

All right. I'm through for today. I enjoyed it. Enjoyed it. Had a good time.

KEATING: Well, since he's through for today, I guess this will have to be my last. I'd enjoy going on for another hour solo, but that hardly would be fair.

I'm going to turn to the subject of the brethren of the Lord and what that means, particularly with reference to whether Mary was perpetually a virgin. That's the Catholic position, of course, that she was a virgin both before and after, even during, Christ's birth. Several verses refer to people called Christ's brethren. Fundamentalists conclude that these people are the actual blood brothers of Christ, brothers german.

The word "brother" had a wide meaning in the Bible. Lot is called Abraham's brother even though he was his nephew. Jacob is called the brother of his Uncle Laban. Sis and Eleazar were the sons of Moholi. Now Sis had sons, and Eleazar had daughters, and we're told that the daughters married their "brethren" who were the sons of Sis, but they really married their cousins. Sometimes the word "brethren" meant kinsman as in 1 Kings 10:13 or just a friend or just an ally as in Amos 1:9. The ambiguous usage was there because neither Aramaic nor Hebrew had a word for cousin in our sense of the word. When the Septuagint translation was made, Hebrew to Greek, the translators used the Greek for brother even though a Greek word existed for cousin. They made a transliteration of those terms rather than a translation.

At the Annunciation, Mary asked the angel, "How can this be since I know not man?" The Catholic Church understands this to imply a vow of life-long virginity. Certainly Mary knew the rudiments of biology. She knew where babies come from. Her comment would have made no sense at all if it was her intention to have several children. She wouldn't have to ask how could that be. It's obvious how it could be, the way everybody else had children. We note that when Christ was found in the Temple, he was called *the* son of Mary, not *a* son. The Greek there implies an only son.

What's more, those who are called the brethren of the Lord are never called Mary's sons. It's a rather odd usage if they were her sons. Something that a lot of us miss is that the brethren gave Jesus advice: leave Galilee, go to Judea, preach there. If Mary had children after Jesus—obviously not before since we know he was the firstborn—then they must have been younger than he. In Oriental societies today, as in the Palestine of ancient times, it is improper for a younger son to give advice to an older, but it would be okay for younger, more distant relatives or friends to do so.

There are two objections, based on one verse, to Mary's perpetual virginity. The verse is Matthew 1:25: "Then he knew her not until she brought forth her firstborn son." First look at "until." 2 Kings 7:23: "Michal the daughter of Saul had no children until the day of her death." This doesn't mean she had children after her death. Here, "until" tells us she never had any children. When the raven went forth from the ark in Genesis 8:7, it did not return "until the waters were dried up on face of the Earth," but we read on and find it never returned at all. We are told in Deuteronomy 34:6 that the burial place of Moses was not known "until the present day," but it still is not known. Here is a reference to a deuterocanonical book, 1 Maccabees. You don't accept it as inspired, but it shows usage of the word. 1 Maccabees 5:54: "And they went up to Mt. Sinai with joy and gladness because not one of them was slain until they had all returned in peace." It doesn't mean they were slain after they came home from the battle.

The word "until" in the Bible does not have the same meaning or implication it has today. Our natural implication is that if something didn't happen "until" now, then it will happen later. The Bible's use of the word does not imply that, as these verses show.

The other complaint is the term "firstborn." The firstborn is the child that opens the womb. Firstborn sons had to be sanctified, Exodus 34:20. There wasn't any reason to wait for a second son to come along before you could call the first one the firstborn. The first son you had was the firstborn from the moment of his birth. Archaeologists found in Egypt a funerary inscription which says, "This woman died giving birth to her firstborn son." Obviously he was her only son, so firstborn doesn't mean there were later-born children. Firstborn is a term of art because under the Jewish law there were certain responsibilities for the firstborn son.

So who were these brethren? Look at Matthew 27:56. Among them, at the cross, "were Mary Magdalene, and Mary the mother of James and Joseph, and the mother of the sons of Zebedee." Mark 15:40 says, "Among them were Mary Magdalene, and Mary the mother of James the less and of Joseph, and Salome." Compare those two to John 19:25, "Meanwhile his mother, and his mother's sister, Mary, the wife of Cleophas, and Mary Magdalene, had taken their stand beside the cross of Jesus."

If we compare those verses, we find that Mary, the mother of James and Joseph, must have been the wife of Cleophas, but James is elsewhere described as the son of Alphaeus. So does that mean this Mary, who is not the Virgin Mary, but a different Mary, was at once the wife of Cleophas and Alphaeus? There are two possibilities that scholars have mentioned. One, she could have been widowed and remarried, but more likely is that Alphaeus and Cleophas were the same person in that the Aramaic for Alphaeus could be rendered in Greek as Cleophas. Just as Saul took another name, Paul, so Alphaeus also could be called, in Greek, Cleophas.

The early Christian writers, post-New Testament, speculated that this Cleophas was the brother of St. Joseph, the spouse of the Virgin Mary. Maybe, maybe not. If he was, then James would have been the cousin of Jesus. And in any case, there simply isn't anything in the New Testament which mandates that these people were brothers german to Jesus. So why, Catholics will ask, why do Fundamentalists bring this up? I'm surprised that nobody really brought it up earlier today.

I think there are two reasons: one is a dislike of celibacy in many quarters, the argument being that for Mary and Joseph to have been celibate would have been an unnatural family situation. It was unnatural anyway, having the Son of God in the family. Obviously this is a family which we cannot compare to any other family. It was established for a particular purpose, to nurture the Son of God.

The other reason is that I think some people hope to undermine respect for Mary by saying that basically she's like the rest of us. Furthermore, I think that a careful perusal of the New Testament will show that there isn't any indication there that she ever had other children. Certainly none of the early Christian writers ever suggested it. There is every indication that Jesus was her only child and that those called the brethren were his cousins. Thank you.

MODERATOR: Okay. I think we've about worn everybody out sufficiently. Let's stand and have a word of prayer, and we'll be dismissed.

BOOK 2

High Desert Showdown

Karl Keating vs. Jim Blackburn

Introduction

For decades U.S. Route 395 was the only north-south highway in eastern California. It still is. There have been few changes to the route or to the towns along it. The largest town is Ridgecrest, population 28,000. It has the distinction of being within a two-hour drive of the highest and lowest points in the contiguous U.S., Mt. Whitney (14,505 feet) and Badwater Basin in Death Valley (282 feet below sea level). Ridgecrest is as large as it is chiefly because it is home to Naval Air Weapons Station China Lake. The town's population is a cross-section of America: urban and rural, well educated and not, financially secure and financially precarious. It displays much of the panoply of American Christianity.

One day I received a plea from Catholics who lived in Ridgecrest. Would I come to town to debate a Fundamentalist minister, the pastor of Watchman Baptist Church, who was riling the local populace? Townsfolk were beginning to turn against one another. The Catholics were at wit's end. None of them felt equipped to deal with the man, who was inflaming emotions in a way not seen before. Sure, I said. I had been wanting to visit the high desert again, and this would be a good excuse.

I was asked to begin with a lecture given at the military base's chapel the evening before the debate. In the lecture I spoke about the Bible as understood by the Catholic Church, how it is the pre-eminently Catholic book, how the Church decided upon its canon, and how it ought to be interpreted by Catholics and non-Catholics alike. I had the leisure of making the positive case for the Catholic Church, anticipating objections without having to discuss them directly.

I explained that the Bible isn't so much the book of the individual Christian but the book of the Christian Church. It—particularly the New Testament—was composed by Churchmen, and it was the Church that decided that the Bible's constituent books were inspired and that other books claiming inspiration were not. It was the Church that was given authority by Christ to interpret the Bible, I said, and it was necessary that there be a reliable and consistent—even infallible—interpreter, as demonstrated sufficiently in our own time when even people of the same denomination elicit contradictory understandings from the sacred text. If Baptists often enough disagree among themselves, and if they disagree with other Protestants on many matters, doctrinal and procedural, and with Catholics on even a greater number—how can a Christian know for certain what the Bible means if he is left to his own devices?

The evening lecture was the preparatory event. The main event was the next day's debate, the topic of which was "What Is the Truth about the Catholic Church?" The debate was held on the campus of Cerro Coso Community College, a small school serving students who live within a huge district of 18,000 square miles. Many of Pastor Jim Blackburn's congregants were in the audience. He had prepped them over the preceding weeks. They expected fireworks from him, but apparently many of them got more than they could deal with. So bitter was he toward the Catholic Church during our exchange that he lost much of his following over the following days—but not, apparently, his animosity. After I departed Ridgecrest he volunteered to write a column for a neighboring town's newspaper. The editor happily gave him space, small-town newspapers always being in need of copy. The column turned out to be crassly anti-Catholic. Catholics living in the area asked the editor to yank the column. He refused, saying he liked Blackburn's opinions. The Catholics showed the column to the newspaper's advertisers, asking, "Is this the kind of newspaper you should be advertising in?" Most didn't think so, and they promptly removed their ads. A week later, Blackburn's column was gone. Not long after that so was his church, which was unable to survive with its reduced membership.

Whatever became of Blackburn I can't say. I lost track of him and sometimes have wondered where he went, whether he remained in ministry, whether his prejudices against Catholicism ever softened. I suppose not, based on probabilities. I have yet to meet a once-Catholic-now-anti-Catholic who developed a bit of a name for himself by attacking Rome and then realized that he had blundered grievously, repented, and returned to the Catholic Church. There must be some such, but I haven't met any. I have met any number of pew sitters who, originally Catholic, eventually returned to the faith of their upbringing, but professional anti-Catholics, those whose reputations were built on attacking "papistry"? No. If professional anti-Catholics who once had been Catholic rarely do an about-face, how much rarer must it be for professional anti-Catholics who had been brought up Fundamentalist and had imbibed confusions and fantasies about Catholicism from youth? Apples still don't fall far from their trees.

Jim Blackburn's church may not have survived the debate and his publishing escapade, but the ideas he expressed no doubt remained behind in Ridgecrest. People come and go while ideas, even bad ones, perdure. He was just another in the long parade of Fundamentalist preachers who found success—if only fleeting—in taking on the Church of Rome. He made anti-Catholicism his avocation, perhaps thinking thereby to attract an ever-increasing band of loyalists to his church. The attempt backfired, but not before he got off salvos that may have pleased as many as they irritated.

My opponent in this debate may have disappeared down the collective memory hole, but there remain thousands like him across the country, some shepherding small churches, others leading substantial ministries that boast presences online, on the air, and in print. There are not enough Catholic apologists even to begin a game of whack-a-mole. An anti-Catholic in one town might be countered successfully, but there remains another in the next town over. This is as true in urban as in rural areas. Most of the professional anti-Catholics I have dealt with over the years more likely might be called city slickers than country bumpkins, even if most of them sported—or at least affected—that Southern drawl commonly associated with Fundamentalist preachers, even those who never seem to have visited south of the Mason-Dixon Line.

I don't remember Jim Blackburn's voice. He may not have had the dulcet tones of Alabama, but his arguments were representative of an anti-Catholicism that may have become less common over the last few decades but that still has force and still attracts adherents by its assertiveness if not its cogency. But judge for yourself as you read the debate.

Debate Transcript
Karl Keating vs. Jim Blackburn

MODERATOR: We will begin with opening remarks of fifteen minutes by Rev. Blackburn.

BLACKBURN: Let me preface my statements. I'm trying to give you my heart a little bit, okay? I'm a man, and I'm subject to emotions. And as the moderator said, this is material that can get people riled. It can get them to speak very hotly, and I'm a person who can get speakin' hotly. But, please, if I should slip, I'll try not to, don't take it personally. I do not hate Catholics. I've spent 17 years of my life, my adult life, not as a child, 17 years of my adult life, in the Catholic Church. I do not like Catholicism. There is a difference between the teachings of the Church and the members of the Church, because I know what the teachings go to and what they have led to and where they will lead to, eventually.

Now, there are a number of reasons that you are gathered here today. Some of you are here in hopes of seeing your champion dispose of a Fundamentalist. Some of you are here hoping the Fundamentalist will dispose of the Catholic champion. Some of you are here just out of curiosity, and quite probably some of you are here to hear the truth, to discern what is the truth. There is only one truth. I'm sure it was a slip of words, last night when Mr. Keating made the statement that some things are truer and some things are less true. Of course, we know that's impossible. You either got to be true or you got to be false. You can't be truer or less true.

Another thing, I want to set the stage for this. Again, I apologize if I get a little strong in my words. I shook hands with Mr. Keating, but Mr. Keating and I are not friends. We're not even buddies, we're not chums, and we are not Christian brothers. We will treat each other civilly here today, because the issue is not Mr. Keating and Mr. Blackburn. The issue is truth. What is truth? You see, both of us cannot be right. One cannot be more right than the other. If one of us is right, the other one is totally wrong, and this is the whole issue that we're going to deal with. We are not separated brethren. Some of you don't know this, but years ago a Christian was not looked upon as a separated brethren, and a Catholic was not looked upon as a Christian. As Mr. Keating made reference last night, if you ask a Catholic, "Are you a Christian?" they'd say, "No, I'm a Catholic," because there was a great distinction between them. If we went back hundreds and hundreds of years, people who hold my position would be killed by the Catholic Church. They would never be looked upon as separated brethren. So, let's really see what the issue is today.

There are people here today, as the moderator said, who've got some prejudiced minds, and before this day is over, you'll probably be more prejudiced toward me. That's neither here nor there. The truth, when it comes forth, does one of two things. It either softens your heart or it hardens your heart. This debate is a result of some articles that were printed in the paper. And no one has come forth to refute the articles, which were referring to me, because I just gave the truth. I just gave history. I just gave the doctrines. No one came forth. I answered an invitation to come to a Bible study at a Catholic church, and I went to the Bible study. Not only did they not ask me back, but when I came the next week they were holding it somewhere else and didn't even let me know where it was at.

I don't want to get excited, but I want to tell you something. It is a reproach to any leadership that they have to hire somebody to defend their doctrines. You can come to my church, and I can open the book, and I can defend my doctrines. I can take my book, the Bible, and I can defend my doctrines. It is a reproach, and I do say a reproach, because I've been called an embarrassment to the Protestant clergy here in town. That a man [the local Catholic pastor] who leads a flock cannot teach a flock—he has to have somebody such as Mr. Keating come in and explain the doctrines to you people of the Catholic Church, so you will know what you believe. That's kind of a sad status of affairs.

Mr. Keating is very skilled in the art of words. There'll be many issues that he'll not touch upon or deal with, but he'll go off to the right or off to the left when asked a direct question. In his book *Catholicism and Fundamentalism* he touches very lightly on a major issue which to me is a focal point of the Catholic Church. In the horrible, horrendous murders that she committed throughout the Dark Ages on Christians and non-Christians alike who would not adhere to her doctrines or not adhere to the pope's supremacy.

For example, the St. Bartholomew's Day massacre in the 1600s. The only sin of the Huguenots was that they would not acknowledge the pope as the supreme authority. And so, on a Sunday when they were all in church, they were killed, massacred, the whole town was. Now, he touches lightly on this. I say lightly because of this fact. He focuses more on the erroneous data and the erroneous numbers that the historian gave. If you will take notice of how often Mr. Keating does this tactic, then you will get to see what this is all about today, what we are talking about.

How many of you here were at the seminar last night, the meeting? Great. I want to ask you a question. If I asked you to take your brains out, your mental capacity, and set it in your back pocket and sit down on it, and then open your mouth and let me shovel some stuff into you, how many of you would agree to that? Well, you know what you did last night? Exactly what I asked you to do now that you said you wouldn't do. Now, I will prove this today. I'm not making idle statements.

Last night the statement was made about the assumed vow of chastity that Mary made. Now, I want to ask you something because he made a big joke out of this. You know, like, when the Holy Spirit told Mary she was going to have a child, she says, "Well, I know that. Any Jewish girl who is going to get married is going to have a kid. That's no big thing." He said, so, she must have said, "How can this be that I know no man?" because she made a vow of chastity. Now, let me ask you something. I want you to raise your hand. I want you to be honest with me. How many of you would have married your mate if he or she had told you that they had taken a vow of chastity? One of you. Well, good. You're honest. I respect that.

Let me tell you something. Joseph wouldn't have married Mary if she'd taken a vow of chastity. But regardless, see he stopped right at verse 34 of Luke. If you will go to verse 35, you find the Holy Spirit explaining to Mary how this can be that she has not known a man and she is going to be pregnant. Because it wasn't time for her to be married yet, and she knew she couldn't commit any of those things without being put away and the Holy Spirit said, "It's simple Mary. The Holy Spirit is going to come upon you and you shall conceive." And he explained to her that she was going to get pregnant by the Holy Ghost. She didn't make a vow of chastity. Before this day is over, I'll take you through the Scriptures, show you the subterfuge that he used to disprove that she had children. And I'll show you that she did have children. I don't have to play with your mind, the Bible says it, and it says it so clearly, and so plainly—it's irrefutable.

Now, there are three types of people here today. Some of you are what we call unwittingly ignorant. You don't know that you don't know. Lots of us in this world are that way. All of us are that way about various subjects. There is a lot of things I don't know about. I'm unwittingly ignorant.

There are those who are knowingly ignorant. They know they don't know what they should know to do what they want to do, and they don't know how to go about it. This is especially true in the area of religion. Many of you people believe what you've been taught, hoping and praying that what you've been taught is true. And this man has come in to affirm to you that it is true, but he's the only assurance you have. If he is lying to you you're in a world of hurt. If I can prove to you that he has been lying to you, you have to make up your mind what's the truth here. Not, is Mr. Blackburn sharper than Mr. Keating? Did he do a better job of putting him down? That's not going to happen. I don't know enough about this man to discredit him, but I do know enough of what he's been doing to discredit the teaching.

Finally there is what we call the willingly ignorant. Those are people who say, "I don't care. I'm going to believe this way, nothing is going to change my mind. I was born a Baptist, I was born a Catholic, I was born a Mormon, I was born this or that, and I'm going to live that way, and I'm going to die that way." That's being willingly ignorant, in spite of the material that's brought before you, the facts that are brought before you, you've chosen to remain that way.

I want you to take a look at something. He said this last night, if you remember, that Mary's offering, when she came on the eighth day after Jesus was born for circumcision, was the offering to redeem the son. He used the Scripture in Leviticus to tell you that the first one has to be redeemed. Well, if you bothered to read your Bible, if you would look in Leviticus, you would find that in chapter 12:6–8, you were to bring a lamb but also you were to bring a sin offering and a burnt offering which was a pigeon or a turtle dove, because a woman who had a child was unclean. If you had no lamb, if you were from a poor family, you had to bring two pigeons or two turtle doves; one for a sin offering and one for a burnt offering. You will see, in Luke 1, that Mary and Joseph brought two turtle doves or two pigeons. Why? One was for her burnt offering because she was unclean after she had the baby, and the other was for a sin offering because they didn't have a lamb to redeem their baby. Now, that's in the Scriptures. Says it plain. I don't have to play with your mind and give you assumptions.

MODERATOR: Thank you, Rev. Blackburn. Now, we will have the fifteen minutes of opening remarks from Karl Keating.

KEATING: Last night, when I spoke at the base chapel [at Naval Air Weapons Station China Lake], I was able to give an explanation from the Bible of quite a few Catholic beliefs. I had the luxury of giving the positive side of the Catholic faith. Today, I'm on the defensive. The topic is, "What Is the Truth about the Catholic Church?" Mr. Blackburn has begun by saying there isn't much truth in it. He said a lot of other things, some of which I'll rebut at the appropriate time.

I was asked out to Ridgecrest some time ago. I was told that in this community there has been considerable anti-Catholic sentiment stated in the press, whether in letters or in ads, much of it crude, all of it wrong. Crude? Yes, such as the insult given to those of you who were at the seminar last night, the suggestion that you checked your brains at the door and that that's how the Catholic Church works. Apparently that also applies to the many Protestants who were there last night. So, if you're Protestant and you were there last night, you have to feel as insulted as the Catholics.

I've never found in the many seminars that we've given that anyone— Catholic, Protestant, Mormon, Jehovah's Witness, agnostic—checks his brain at the door. People come to find the truth, in love. They don't always agree, but that's why they're there.

Mr. Blackburn said, "There's a great reproach against the local Catholic Church, that it had to hire an outsider to come in and explain the Catholic religion." Let me make it clear. The Catholic Church doesn't pay for my organization. When we go around the country, we don't ask dioceses to fund us. We are not employees of the Church. This is precisely why we are a lay organization. If a priest were doing this, to the frequency that we are, people such as Mr. Blackburn would say, "Ah, you can't be telling the truth because you get a salary from the bishop." Couldn't the same complaint be made against a Protestant minister, getting a salary from his congregation? But I wouldn't bring up such a silly complaint.

"By their fruits you will know them." If you look around you'll find that there are no active anti-Episcopalians, no active anti-Methodists, no active anti-Quakers. No one takes out ads in the newspaper to run down these other religions. No one writes mean-spirited letters full of all kinds of exaggerations about these religions, but a lot of anger is vented at the Catholic Church, especially by ex-Catholics. It's much like the fellow who jilts his girlfriend and then, to make himself look good, bad-mouths her. We've all seen that happen. And here leaving the Mother Church, which is the Church that Jesus Christ founded, we find many people making it their profession or their avocation to spread false information about the Catholic faith. There is often little concern for the truth. What usually happens is that a partial truth is connected to a substantial fabrication. You can't get along in this country telling straight out lies. Nobody would believe that. But if you get something that's partly true, but misstate the facts, you can make headway.

I'll give you a couple of examples. Did you ever hear the story of the Catholic Church chaining the Bible so that Catholic lay people couldn't read it? It's true that the Church chained the Bible. Now, why did it do that? To keep it away from the people? No. To keep it *for* the people. Have you ever been in a telephone booth and found there a telephone directory? It's chained isn't it? Why? To keep it away from the people who want to use the telephone, or to keep it there for their use? Well, it's obvious. To keep it there for their use. In olden days, when Bibles were hand copied, a Bible would cost, in today's terms, as much as $10,000. It might be the only book in a town. It would be left on a table near the pulpit in the church for all to read but chained to that table so no one could steal it. As a matter of fact, after the Reformation in England, a country where Bibles had been chained, the Protestant Reformers ended up chaining many more than the Catholics ever had. As you see, when that charge is given by itself, it looks very black against the Catholic Church, but, when you look at the facts, you see it makes a lot of sense.

Let's go on to another topic, the Inquisition. The comment was made that millions of people, uncountable numbers of people, have been killed under the Inquisition and at other times by the Catholic Church. I deal with this question in my book. Reputable scholars will acknowledge that about three thousand people died during the centuries of the Inquisition. I'm not defending that, but that's the approximate number. Catholics and Protestants came up with that figure. I'm sure that Mr. Blackburn will not defend the fact that during early Reformation England, 800 people a year were burned at the stake for witchcraft. Of course, they weren't witches. In fact, there were many more people killed in England alone than during that entire Inquisition.

That the Protestant Reformers in England engaged in a punishment that we find horrible doesn't argue against the Protestant position. And the fact that six centuries ago some Catholics engaged in similar activities doesn't argue against the Catholic faith. All it argues for is that there are people on both sides throughout history who often lacked a sense of proportion and who sinned. Some of those people had positions of power, and they were able to exert their influence on others, even to the point of execution.

Swipes at Catholic history are a quiet acknowledgment that the Fundamentalist side has no history to talk about. Fundamentalism as a religious movement can be traced back only about a century. The name itself exists only since the time of World War I. It is not the same as Reformation Protestantism. Luther and Calvin and Zwingli would not agree with Mr. Blackburn, in his positions, and their positions are less than 500 years old. They're not the positions of the historical Christian Church. Whatever else you can say, if you say the Catholic Church cannot be the Church of Jesus Christ, you must admit that none of these upstart churches could be the one he established—unless, perhaps, you take the position of the Mormons, that his Church entirely disappeared and many centuries later popped-up with the advent of a new prophet, but I don't believe you take such a position.

It was suggested that, if one side is right, the other cannot be partially right. It must be totally wrong. That doesn't make sense. Consider, say, two political candidates, one with whom you agree entirely. Does that mean you disagree entirely with everything the other candidate professes? Very unlikely. Probably the two candidates agree on most things and differ on a few major or minor matters. Much the same when it comes to a question of truth. What I said last night, and what already has been misrepresented, is that only from the Catholic Church will you find the fullness of biblical Christianity, because it alone is the Church that Jesus Christ established. The Catholic Church always has acknowledged, not just since Vatican II, that other churches maintain truth in greater and lesser degrees.

For example, the Eastern Orthodox churches split off from the Catholic Church in 1054. The Eastern Orthodox believe the same things we do on almost every point. There are few points on which they disagree with Catholic teaching. The Catholic Church never claimed that everything those churches taught was incorrect. Not at all. That's not the Church's position. When it comes to Protestants, every Protestant church, in greater and lesser degrees, teaches truly, which is to say it teaches many things that are true but some things that are not. For example, almost every Protestant church teaches the

Trinity. When it does so, it teaches just the way the Catholic Church teaches. Some Protestant churches teach the imminent Second Coming of Christ, a theory that happens to be incorrect. To that extent, those churches teach something that is not true, but the fact that those churches teach some things that are not true doesn't mean that everything they teach is untrue.

I hope, as this afternoon continues, there's going to be a real effort to talk about truth and light, not falsehood and mere heat. Thank you.

MODERATOR: Thank you Mr. Keating. And now we will have a ten-minute rebuttal from Rev. Blackburn.

BLACKBURN: My telling the truth does not make me a bad person, folks. I didn't start this little charade, this little put-together. It was his group that put an article in the paper that said, "Jesus is not going to return," as he just said. That those of us who believe in the pre-millennial return of Christ are not teaching the truth. Well, listen, if Jesus isn't coming we have no hope. But that's what he said. And I just responded to that article, and I got called all kinds of names, and all I did was to respond to him. I have copies of every article in my scrap book if you'd like to see and find out the claims that I made. There is not a one that can't be backed up by historical fact.

Secondly, he talks about reputable scholars who will say there were only about three thousand killed. Listen, there were twenty or thirty thousand killed in one city. What do you mean three thousand killed in a span of time?

Now, let's go on a little further here. Fundamentalists can be traced back a hundred years. Can you imagine that? Folks, we can go back to Genesis 3 and find a Fundamentalist by the name of Abel who brought forth a bloody offering, and his brother tried to bring forth a bloodless offering, and God said, "I'll have nothing to do with that bloodless offering." We can trace Fundamentalism back from Noah to Abraham, from Abraham to Isaac, from Isaac to Jacob, to Israel, all the way up to Christ, and to the Church that Jesus Christ established that still carries on Fundamentalism and the truth of the Gospel.

The Catholic Church is not the Church Jesus founded. She came right in—you pick her history up—and became formalized around the year 300 or

325. You find the very thing that she did was start, again, to kill those who would not align with her. Why? Because she had the secular arm on her side, just like the Jews did. They had the Romans' secular arm on their side so they could arrest somebody and get the secular arm to kill him. It's just what happened throughout Catholic history. It's going to happen, again, one of these days when the secular arm and the religious arm unite again.

He made a statement last night, if you recall. He said that the beast in revelation was Nero. Did I misunderstand him, or did he say that? He said it was Nero, didn't he? Did you know that Nero reigned in 64 A.D.? Did you know that John, who wrote Revelation, wrote it after 64 A.D., and the Bible says there that he looked upon the beast and he was amazed. He couldn't believe that Christianity "had come to this cause." Why would John be amazed if he knew it was Nero who was already dead? Uh-uh, folks, something is wrong with that theology there.

Let me ask you something here. And I'm just going to read it to you because I know most of you don't have a Bible, or you don't have it with you, and I'm not trying to be sarcastic, but it tells us this. It says in John 1:13, if you want to take a note. It says, "which were born," speaking of men "born again." See, he says that we cannot find a born-again man before now. Let me tell you what. In 1 Peter 1:23 it says, "Who were born again, not by corruptible seed but by the word of God that liveth and abideth forever." I can take you back at least eighteen or nineteen hundred years and tell you there were born-again people there. And there still are. And they're getting them every day. And, praise God, if God opens any ears up here today, there'll be some more born again before this thing is over with.

I've been baptized, I've been confirmed, my kids were confirmed, I even took on the name when we went through confirmation. My son over there, who's with us, was confirmed. His name was John, my name is Jim. He took on the name of St. James, and I took on the name of St. John when we got confirmed. Listen, it didn't mean a thing. Neither one of us were Christians. We went through the rituals. There was a lady there last night that made a statement. She said, "I wish you could help me tell my Fundamentalist in-laws that the sprinkling baptism my baby has received is just as good as the dunking that they have in the Baptist church."

Let me tell you something: she's exactly right. The sprinkling baptism is just the same as the dunking baptism. There is no difference because neither one of them affects salvation. Neither one of them does a thing except get the baby wet. There is nothing in baptism that is sanctimonious [sic] and holy. Now, I know he is going to tell you the holy Church tells you differently, and I know she does, but there is nothing in the Scriptures that tell you that. If you would search out baptism in the Scriptures, you'd find the only ones that ever got baptized were those who believed. Folks, an eight-day-old baby cannot confess its sins and believe, and you can't confess them for him and make him believe.

If this gentleman is wrong about the teachings that he's teaching you, if they are anti-scriptural and he's teaching basically what the Catholic Church does teach—if he's wrong, you folks are in a lot of trouble, because you trusted the Church to be right. You'll not be able to stand before God one day and say, "My priest taught me, and I believed him, so it's his fault, not mine." Not when we have this book.

Before this day is over, I'm going to read you some things. You're not going to believe your ears, but it comes from the Catholic book. It comes from the Catholic Church: her beliefs, her teachings on the Word of God. You're going to have to make up your mind about it. I'm not going to do little verbal run-arounds with him. I'm concerned about presenting the truth. And if I can just get you one little truth that will make you stop and think, then I've done something. Now, I don't imply that you came in there and sat on your brains, but if you bought what he said last night, yes, you did.

MODERATOR: Thank you, Rev. Blackburn. Now we will have a ten minute rebuttal from Mr. Keating.

KEATING: So many errors, so little time.

Mr. Blackburn said the Bible says nothing about baptism doing anything to you. In my Bible, I find in the Epistle to Titus 3:5-7: "He saved us by the washing and regeneration in renewal in the Holy Spirit, so that we might be justified by his grace." What is the washing of regeneration? That's baptism. That's how Paul uses that phrase. The footnote to these verses in the Revised Standard Version, which is a Protestant translation, says that this is a brief and clear statement of the doctrine of justification. It explains that it is through baptism the soul becomes regenerated and the person becomes justified in God's sight.

Look at Acts 2:38: "Repent and be baptized every one of you in the name of Jesus Christ for the forgiveness of your sins, and you shall receive the gift of the Holy Spirit." Notice the sequence. First, repent. Then, baptism, which provides forgiveness. Then you get the Holy Spirit, which is to say God's grace. Baptism actually produces the forgiveness. That's what the Bible teaches. That's not what some Protestants teach, but they overlook certain passages of the Bible. They overlook history too. Did you catch the comment that the Catholic Church began in 325? That was it, just a bland phrase thrown out. No support. Why no support? Because there is no support. I give much of a chapter in my book to this type of Fundamentalist history. It's not enough just to make the claim.

What they say is that in 325 Christianity became legal, and then pagans rushed into the Church with their pagan ideas, corrupting it, and the Christian Church became the Catholic Church. If that were true, it would be only after 325 that we would see any alleged Christians professing distinctively Catholic beliefs, such as belief in priestly ordination, the Real Presence and the sacraments, confessing to a priest, a hierarchy in the Church, and the veneration of saints. We should expect those to come up only after 325 if this theory is true. But look at early Christian writings—I quote them at length in *Catholicism and Fundamentalism*. All these things, all these peculiarly Catholic beliefs, were believed in before 325. So the whole theory is out the window.

I know that Mr. Blackburn has my book. Perhaps he's not got to that chapter yet, but I hope he continues to read it because I explain there, for Protestants as well as Catholics, why that was the case. He said the Christianity of the New Testament really was Fundamentalism. Even Adam was a Fundamentalist, even Paul was a Fundamentalist. This is nonsense, ladies and gentlemen. Fundamentalism as a religious term denotes a particular set of beliefs that were not held, as a set, by any Christians until the last century or so.

I acknowledge that Fundamentalists have mostly truths in their religion, but they also have beliefs that are inventions of recent years. And you can't get those new beliefs from the New Testament. I notice one thing always happens. It's claimed this or that New Testament passage means the same as what Fundamentalists today teach. The connection is never drawn very well. Nothing is said of the intervening 1,900 years. Why? Because you will not find evidence, especially in the first 1,500 years, of anybody believing those things. If they were believed by the New Testament authors, we should expect them to be written about by writers in the first, second, and third centuries, but we don't find that.

Mr. Blackburn suggested that last evening I said that Jesus would not return. No, I didn't say that. Maybe he didn't tune in a few days ago when I had a radio debate with Dave Hunt, who is one of the most popular dispensational pre-millennialists in the country. Dave and I talked about this very question. The Catholic position and the majority of traditional Protestant positions since the Reformation—the position, really, of all Protestants until the last few decades—has been that Jesus would return at the end of time but that his return is not imminent. We find that people who are influenced by this dispensational school have a tendency to see the Second Coming right around the corner, and they always are trying to put America in a key place in the Book of Revelation.

Of course, America is not mentioned in Scripture. Years ago Hal Lindsey in his *Late Great Planet Earth* predicted that 1975 would be the time and that didn't happen. Then 1981 was to be the rapture and the tribulation. That didn't happen. Our Lord said we're not going to know the day or the hour. He did say he would return. The Catholic Church has always taught this, but we don't know when that will be. There is no teaching in the Bible about seven so-called dispensations. That was an invention, in the nineteenth century, by John Nelson Darby of the Plymouth Brethren denomination. His theory was unknown by Christians before his time, Catholic and Protestant. He simply made it up.

What about Mary's sin offering? Did she make the sin offering? Yes, she did. Does that mean that she committed sins? No. Perhaps Mr. Blackburn forgot what Jesus did when he commanded Peter to throw the line in the water and bring out a fish. In the mouth of that fish was a coin. "Render to Caesar," he said, "what is Caesar's, to God what is God's." Remember something else Jesus said. He did this not because he was under any obligation to do so, but he did it to conform with the law, to do all that was in the law so as not to give scandal to others. Mary, of course would do the same, because the townsfolk didn't know our Lord's status. Mary and Joseph didn't go about and say, "This is the Son of God. The conception was miraculous, the birth miraculous." No. The people thought the child was Joseph's own. Jesus and his parents were concerned to fulfill the law in all ways so as not to give scandal to anyone. And they did that. Jesus perfected the law, but he never violated the law.

Joseph wouldn't have married Mary, we're told, if he had known about her vow. The Bible doesn't say that anywhere. The Bible doesn't hint that anywhere. This is just a conclusion drawn out of thin air. If you can swallow the fact that God takes human flesh, which is the biggest miracle of all, you can swallow the very minor inconveniences that the Holy Family might have had inasmuch as it was not the average family on the block. It was not like yours or mine, with average kids. Its one child was a special child.

I'm saying that, yes, God would have provided specially for Mary. I explained last night that Mary had to be married, else, at the birth of Jesus, she would have been stoned to death because the crowds would have thought she had committed fornication or adultery. She had to be married. Is it beyond possibility that someone such as St. Joseph could have so much love for God and for Mary that he would enter into such a marriage, rather than a normal marriage? Is it possible a man could do that? I think St. Joseph, under God's grace, could do such a thing and did do such a thing.

MODERATOR: This next segment, we're going to have a cross-examination. We will begin by Rev. Blackburn asking Mr. Keating a question. He will have 30 seconds to ask the question. Mr. Keating will have two minutes to respond to the question, and then we will allow one minute rebuttal on the part of Rev. Blackburn. Then we will alternate.

BLACKBURN: I'll ask Mr. Keating, because I want this defined for my understanding. In his book—and by the way, I have read all of his book. I've got footnotes all over it. In fact, I have to buy his book from the guy who gave it to me because I've got so many footnotes in it, I can't give it back to him. I scratched his book all up, writing in it. So, if you see me purchase one, I'm not buying it because I'm interested in it, but I owe it to the guy who gave it to me.

Could you please define, because you make the statement on page 275, paragraph 3, that although the Scripture is completely silent on the Assumption of Mary, because the Church teaches it as being true, we are guaranteed that it is true? Now, I want to know what that church is that you are talking about, that guarantees it. Please don't say it's the Catholic Church. I need the definition of that church that makes these decisions, makes these theological interpretations out of where there is nothing.

KEATING: In my book, I'm referring to the Catholic Church when I use the shorthand "the Church" with a capital C. Reading my book, that's clear. This Church is precisely the Church that Jesus Christ founded. It is his body extended throughout time and history. It is that vine of which he spoke, that kingdom of which he spoke. Does it have an institutional aspect? Yes, it does. It has a human aspect, because we are members of this Church. But Jesus Christ is the ultimate head of this Church because he founded it. He granted to it his own authority and his own power, and included in that power was the power to teach truly. The Christian Church had to have that power. The one thing it had to have is infallibility because souls and their destiny were at stake, were the Church to teach in error. He gave that power to the Church because he himself had it. That power allows the Church to explain and to work out the doctrines given by Jesus to the apostles, passed on to them through Sacred Tradition down to our own time.

There may be something, such as the Assumption, which is not explicitly mentioned in Scripture, certainly not by name. Of course, the Trinity is not mentioned by name either. Does this argue against its actuality? The Bible does not claim to be a catechism or theological treatise. It wasn't even written for non-Christians. Every book of the New Testament was written for people already Christian. Much of the latter part, the epistles, were written to Christians who were having problems, confusions. The New Testament, in no place, claims to be a complete delineation of all Christian teaching.

MODERATOR: Brother Blackburn, you have one minute.

BLACKBURN: I didn't get my answer. I got the same thing I got last night. Am I right or wrong?

VOICE: You're wrong.

BLACKBURN: Okay. Then you tell me what the church is folks, because he sure didn't tell me. He just said it's the Catholic Church. What is that entity that makes the decisions that you believe? That's all I'm trying to find out. I see a segregated aspect. The pope, the priests, the bishops, the intellectuals, the theologians tell you how you can become a member of the Church. The Bible says that we are members in the body of Christ. I see that the church that Christ puts forth is led by the Holy Spirit. But we, evidently, don't have it because we have to look to them for leading, and that's anti-scriptural. The Bible tells us that the anointing that we have will teach us and that we need no man to teach us.

KEATING: My question to Mr. Blackburn is this: if Mary did have children, other than our Lord, why was there no mention of her having other children in any writing outside of and after the New Testament, by any person claiming to be a Christian, whether heretic or Catholic? Why was there no claim at all until the year 380 when Helvetius made the claim?

BLACKBURN: This is an easy one, folks. The people who conquer usually write history, so what history we have, we have the Catholic Church's because they conquered the Christians, so they burned all the books and the Bibles and the history. You've not studied what I have. Let me tell you something. Look at John 19:25, which he used last night, about the three Marys at the Cross. It explicitly gives those three Marys: Mary Magdalene, Mary the wife of Cleophas, and Mary the Mother of Jesus. You find those three Marys at the Cross with their sons James and Joseph.

Now Mr. Keating used the son James to show you the ambiguity of it that James could be the son of this or that. Why didn't he use Joseph? I'll tell you why, because every place you find Joseph in the New Testament outside the Joseph of Arimathea, Joseph the Levite, and the husband of Mary, you find this one particular Joseph with Mary the Mother of Jesus. Identification. It just seemed so natural, since her husband was named Joseph that her son would be named Joseph. She had no choice in Jesus. The angel said he is already named. But you find this Joseph in Matthew 13:53. Everywhere you find Mary, the mother of Jesus, you find her son Joseph.

KEATING: Please note that, by default, he proved my case. He did not name any writer between the time of the New Testament and the year 380 who claimed at all that Mary had children other than Jesus. There are none. He claims that all the writings were destroyed. We have lots of writings from heretics in those centuries. Lots of writings that are in libraries. They weren't destroyed. We have writings which are against every other Catholic doctrine. Why not this? The claim is that the Catholic Church destroyed the Bible. I would like to point out to Mr. Blackburn that, were it not for the Catholic Church preserving the Bible, you wouldn't have one at all.

BLACKBURN: You got that backwards. Let's not get into a shouting match. I'm about to shout myself already.

MODERATOR: Ladies and gentlemen I would like to caution you, please, to keep your comments to yourself. I know how difficult that can be, but the amens, hallelujahs, hooray brother, whatever, please keep them, because once it starts and we open the door, we could end up having a real rhubarb. That's not what we're here for. We're here to let these gentlemen explain their positions. So, I will ask you, again, please withhold any comments. Thank you. Rev. Blackburn.

BLACKBURN: I would ask Mr. Keating to explain again as he did last night, because I didn't get it clearly, when he talked about praying in vain repetitions, if he would please clarify that for me.

KEATING: My remark last night was that the reference can't be used against the rosary because the essence of what Jesus was saying happened to deal with the word "vain." I explained at some length why the prayers of the pagans, the heathens, were vain because they were praying to gods who did not exist. That's why they were vain. Jesus did not condemn repetition in prayer. In fact, he repeated prayers himself in the Garden of Gethsemane. I said, if you are to say that he condemns repeated prayer, you must conclude that he is a hypocrite, which just cannot be the case. The other thing I would point out is the claim that the prayers in the rosary are prayers you ought not to say, yet the Hail Mary is a prayer composed from clauses taken out of Scripture. The Our Father, of course, was given to us by our Lord. There is nothing in the rosary at all opposed to the Bible.

BLACKBURN: Last night he gave us a little clear example when he started talking about how they would name Jupiter and call him all kinds of names, all the names named for the gods. And they would go through all these names, and names, and names, until they finally got through all the names and then they would make the request right quick. You termed that vain repetitions. I'd like to read you something from the 1959 Catholic missal. It's called a litany. I think there must be forty different names that they put here to Jesus. And then they finally say, "Be merciful, and save us from all sins," and so forth. That's the same situation, folks. It's vain, repetitious prayers. And it's not just a prayer, it's a programmed prayer. Not something from your heart, just say this over and over and all these blessings come from it. That's vain repetition.

MODERATOR: Next question.

KEATING: Let me glide into a question that is similar to a previous one. Perhaps I can get a more direct answer. If Jesus is not present, really, in the Holy Eucharist, why was there no written opposition to this by any Christian, or alleged Christian, until the eleventh century, with Berengarius of Tours? If the Real Presence was an invention, why did no Christian write against it until that point?

BLACKBURN: We have your statement that no Christian wrote against it, but we don't know that for a fact. Just as there is much history we don't know. But I think because it was so silly nobody considered that anybody could possibly believe something like that. Look in John 4 and you'll find that Jesus is talking to the woman at the well, and the disciples come to him and ask him about getting something to eat. He said, "I have meat that you know not of and my food is to do my Father's will." Now if you want to tell me that when Jesus worked, he got physically nourished, then I'll accept that when Jesus passed the bread out, that they really ate his body.

KEATING: I think the honest person has to say there is something wrong with a religious position that works by conspiracy theory, that says, "Oh, I can't find any opposition to your point in history, or any support for mine, because it must have all been destroyed." That's somewhat like those people who go around nowadays saying, "Oh, the Holocaust never happened under the Nazis" and that all the evidence was faked. Or "Neil Armstrong never made it to the Moon, and it was all done in a studio in Hollywood." There are people who think that, but I don't think they're credible, and there are people who think that, conveniently, all the tough things disappeared in history. I don't buy that either.

MODERATOR: Your question, sir.

BLACKBURN: Would you please explain to me what an indulgence is?

KEATING: An indulgence is a grant of God's own merciful benefaction to a soul in purgatory by which that soul is cleansed more quickly of that self-love that still remains in it and that prevents it from going into heaven and enjoying the Beatific Vision. An indulgence, some people say, was a thing which prompted the Protestant Reformation. In fact it was not. True, Luther did have some complaints about indulgences in his Ninety-Five Theses, but that wasn't the cause of the Reformation. The ultimate cause for Luther and for Calvin was the question "Where does authority lie?" Not the question of indulgences.

At the time of Luther were there people who were misrepresenting what indulgences were? Yes, there were, and popes came out and condemned them. But remember in those days there were no telephones or telegraphs. Communication was slow and the papacy, really, quite weak. It was not always able to straighten out people who were going off onto their own tangents, such as Friar Tetzel in Germany. Luther had a legitimate annoyance, but I'm afraid in his case he threw out the baby with the bath water. Indulgence is a historical and true Christian doctrine. It's an example of God's great mercy to sinners.

BLACKBURN: Never did get a clarification of what an indulgence is, but I understand it, from my experience, was that if you sin you could build up things that would take care of some of your sins. So if you had 45 indulgences, they might be good for one venial sin or two venial sins. I don't know the amount, but in essence, you could buy off your sins with your good works. Now I don't know if that's what he's trying to say, but he's saying that something happens in purgatory, that if you have indulgences you evidently don't suffer as long. So they must be buying them off. And I don't find any place in Scripture where it says you can do things to build up against the sins you're going to commit.

KEATING: Scripture doesn't say and the Catholic Church has never taught you could do things to get a reservoir of brownie points so that you could have certain sins you don't have to worry about.

MODERATOR: This is your question period.

KEATING: Sorry. This is my rebuttal, is it not?

MODERATOR: No, this is your question.

KEATING: Then I will switch my question. My question is this: the Bible nowhere lists its own contents. It doesn't list the books that make it up. How does the Bible Christian know what books belong in the Bible and what books don't belong in the Bible?

BLACKBURN: Primarily, we know that the books of the Bible were canonized and, I'm not even going to get into the silly argument, the Catholic Church, they're the ones that did it, so they're responsible for the Bible. We know that's not true. God is. But, we can tell through the harmony of the Scriptures. There is not a passage from Scripture or a document in the Bible, or a book in the Bible that you can't find the harmony. This is one of the criteria when they made up and canonized those books that they wanted to be in the Scriptures: did they harmonize with the rest of the Scripture? This is the reason, and I'm sure Mr. Keating knows, but will not admit it, that the Apocrypha part of the Catholic Bible is not accepted by Bible scholars because it doesn't harmonize with the rest of the Scriptures. It actually conflicts with it. But, the books are made up by study of the Scriptures, affirming that they are God's word by the authors who were the apostles, and the harmony of it. We know that there was a book or a letter written by Paul to the Corinthians. There was a third letter to the Corinthians, but for what reason God chose not to have it stay in existence or have it put into the Scriptures, I don't know. God did that. You see, God has said that he will preserve the Scriptures, his word.

Now, I note Mr. Keating uses that to say that's the Church. But the issue there is in Isaiah 51:19, I believe: "The word that I put in your mouth and my spirit will not depart forever from your children's mouth," and so forth and so on. God preserved his word. And if you would look through the

Scriptures under preservation, you would discover God has done exactly that because he's promised it over and over. It's not in mankind's ability to preserve God's word. We're so full of errors and mistakes. So you have to look at the harmony of it and then you'll know which books are which. It's easy to do, if you want to study. But I know it's a scholarly job and most laymen don't do that. I tell you this much, don't even believe what I'm saying today without studying it out for yourself. I ask none of you to believe me on my word.

KEATING: The problem with the harmony theory is that it simply won't work. Take, for example, the Didache, the teaching of the twelve apostles, written about the year 70. Nothing in it is objectionable to Protestants. Yet it was not put in as an inspired book of the Bible. It harmonizes perfectly. Take, for example, the book of Philemon, the epistle to Philemon. Read it for yourself. You'll find almost no doctoral content in it. Why would somebody put that in—because it harmonizes, because it simply doesn't contradict? In that case, you would have put in all sorts of other books. No, there had to be some judge to make the decision which books belong in the Bible. That was the Church that Christ established.

MODERATOR: Your question, Rev. Blackburn.

BLACKBURN: In your book you use the theologian Tertullian five times. Four of those times you use him as an authoritative reference to the sign of the cross, doctrinal issues or the development of doctoral issues, the papacy, and so forth and so on. But on the fifth issue, it comes to him refuting the perpetual virginity of Mary, and you dismiss him as a heretic. How can that be, that he can support you on one end but he can't on the other?

KEATING: When I refer to Tertullian—for example, mentioning the sign of the cross—I did it to show that there were Christian writers saying that that was already an old custom, to show that you can't very well go about saying, "Oh, this was invented in the Middle Ages." Tertullian did not write everything accurately. Others did not write everything accurately. My point in quoting Tertullian and many other early writers is just to show these things were believed by somebody at that time, as disproof of the notion that they were invented many centuries later. It's a very simple thing. Look in the book. Look at the references to him and to others. That's all I was doing, to show that the notion that the Church started after 325 just falls apart.

MODERATOR: One-minute rebuttal.

BLACKBURN: I can only say this: if I cannot accept the man's testimony because his credentials are bad, I cannot use him as a witness.

KEATING: Let's go back, if we may, to the question of repetitious prayer. Mr. Blackburn, you said we ought to avoid prayers, such as litanies which are praises of Jesus, because they are programmed. They are set prayers, which they are. Are we also, therefore to avoid the Our Father, which is a programmed set prayer?

BLACKBURN: There are so many doctoral issues set forth in the Our Father that you could say it, just one aspect of it, and pray on that for a long time. The disciples said, "Teach us how to pray." They knew how to pray. They're not asking for the instructional manual. They're talking about how do we revere God in our prayers. He said, "well you start off with 'hallowed be thy name,'" because if the name isn't hallowed, then you can't come into God. And it goes on, "We're pleased that your kingdom come, and that it be done here on Earth as it is in heaven." And it's a plea, again, for God to come and reign and rule. It's not a vain repetitious prayer, and that isn't our Lord's Prayer, by the way. Our Lord's Prayer you'll find in John 17. This is just a prayer that Jesus instructed them on how to pray. The Lord's Prayer is in John 17. It's not vain, repetitious.

KEATING: Just as we can meditate on the words within the Lord's prayer, we can meditate on any set prayer and its phrases in praise of God. And that's what we ought to do. I guess Mr. Blackburn agrees with me that there are programmed, set prayers that are good. That's a wonderful admission on his part.

MODERATOR: Question, Mr. Blackburn.

BLACKBURN: You tell me that the pope cannot make an infallible statement, *ex cathedra*, infallibly in the Church, because the Holy Spirit prevents him from doing such. But in 352 you had Pope Liberius, and when he was deposed, Felix took his place, and both of these adhered to and swore to the doctrine of the Arians, who taught that Christ was created and was lower than the Father.

KEATING: You got the facts wrong. The document that Liberius signed was written by Semi-Arians. That's different from Arianism. The Semi-Arians had an ambiguous phrase, not a heretical phrase. Liberius did it under coercion, political coercion. He was arrested and would not be released until he signed it, and the Catholic Church has always taught the pope does not teach infallibly unless he teaches freely. If he is tortured into signing something, it doesn't count. That's the same rule we have in courts of law in this country. Even if it had been a free signing, he was not teaching publicly something for all Christians to hold. Liberius, as I mentioned in my book, is one of only three potential cases to argue against papal infallibility. As I explain, they all collapse.

If popes have been teaching fallibly for all these centuries, you would think that they would come up with exactly contrary positions. Some pope would teach, for example, that the Resurrection never happened. That's what you need to show to disprove papal infallibility, but you can't show anything like that. You'd expect it out of normal human beings not under the protection of the Holy Spirit, but in fact the popes, in their official teachings, have never contradicted one another.

BLACKBURN: The Bible tells us in Isaiah that we are to compare Scripture with Scripture, line upon line, precept upon precept when we study the

Scripture. It is not for us just to grab something up. You can reason things together. You can point them out. You can't take things out of context. This gentleman took the Church of Christ's position on baptismal regeneration in Acts 2:38: "Be baptized and repent for the remission of sin." There is a counter verse to that, in Luke, where two men are healed from leprosy, and they start going back and Jesus says, he says, "Go to the priest and make an offering for your healing." Now, if we take the word "for" in that context, then it means go make an offering so you can be healed, but he was already healed. The context of the Scriptures is go make an offering to the priest because of your healing. It's the same thing in Acts. You repent because of your sins, and you get baptized because you repented. Baptism never washes away. Look at Ephesians 5:25-26. It says, "He gave himself for the Church and he cleansed it by the washing of the water of the Word." You get it from studying the Scriptures, comparing Scripture with Scripture, not coming with these things, "Well, the Scripture doesn't talk about this."

KEATING: Even if you say we must compare one passage with another—which, of course, you should do—you're still are left with making an interpretation. No book can interpret itself. Interpretation is handled only by a person, an agent. You must do it with your mind and your heart. The Fundamentalist interprets the Bible on his own, and within Fundamentalism we find people at odds with one another. Post-millennialist against pre-millennialists and post-tribulationists—all these kinds of things. They're all born-again Fundamentalists. They disagree because they tried to do it on their own without a guide.

MODERATOR: Next question. We'll have time for two more. One from each of you.

BLACKBURN: Sir, you made a statement last night that it was okay to make statues, graven images. The Bible specifically says that you are not to make unto yourself a graven image. So would you reconcile how you can make a graven image when the Bible forbids it?

KEATING: What is a graven image? An image of some created thing worked by human hands. That's all it is. I mentioned that God told the Israelites in Exodus 25 to make images to adorn the Ark. He told them to make statues. It was commanded by God and therefore approved by God. I take God's word for it.

MODERATOR: Rebuttal.

BLACKBURN: I wish you really would. Now, God said to make the image, and if you'll look in Hebrews 8:5, you'll find that the Temple was a shadow of things in heaven, and no one got to go in and worship the images, or bow to those images, or do anything to them because the high priest went into the Holy of Holies. Nobody else could go in. They were an example or a type of the mercy seat where Jesus, when he ascended to heaven, sprinkled his blood on the mercy seat. But we are not allowed to make images or bow down before them. Now, I spent 17 years in the Catholic Church, and I've walked down the aisle and seen Jesus hanging on the cross, with the statue of the Virgin Mary, and bent down to do my genuflection, folks. The Bible says, no. Now, if he's going to take the Bible's word on it, he ought to practice what he preaches.

MODERATOR: Final question, Mr. Keating.

KEATING: I'd like to know why anti-Catholic Fundamentalists are so reluctant to look at and to appeal to early Christian history and writings? Why do they shy away from them and never use those writings to bolster their own position?

BLACKBURN: If you have a pencil and paper, write down these verses: Deuteronomy 4:2, Proverbs 30:5-6, Revelation 22:18-19, and Matthew 4:4. The Bible says, "Add not to the word, take not away from the word." It says it three times, and then it adds this: when the Devil was testing Jesus, Jesus said, "Man shall not live by bread alone but by"—and I'll paraphrase Mr.

Keating here—"some of the words in the Bible." No, the Scripture says, "Every word that proceedeth forth from the mouth of God." If it's not in the Scriptures, it's not legit. If you have to pervert the Scriptures to make it fit, it's not legit. I don't need anybody's Christian writings. I have the testimony and the word of God himself. Why do I need some man to tell me, "Well, he did this and he did that," even though it's contradictory to the word of God? I don't need that, nor will I practice it.

MODERATOR: One-minute rebuttal.

KEATING: I notice that you were free in making allusions to later Christian history and writings. Are those adding to the word of God? No. No Catholic claims that the early Christians, in the first, second, third centuries, wrote things that are being added to the word of God, when we merely appeal to them for evidence of what the early Christians believed. What did the first Christians understand the Gospel to be all about and to teach? That's a good way to find out the proper interpretation. But if we close our minds to that, put blinders over our eyes, we are cheating ourselves, and we are liable to come up with the wrong conclusions. That happens a lot with Fundamentalism.

MODERATOR: We're going to have now a 30-minute question-and-answer period. The first question will be to Rev. Blackburn. Then we will alternate. Rev. Blackburn will have two minutes to give an answer. Then Mr. Keating will have a one minute rebuttal period. We will continue like this for 30 minutes.

QUESTIONER: Rev. Blackburn, you stated that there is no problem with an individual interpreting Scripture on his own. I ask you this then: as of 1500, there was one Church, the Catholic Church. Since then the Bible's been turned loose into everyone's hands. Now, we've got over three thousand Christian churches, all stating to be the one and only Church. I'll say three thousand even. That means two thousand nine hundred and ninety-nine say you're wrong. Seems to me that your theory has some fallacy to it.

BLACKBURN: Now, there can be three thousand, there can be ten thousand churches that say they are following Christ, and that's very possible. You see that Paul wrote to the churches in Galatia, he wrote to the churches at Corinth, the churches in Macedonia. He went to a number of churches. They are individual, local bodies, they're all autonomous. Nobody has a rule over anybody. If you want to check this out, look in Acts 15, where they have the big convention about what should we do, because some of the people were teaching that you had to be circumcised and keep the Law in order to be saved. The apostles got together and the rule went out, that they should abstain from meat, from blood, and from fornication. No other things. The churches are free to rule their own. There is no hierarchy, there's no ruling political body that tells you what to do. They can follow after Christ.

They are not the church of Christ per se, in that they are the only entity, such as the Catholic Church puts herself. But they're all churches that are following the Scriptures. They're not all known as Baptists, as Mr. Keating has referred to. Some were called the Anabaptist, some were called the Albigensians, some were the Donatists, some were the Montanists, some were the Waldensians, some were Huguenots, some were Paulicians, but it was the doctrines that they followed, and contrary to his word, you can trace them all the way back to Christ's time from today. You cannot trace the doctrines that are being taught today erroneously back to the apostles. The apostles never baptized babies. The apostles never taught baptismal regeneration. The apostles—

QUESTIONER: You didn't answer my question.

BLACKBURN: Okay. I'm sorry. I did not. The question was the amount of churches. There can be three thousand, there can be ten thousand churches that are following Christ.

MODERATOR: Karl Keating has a one minute rebuttal.

KEATING: The word church is used in two different senses in the New Testament. In Matthew 16:18 our Lord says, "Thou art Peter, and upon this rock I will build my Church," singular. He founded one Church. But Paul writes to many churches. What does that mean? Did Jesus found more churches? No. The Church, itself, is manifested in local communities of Christians. That's all it means. Today we use the term "church" for the actual building. It could be used in many senses. The fact is that these heretical groups that Mr. Blackburn listed did not all teach the same. The Albigensians believed in ritual suicide and that fornication was permissible, not immoral, and that marriage and the body are evil. You can't trace those teachings back to Jesus.

MODERATOR: Question for Mr. Keating.

QUESTIONER: Should Protestants and Catholics living today strive to keep all of the Ten Commandments including the Saturday Sabbath?

KEATING: Catholics and Protestants, of course, should do their utmost to maintain God's commandments, but it is not a doctoral matter what day of the week we worship God. In the book of Acts we find that the first Christians are meeting on what we call Sunday, when the Jews were meeting on what we call Saturday, the Sabbath, the last day of the week. This is purely a disciplinary thing. The early Church changed it. There was no complaint about it until many centuries later, at the time of the Reformation, when some Sabbatarian sects came up, and now we see, for example, the Seventh-day Adventists who say, "No, you have to go back to Saturday because that's what the Bible teaches." Well, that's strange because we had more than a millennium of Christians who did not teach that at all. As I said, it is merely a disciplinary decision as to what day of the week one is to worship God corporately, socially, in union. It could have been any, but the early Christians chose Sunday to be that day.

BLACKBURN: In the New Testament, all of the commandments are reiterated except the one to keep the Sabbath holy. If we study the Scriptures, we find that Jesus is our rest. In him we find rest, the Sabbath. He told the religious leaders that I am the Lord of the Sabbath and the Sabbath was made for man, man wasn't made for the Sabbath. Worship, mostly, is on Sunday. If people want to worship on Saturday, fine, as long as it doesn't become an issue of salvation, and some people make it an issue of salvation, that if you don't keep that commandment you can't be saved. That's not scriptural.

MODERATOR: Question for Rev. Blackburn.

QUESTIONER: Rev. Blackburn, you said that you were a Catholic for 17 years and this was not a childhood Catholicism. Would you please tell us the age at which you became a Catholic, the year that this happened and where it happened and what caused you to leave?

BLACKBURN: I became a Catholic in 1959 when I married my wife, who was born in a Catholic home, raised in a Catholic home, and attended Catholic schools, and so I converted to her religion. I had been raised as a Baptist. And I'll tell you why I converted to her religion, because a priest told me that as long as you don't over-indulge you don't sin. I liked to drink and I liked to party, and I liked to do all those things, and he told me that you can do anything you want to do as long as you don't do it to excess. So I converted to Catholicism. In 1977, we had a tragedy in our home that the Church could not meet. It could not heal, could not help. I found Jesus Christ, and so did my wife, and he healed, and he helped. From that day forth I started examining. It didn't matter to me what I believed because I had the Church taking care of me. She sheltered me, she took care of me and made sure that she was going to get me out of purgatory if I was bad. She was going to do all these things for me, and then I got to studying and discovered she couldn't do a thing for me, but Jesus could. That's the reason that I abide him today.

KEATING: Naturally, I can't rebut an individual's conversion story. I just want to refer, if I may, to one point he brought up about what the priest had said. To the extent I understand it, the priest was correct. Such things as drinking alcohol or smoking or gambling are not, in and of themselves, sins unless taken to extremes. Our Lord himself drank. He was accused of being a drunkard. He made water into wine after the guests had finished off the usual quantity of wine. Everybody had had some. He made more wine for the wedding. He was accused of being a drunkard because he was seen drinking wine. The Bible teaches is that these are good things if used properly, but anything can be misused.

QUESTIONER: I think you were right when you said that the main issue in the Reformation was authority, not necessarily grievances and indulgences and things like that. And I think the main issue of this debate is: are Catholics really going to heaven? Are Baptists really going to heaven? That's the issue, right? We all want to go to heaven. We don't want to go to hell. The question is, in Acts 2:38, you said repentance preceded the baptism. How does a two-week-old baby repent? If baptism is necessary to save you after repentance, then Catholics haven't been saved if they haven't been properly dunked.

KEATING: God does not require of us what is beyond our natural capacity. He does not require positive affirmation by a young child below the age of reason, what the Fundamentalists would commonly call "the acceptance of Christ as Lord and Savior." A young child cannot make such an affirmation, just as he cannot sin because he cannot use reason yet. Since the child is not able to do those kinds of things, the requirement is not held up to him. Jesus said, "Let the children come to me," and in John 3:5, he said, "You must be baptized. You must be born again of water and the Holy Spirit." That's baptism, and it applies to children. As I explained at some length last night, infant baptism is perfectly permissible and was practiced by the earliest Christians. There is no recorded complaint about it, and it in no way contradicts the Bible.

BLACKBURN: Again, studying the Scripture with Scripture, precept upon precept, you find that being born of water and the spirit refers back to Ephesians 5 where he washed him through the washing—he made him clean

89

through the washing of the word. Born again by the infallible word. If baptism really regenerated people, we would wonder why John baptized all those people. In Acts 19 Paul came upon a bunch of people and all they had known was the baptism of John, and they weren't Christians. Paul preached the gospel to them, and they got saved, and it tells us that they received the Holy Spirit. If baptism had regenerated, Paul wouldn't have had to do that.

QUESTIONER: You mentioned a while ago that if we sin, we can confess it to the priest. In 1 Timothy 2:5 it says, "For there is one God and one mediator between God and man, the man Christ Jesus." And he also said, in 1 John 1:9, "If you confess your sins, he is faithful and just to forgive us our sins and to cleanse us from all unrighteousness." And also, in Matthew 11:28, he said that.

KEATING: He also said in John 20:22-23, to the apostles, "Whose sins you shall forgive, they are forgiven, whose sins you shall retain, they are retained." He gave his own authority to the apostles. He delegated his authority as principal to agent. That's in the Bible. There is no contradiction there. The priest does not forgive sins out of his own human power. He forgives sins only because Jesus has granted him the power. He could not do so otherwise. If you say no to that, you reject what Jesus says in John 20:22-23. There is no way around that.

BLACKBURN: That's a tough piece of Scripture. I realize that. But when we look at the history of it and we look at the facts of the Scripture in that this man that was supposed to be the rock, Jesus called Satan and told get behind me, God never entrusted in man the power to forgive sins. He never has. In John 9 you'll find that it is stated emphatically that only God can forgive sins.

QUESTIONER: Question for Mr. Blackburn. You stated that the Blessed Mother, Virgin Mary, whatever you care to refer to her as, is nothing more than an ordinary woman. Luke 1 states that Elizabeth, filled with the Holy Spirit, said, "Blessed art thou among women and blessed is the fruit of thy womb, Jesus." In that same chapter, it says, "All generations shall call me blessed," referring to the Blessed Mother. Could you state how you could possibly say that she's just an ordinary woman?

BLACKBURN: In the book of Judges we have a story of a gal by the name of Deborah who went to war. Deborah was called "blessed are you above all women." Not "blessed among, but blessed above all." Now we need to clarify something here in that Mary was blessed among women because she was chosen of God to bring his Son into this world. That would be a blessing any woman would love to have bestowed upon her, but she wasn't blessed because she was somebody. God could have used any virgin, and the only reason he used a virgin was because he prophesied that his Son would be born of a virgin. Had he prophesied his Son would be born of a 68-year-old grandma, he would have been born of a 68-year-old grandma, and they would have said of her, "Blessed are you among women, because you have given birth to the Savior." No merit on Mary's part whatsoever.

KEATING: When we look at the Greek, we see that the word used to describe Mary implies plentitude or fullness of grace, not just that she was a lucky gal because she got to give birth to the Savior. This is a quality inhering in herself, a condition of her own being—full of grace to the fullest extent possible for a creature. That's what the Greek implies, and that's what Christianity has understood consistently. Appeal, for example, to the Eastern Orthodox churches. They broke off, as I said, in 1054, but they teach this exactly.

QUESTIONER: Sir, please correct me if I heard you wrong, but I heard you say that there was an authority about the graven images from God. But in Exodus 20:4-5, it reads, "Thou shalt not make unto thee any graven image, or any likeness of anything that is in heaven above or that is in the earth beneath or that is in the water under the earth." And verse 5, "Thou shalt not bow down, exalt them nor serve them, for I, the Lord thy God, I am a jealous God." Which is correct—what you have told us, that there was an authority from the Lord about graven images, or what we just read?

KEATING: You're putting the wrong spin on Exodus 20:4. Look at Exodus 25:18. That's where God told the Israelites to put statues on top of the Ark of the Covenant. He said, "Make them." The Ark, of course, was the object in which the Ten Commandments were kept. In the Temple that the Jews had in Jerusalem the priests would prostrate themselves in the Holy of Holies, bowing down before things created by men. In your wallet you probably have pictures of your family. Those are graven images. I don't think you would make Exodus 20:4 so extreme as to say those are condemned by God. No, what God says is, "Make no graven image that you then worship." In Exodus 25 he told the Israelites, "Put these statues on the Ark." They didn't worship the statues, which reminded the Israelites of God.

The verses can be put together, if you understand their proper meaning. If you take one verse alone, and then take off on a tangent, you will misunderstand what God is saying to his people. You have to take the whole together, and then you'll see that there is nothing wrong with making a statue or other graven image. What's wrong is worshipping a false god or worshipping that very statue. That's idolatry, and that's condemned.

BLACKBURN: I'm not going to ask you how many of you have bowed down before the Virgin Mary and prayed to her. I'm just going to tell you there are words in those commandments that say, "Thou shall not make unto you any graven images." God meant exactly that. Not make unto you any graven image. Something that you're going to look upon and think has got some kind of spiritual powers. That's totally anti-Scripture. And you'll find if you look in Romans 1 that that's exactly what people with the mentality of the religious have done. It says they started worshipping the creature rather than the Creator.

QUESTIONER: Mr. Blackburn, I wonder if you believe in the healing of the body, of going to the elders of the Church or others to be prayed over, perhaps with laying on of hands and that through God's power healing can come down. If you do believe in that for the body, why can't you believe in the healing of the soul through God's power by going to the priest to pray with you?

BLACKBURN: In James 5 we have what this lady was discussing, the scriptural admonition and the way to deal with people who are sick. The elders of the church pray over them, heal them, pray for them, so forth and so on. I have no problems with that whatsoever. That's scriptural as can be. The healing that this lady is talking about—correct me if I'm wrong—is referring to the Virgin Mary, being pure and whole.

VOICES: Forgiveness of sins.

BLACKBURN: Forgiveness of sin. Oh, the priest? Well, first of all, if he didn't die for my sins, he sure as heck can't forgive them. If we give this man the power to forgive as implied there, he also has the power to withhold. Now, with that power to withhold comes tremendous power. In all clear honesty, if I had the keys, I don't know if I wouldn't own the world also because human nature—the Bible tells us in Jeremiah, that the heart is deceitful above all things. God would never trust man, carnal man, with the right to deny or open up the gates of heaven to another man. That's where corruption comes in and has come in. You could sell that power. Look in Acts 8 at Simon the sorcerer. That's exactly what he wanted.

KEATING: I see some residual Catholicism here. Mr. Blackburn is supporting the basis for the sacrament of the anointing of the sick, in James 5, also known as the last rites. I'm glad to hear that. I see no problem at all in granting that God has given human beings his own powers to heal bodily and also given them power, his own power, to heal spiritually.

QUESTIONER: I address this question to Mr. Keating. Sir, you did mention earlier that Mary is sinless. How could you explain in Luke 1:47 when she said, "My spirit rejoices in God my Savior"? And Romans 3:23 would say, "For all have sinned and fall short of the glory of God"?

KEATING: Even Fundamentalists say that young children cannot sin. Thus what was being said there by Paul wasn't applied to all human beings. It wasn't applied to young children. They weren't mentioned by exception. Mary didn't have to be mentioned by exception either. We say Mary was immaculately conceived, that the stain of original sin was not on her soul as it was on our souls. Here's the difference. You have a pit. A man is going along, he falls in. You save him by pulling him out after he falls in. Another man comes along, and before he falls in you grab his sleeve to prevent him falling in. In each case, a man has been saved—one after the fact, the other by anticipation. Mary was saved from the stain of original sin by anticipation. The rest of us have been saved from the stain of original sin at baptism, after the fact. She is saved by Jesus Christ just as we are. It came at the moment of her conception; for us it comes some time later.

BLACKBURN: The words of our Lord Jesus Christ concerning the exalted position of his mother: "And it came to pass as he spake these things a certain woman of the company lifted up her voice and said unto him, 'Blessed is the womb that bore thee and the paps that thou has sucked.'" But he said, "Yea, rather blessed are they that hear the word of God and keep it." Do you understand that Mary was conceived in sin, her children were conceived in sin? If she had an immaculate conception then also Joseph was born without sin too. Then Joseph's children were born without sin and on and on it goes. You're missing the fulfillment of Scripture, and you are taking Christ out of the picture. Christ wasn't holy because he was born of a virgin. He was holy because he's God's Son.

MODERATOR: This will be our last question.

QUESTIONER: You mentioned earlier that Catholic doctrines actually started earlier than the third century. Now I agree. In fact, we find confession to a priest, the worship of the queen of heaven, and even God in the bread all in Babylon, which God harshly condemned throughout Jeremiah, in the Old Testament. So what's your response that God already condemned these practices, and now they are found in Roman Catholicism?

KEATING: You have the facts wrong. Some Unitarians claim, "Oh, the Babylonians taught three gods therefore they taught the Trinity and therefore it's not a Christian doctrine. No, the Babylonians never taught the Trinity. This is the alternative Fundamentalist history, the Babylonian one. The standard Fundamentalist history concerns the year 325. In this Babylonian alternative, everything came from Babylon. It's a wonderful theory. It's like some people said, "All the evil in the world comes from Jews who are bankers," but that's not factual. This Fundamentalist theory concerning Babylon is simply not historical, not factual.

BLACKBURN: There's a tremendous book out by [Alexander] Hislop called *The Two Babylons*. Read it for yourself, and you decide for yourself. It's the most exhaustive documented work. It's the driest material you'll ever read, but you'll just see her. She just sits right in the middle of it, the Catholic Church.

MODERATOR: Thank you gentlemen. We will now have a closing statement, first by Rev. Blackburn for fifteen minutes and then by Mr. Keating.

BLACKBURN: Now I'm going to read to you, and what I'm going to read to you is Catholic material—Catholic words, the Church's teachings, whatever else you want. I don't want to discolor this, and I'm not trying to fault this man, okay? But Mr. Keating said earlier that the Catholic Church is the only Church with unity. Now, this is an article out of the *Los Angeles Times*, and it says right here, "Gay Priests, a Dilemma for Catholics." And this gentleman in the article finally says, "I cannot personally hold the Church's teaching on homosexuality, teach it or preach about it, I have to be disobedient in that regard." We know that there are nuns and other women of the Church who are fighting for birth control. They're fighting for the priesthood. It's not a church in unity by any means.

But now, let me ask you something. What would it matter if Mary was a perpetual virgin? What effect would it have on the Scriptures? None whatsoever. She wasn't. But I want to show you that she's more than highly venerated, and I want to read from Pope Pius IX, who was pope from 1846 to 1878. Now, I'm just quoting, folks. Don't get mad at me. "God has committed to Mary the treasury of all good things in order that everyone may know that through her are obtained every hope, every grace, and all salvation, for this is his will that we obtain everything through Mary." Pope Leo XIII: "As no man goes to the Father except through his Mother." St. Alphonsus Liguori in the *Glories of Mary*: "Mary is called the Gate of Heaven because no one can enter that blessed kingdom without passing through her."

This deals with what the Church really believes about the Bible. And what I'm going to do is quote exactly what the Church says. I'm quoting it out of this book, which is the New American Bible Catholic edition. And it starts out right here. This is in the Dogmatic Constitution on Divine Revelation from Vatican II. And it says this. "Those divinely revealed realities which are contained and presented in Sacred Scripture have been committed to writing under the inspiration of the Holy Spirit." I agree with that. "For Holy Mother Church holds that the books of both the Old and the New Testament, in their entirety, with all their parts, are sacred because written under the inspiration of the Holy Spirit. They have God as their author." I agree with all that. "Therefore, since everything asserted by the inspired authors or sacred writers must be held to be asserted by the Holy Spirit, it follows that the books of Scripture must be acknowledged as teaching solidly, faithfully, and without error that truth which God wanted put into the sacred writings for the sake of our salvation." It quotes 2 Timothy 3:16-17, "All Scripture is given by inspiration of God."

Then it goes on. "The plan of salvation foretold by the sacred authors is found as the true word of God in the books of the Old Testament. These books, therefore, written under divine inspiration, remain of permanent value. God, the inspirer and author of both Testaments, wisely arranged that the New Testament be hidden in the Old Testament and the Old Testament be made manifest in the New." Tremendous words. It's true. "The Church has always and everywhere held and continues to hold that the four Gospels are of apostolic origin. Holy Mother Church has firmly and with absolute constancy held and continues to hold that the four Gospels faithfully hand on what Jesus Christ really did and taught until he was taken into heaven. Besides the four Gospels, the canon of the New Testament also contains the epistles of St. Paul and the other apostolic writings composed under the inspiration of the Holy Spirit by which, according to the wise plan of God, those matters which concern the Lord are confirmed."

Folks, I don't disagree with a word of that. Now, let me read you something else and see if you applaud. "In the congregations, mainly in the cities around the Mediterranean, they found scores of narratives about Jesus. The writers took these narratives and frequently remolded and refashioned them to bring out the lesson they wanted to teach. Moreover, some of these accounts may be adaptations of similar ones in the Old Testament. In the conflict stories of the Gospel, it is usually"—get this—"Jesus who is in conflict with his opponents, those Jews who did not believe in him." Was Jesus involved in these conversations? Did he answer exactly as related in the Bible?

Listen to these words. "It is not certain. Since we do not possess a biography of Jesus, it is difficult to know whether the words or sayings attributed to him are written exactly as he spoke them." Another question is, did Jesus sit on a hill and give the beatitudes? Now, listen to this. "The ancient tradition that the author of the Gospel of Matthew was the disciple and apostle of Jesus named Matthew is untenable. The unknown author, whom we shall continue to call Matthew for the sake of convenience—" blah, blah, blah.

Then we go into the Gospel of John. "Although tradition identified this person"—and Mr. Keating loves tradition—"the writer of the Gospel of John as John the son of Zebedee, Jesus' apostle, most modern scholars find that the evidence does not support this." But I just read that she has always held onto this and still does. Now, let's go on with this further. "Most scientists hold that the human species have developed somehow from lower kinds of life." That's called evolution, for those who don't grasp it. "This knowledge helped Christians to re-think the how of God's creative activity and to understand that Genesis chapters 2 and 3 are not a lesson in anthropology but an allegory." Now that's what your church believes. And if that's what you want, great. That's strictly up to you. And if you believe that we evolved, well, that's too bad for you, because the Word of God stands firm today that he created us, and I don't have an ancestor that came from a monkey or an elephant or anything else, and I'm sorry about you. Now, if you want to honor the Virgin Mary, just go right ahead.

Now, I just want you to know this. I believe and I know that the truth was presented to you today, and Jesus said, "Do you hate me because I've told you the truth? Why are you trying to kill me?" And they didn't know what to do. But that's what they were trying to do because he told them the truth. And he said, "He that rejecteth my words and receive not me has one that judgeth him. My words in the last days will be used to judge him." You've heard enough today to know the truth. Now, you can keep your mind closed, you can refuse to look this up and study it out for yourself, you can trust in Mr. Keating, you can trust in your priest, you can trust in the Church, that Mary was assumed up into heaven and that she made this vow that is non-scriptural. You can have all of these if you want, but I want you to understand you've made a god out of Mary.

In chapter nine of his book, pages 121 through 125, Mr. Keating deals with inspiration of the Bible. We can go back through prophetical observations or fulfillments, archeological facts, scientific data, historical facts, and we can prove that the Scriptures are true. When they dug up the Dead Sea Scrolls, they found out that the book of Isaiah that they found, except for, I believe, three punctuation marks, was identical to the book of Isaiah in the King James Bible. We can go through and validate these things. If I had, for instance, an orange here in my hand, I'd say, "this orange speaks for itself, it's an orange." We have the taste of the orange, the color of the orange, the texture of the skin. The orange has evidences within itself that it is an orange. If it said I'm a lemon, we could say, "Oh, no you're not." We can prove it. The Bible has evidences to support itself, that it is what it says it is, the inspired word of God, the infallible word of God. Mr. Keating says, "No, no, no, we do the same thing as you do, to certain extents, but then we stop and we say that the Church says it's the inspired word of God. And now that the Church has said it, you can use it. But until the Church says it's the inspired word of God, it's not inspired." Folks, that's like saying this orange here is an orange, and you know it, but you cannot believe it is an orange until I tell you that it is an orange. You can't weigh the evidences within it yourself. You have to accept my word.

Now, let me show you what they've done with that. First of all, God said, "All Scripture is given by inspiration of God." God said it's inspired. Mr. Keating says the Church says it's inspired. Don't believe God, believe the Church. Jesus said, "I am the way, the truth, and the life." The Church says, "No, you can only attain salvation through me!" So God's out, and the Church is in. Jesus is out, and the Church is in. The Bible says that it is the Holy Spirit that guides us and teaches us into all truth. They say, no, the Church does it. So now they've kicked out God, they've kicked out Jesus, and they've kicked out the Holy Spirit. The Trinity doesn't remain, but who does? Mary?

Let me show you how great Mary is, while I've still got time here. It tells us this in a 1919 Carmelite devotion to the Virgin Mary. It says right here about their scapular that if you are wearing this little scapular with a picture of Mary on it, she'll pull you out of purgatory on the first Saturday after you die. Isn't that something? It's totally unreal. I can't believe this. It says, "To whom should they turn but to Mary who never forsakes her children?" I got news for you. Mary may be your mother, she's not mine. Let me give you one other thing. This is real bad, I know, but I'm kind of a bad guy. When you call Mary the Mother of God, the daughter of the Son, that makes an incestuous relationship. The Mother of God, the daughter of the Father. That's an incestuous relationship. When you call her the Queen of Heaven, she can't be the Queen unless she's married to the King. And there is another incestuous relationship because Jesus is the King. Although you cannot find this in the Scripture, I know the holy Church says it's so, so it must be so. I'll tell you what I'll do. I'll take the book, you take the Church.

KEATING: I agree that the truth was presented to you this afternoon, and I'll continue to present it. The Catholic interpretation of the Bible can be found all the way back historically. Fundamentalist interpretations are, historically speaking, novelties. They only go back a few centuries at best.

Look at such things as the Bible-alone theory, entirely unknown before the Reformation. The absolute assurance of salvation, entirely unknown before that point. Adult-only baptism, some ways into the Reformation. The rapture, even newer than that, from nineteenth-century dispensationalism. The notion that the Second Coming of our Lord is imminent, within our own lifetimes, and that we can figure out the dates. All inventions.

You might have heard about a man named Edgar Whisenant who published a book called *88 Reasons Why the Rapture Will Be in 1988*. He went through, in a Fundamentalist fashion, the books that have prophecy in them, and he concluded that the rapture would occur during Rosh Hashanah in September of that year. Well, September came and went. Whisenant, who sold four million copies of his book, said, "I made a mistake. I forgot there was no year zero. The rapture will occur in September 1989 instead." September 1989 came and went. Our Lord said, "You know neither the day nor the hour." Whisenant said, "Yes, but you can know the week and the month." That kind of playing with Scripture is unhistorical, it's contrary to the Christian faith, and it's indicative of Fundamentalism.

Which is the true Church? There can be only one because Jesus established only one. That Church is historically identical with the Catholic Church, which has unity of doctrine. It always has taught the same. Have there been individual Catholics who have been in error? Yes, in the past and today. There are Catholics who say, "Oh, I don't believe in the Resurrection," but the Church does not agree with them. There are Catholics who say, "Oh, I don't believe in the Redemption," but the Church does not teach that. The Church always has taught the same. Individual Christians will come and will go, will err. The Church does not err. There is complete conformity with biblical teaching in what the Catholic Church teaches. There are unconformities in Fundamentalism.

You can ignore facts. I brought up many of them today, such as what the early Christians wrote. You can ignore facts, but you can't refute them. There has been no effort made by Mr. Blackburn to refute the facts that show the early Christians, and Christians throughout the centuries, believed as the Catholic Church still teaches. "Who hears you, hears me," said Jesus, and he said that to the apostles. "Who hears you, hears me." There are some people who refused to hear Jesus, the apostles, and their successors. They refuse to hear Jesus and instead, as Peter warns, twist Scripture to their own destruction. They overlook or even pervert sections of Scripture when those sections don't match their pet theories or inventions.

Go to a Fundamentalist church and sit in on the services. Do it consistently, for a period of time. See what is preached about. Only parts of the Bible. Many parts are skipped over. In the Catholic Church, in the course of the three-year cycle of readings, you hear almost the entire New Testament read out. We accept it all. You don't find that in Fundamentalist churches.

Something you will not find any preaching about is the latter part of John 6. Do you remember what happens in John 6? In the beginning is a multiplication of fishes and loaves for the five thousand. Jesus miraculously provides earthly food for his people. Then he says, "Now I promise you that you will be getting, miraculously, spiritual food." He says, "If there is to be life within you, you must eat my flesh and drink my blood." What does the crowd say? First the Jews on the periphery say, "How can this man give us his flesh to eat?" They take him literally, not figuratively, not metaphorically. What does Jesus not do? He does not say, "No, you misunderstand, I'm just talking symbolically." In other cases, when Jesus was talking to the crowds, they misunderstood the full import. Even the apostles often misunderstood. So, he took the apostles aside later and said, "This is what I meant." He does not do that here. What does he do instead? Instead of saying, "You misunderstood me, I was speaking symbolically," he repeats himself: "You must eat my flesh and drink my blood."

Then what happens? Some of his disciples, people who had accepted everything he had taught up to this point, say, "This is a hard saying, who can accept it?" And what are we told? That they walked with him no more. This is the only place in the New Testament where anybody leaves Jesus for doctrinal reasons. It was over the Real Presence of Jesus in the Eucharist. What did Jesus not do? He did not correct them. He again said, "You must eat my flesh and drink my blood." He let his own followers depart. And who also did not accept Jesus at his word? Look at John 6:64; it was Judas.

This is where Judas fell. He would not accept this great central truth of the Real Presence of Jesus, under the appearances of bread and wine. Read chapter 6 for yourself. Here Judas falls away. Unlike the other disciples who left, he didn't actually leave in body, but he left in mind and in heart. Later on we're told he was a thief, stealing from the common purse, but that's not what turned him against Jesus. This was the point, his refusal to accept an explicit teaching of Jesus, one that Jesus continued to repeat.

Many Fundamentalists will say Jesus is talking symbolically when he refers to this truth as being "spirit and light." If anyone tells you that, have him show you elsewhere in the New Testament where the word "spirit" is used for symbolic teaching. No place. What Jesus is saying is that this is a high doctrine which you will not accept unless you are a true follower of his. If you are not a true spiritual follower, you will reject the Real Presence of Jesus in the Eucharist. That's what happened to Judas.

We're very blessed as Christians with having an opportunity to accept Jesus fully in all his words. We have no need to pick and choose. We follow the Church that he set up in Matthew 16:18 and follow those constant teachings which the Church has given. But some will not do so. How are we to decide, when so many claims are made? "I am for Christ," they said. "I am for Paul, I am for Apollo." Who taught truly? Scripture gives us many ways to discern.

There is one that I think might be especially appropriate today: to discern which is *not* the true way. And it is this: bitterness is not one of the fruits of the Holy Spirit. It does no good to say this is righteous anger. That's not what bitterness is. Bitterness is an indication that the soul needs reformation. I call upon all of you to go home today, open your Bibles, and read through the sixth chapter of John's Gospel. Pray to the Holy Spirit that he will enlighten you as to the true meaning. If you do that, you will understand why Jesus is truly, corporally present in the Eucharist, and you will begin to see, if this applies to you, a lessening of bitterness against the Church which maybe once you embraced, but now, like a rejected lover, you have cast off. Thank you very much.

MODERATOR: Ladies and gentlemen, on behalf of both of our participants, we wish to thank you all for being here. You've been a gracious audience. Thank you very much. Let's hear it once again for our debaters.

BOOK 3

Tracking Down the True Church

Karl Keating vs. Jose Ventilacion

Introduction

We drove up to the high school campus. There was a small parking lot between us and the gymnasium, where the debate would be held. "Looks like we have competition from a football game," I said. Yellow buses were pulling into the lot, spilling passengers into a large crowd of people milling around on the grass. We turned in behind a bus, and I hit the brakes. Now we were close enough to see the unsmiling faces. Everyone was dressed in Sunday-go-to-meetin' clothes. "I don't think they're here for football," said my co-worker.

"What's going on? The debate isn't for two-and-a-half hours. Where have all these people come from?" They were coming from all over Southern California, expecting to see their hero, a minister for Iglesia ni Cristo ("Church of Christ" in Tagalog), rhetorically smash a Catholic apologist. I was to be the smashee.

We parked the van and walked to the gymnasium. Iglesia men in three-piece suits were speaking into walkie-talkies. Several women were setting up a reception table outside the foyer. Others were checking off names on long lists. At the side door trucks filled with folding chairs were being unloaded. Farther back, people were taking video equipment out of a van. And behind us more yellow buses were pulling into the lot, disgorging passengers, and moving on.

We walked inside, stepped over cables, dodged men carrying chairs. Against the wall opposite the foyer was the raised platform: lecterns, tables, microphones, and, off to the left, an overhead projector and large screen. Video cameras were being set up in a semicircle in front of the platform. Technicians hovered around them, armed with bandoliers of battery packs.

The bleachers had been extended on both sides of the gymnasium. The floor was being filled rapidly with folding chairs, some of which already had been claimed. Several dozen impeccably dressed Iglesia members wore badges identifying themselves as ushers. They greeted people at the doors and took them to seats that seemed to be assigned. The mood of the audience was distressingly expectant, perhaps not unlike the mood of audiences at a Roman arena. These people were looking for blood—mine.

After we set up a book table (we ended up selling almost nothing since Iglesia people are discouraged from reading anything but their own church's literature), I started to look for my opponent, Jose Ventilacion, the minister from the National City, California, Church of Christ. His church is visible from the freeway and gets plenty of stares—and with good reason. Iglesia churches are reminiscent of Mormon temples. They feature multiple pinnacled towers (though none with a trumpet-blowing angel Moroni on top). Some people say the architecture reminds them of the Emerald City in the *Wizard of Oz*. In the Philippines it is said the Iglesia churches are built not so much with an eye to aesthetics but with an eye to necessity.

At the rapture, or so the story goes, Iglesia members will be whooshed into heaven, but only if they're inside one of their churches when the rapture comes. The church building too will be taken up, thus the need for the aerodynamic design. The story may be apocryphal, but I wouldn't dismiss it out of hand. These people believe strange things, and they believe them sincerely—more than sincerely, fanatically. Their fanaticism is not to be taken lightly.

When I sat down at my place on the platform, an Iglesia man took a chair a few feet away, near the stairs. "What are you doing?" I asked.

"I'm your bodyguard," he said. "At our debates in the Philippines, people often charge the platform, and I'm here to protect you in case that happens." I was not comforted. What good would one bodyguard be against 3,500 people trained to hate Catholicism?

I should give a little background about this strange sect. Its founder was Felix Manalo. Baptized a Catholic, he fell away from the Church as a teenager. Later he was influenced by Protestant missionaries who had come to the Philippines. He also must have been influenced by Mormons and Jehovah's Witnesses, since his church's distinctive doctrines seem taken from those religions.

In 1914 Manalo incorporated Iglesia ni Cristo in the Philippines. Within a few years he was teaching that the Christian Church had apostatized in the first century and had ceased to exist. Eighteen-and-a-half centuries later, God instructed Manalo to effect a restoration. Today's head of Iglesia ni Cristo is Manalo's grandson, Eduardo.

The church publishes a monthly magazine. At the time of the debate it was called *Pasugo*, but nowadays, to appeal to people who don't speak Tagalog, it is called *God's Message*. Its most notable feature is its strident and low-brow anti-Catholicism. It is also anti-Protestant. The Catholic and Protestant churches, but especially the former, are tools of Satan, say the writers. Each issue has more pages devoted to debunking Christian churches than to explaining Iglesia's own positions. In a way that's understandable: Iglesia ni Cristo has few positions to explain. This is a sect built not so much on doctrines but on anti-doctrines. The members are told what to shun; there isn't much for them to accept in the positive sense.

Unlike Fundamentalism, unlike even Mormonism and the Jehovah's Witnesses, Iglesia ni Cristo is a true cult. If you had seen the Iglesia people in the audience, if you had seen how they reacted in lock-step to their leaders, you would have understood that. At least that's the impression I got, from my vantage point on the platform.

The gymnasium was preternaturally hot. An hour before the start of the debate the people seated on the folding chairs were fanning themselves. At the top of the bleachers it was hotter still. And on the platform, under the klieg lights, it was hellish. (I went through a quart of water before the night was over.) I wondered if someone had turned on the heaters in the afternoon of this balmy early October day, in order to get the audience on edge. I wouldn't doubt it. The Iglesia folks are sneaky.

Jose Ventilacion and I had negotiated terms of the debate over a period of several months. Each time a change was made in the format, he had to check with authorities in Manila. I had been warned by people who had seen Iglesia debates not to trust Ventilacion. I pooh-poohed the warnings, but I was wrong. The terms of the debate were broken even before I arrived at the gymnasium.

Ventilacion and I had agreed this would be *mano-a-mano*, just the two of us. I was seated alone at my table, but he had two "seconds" at his. Their job was to pass him notes and books to read from while he was at the lectern. Sometimes they did more than that. One of them, himself a minister, was unable to control himself during my remarks. He repeatedly stood up and shouted at me. "I'm not debating you," I shouted back. "I'm debating *him*. Sit down!" (This and other irrelevant exchanges have been edited out of the transcript that follows.)

The overhead projector also wasn't part of the agreement. It was placed on Ventilacion's side of the platform, with two more of his people manning it. When I first saw it and realized that its operators would be acting as yet more helpers, I complained to Ventilacion. He flashed a toothy smile. "If you don't agree to this format, we'll cancel the debate and give our people an instruction." By that he meant he'd just preach to them.

I didn't have much choice. The listeners were mainly former Catholics bamboozled by Iglesia ni Cristo's anti-Catholic rhetoric. They *needed* to hear what the Catholic Church really stood for—and what *their* church really stood for and how it came to be. Besides, five against one had a positive aspect. I was bound to get a certain amount of sympathy, especially if I explained the situation—which I did. But Ventilacion, in the question period following my opening remarks, said I misrepresented the facts, that I had "agreed" to the format. I replied, "If you say, 'If you don't give me your money, I'll shoot you,' of course I'll give you my money." Ventilacion said I shouldn't worry about technicalities, but it was clear *his* people had spent *lots* of time worrying about technicalities. You don't produce a well-orchestrated (well-railroaded?) debate by ignoring the little things.

However meticulous it may be organizationally, Iglesia ni Cristo is remarkably cavalier when it comes to "the little things" of theology. Its positions are just stated, never really substantiated. Its arguments are puerile. For instance, believers in the claims of Felix Manalo say Revelation's references to an "angel" coming out of the "East" or from "afar" refer to a "messenger" ("angel" is taken from the Greek for "messenger") coming from the "Far East." And what is the geographic center of the Far East? Why, the Philippines, of course. Therefore, Felix Manalo was a true prophet: (1) he claimed to be a prophet, which means (2) that he claimed to be God's messenger, and (3) he came from the Far East.

How to respond to such a claim? I started by listing the countries that make up the Far East: China, Korea, Japan, Taiwan, Hong Kong, Indochina, and, yes, the Philippines. "If you look at a map of the Far East," I said, "you'll see that the Philippines is in the southeast corner." The geographic center is in southern China, not in the Philippines. There were laughs from the Catholics and Protestants (a few hundred of them were in the audience), nervous fidgeting from the Iglesia people.

Later on, after having dealt with the main charges against the Catholic Church, I zeroed in on Manalo himself. Iglesia ni Cristo tells its members little about their founder: what I said brought a strange silence to the gymnasium. I explained Manalo's early years and how, as it is now said, he began his church in 1914 after receiving a revelation from God and being informed that he was the new prophet. I asked the audience why, five years later in 1919, did Manalo go to the U.S. to study with Protestants? Why would he study with people he later claimed were "apostates"? Why would a prophet need to study religion at all, after having talked with God?

Then I gave the answer: because Felix Manalo didn't start off claiming to be a prophet. Originally Iglesia ni Cristo was just another Protestant sect, one that borrowed heavily from the American Campbellites. It wasn't until 1922, when there was a schism within Iglesia ni Cristo, that Manalo started to say he was a prophet. He said that because he wanted the members of his fledgling church to take his side, not the schismatics' side.

Iglesia ni Cristo's anti-Catholicism is not very inventive—that, or the attention span of Iglesia people is remarkably short. *Pasugo* brings up the same charges again and again, yet there's no indication that devoted readers tire of hearing the same thing, even in the same words. Two, three, even four times a year there will be feature stories decrying the same Catholic belief or practice. I don't mean stories that mention a topic briefly and then move on. I mean stories that are almost word-for-word identical.

One of the favorite topics is the identity of the beast of Revelation, the symbolic number of which is 666. Most reputable scholars, Catholic and Protestant, say the number refers to the Roman Emperor Nero. Not all agree, but no such scholars say the beast is the papacy. But that's exactly what Iglesia ni Cristo says. In itself that's not surprising. After all, countless Fundamentalists say the same thing. But Iglesia ni Cristo, in *Pasugo*, says it in a most peculiar way. It makes a bold argument which any attentive reader can disprove simply by glancing at *Pasugo* itself.

The argument goes like this. The number 666 is the sum of the letters of the beast's title. The pope's title is *Vicarius Filii Dei*, Vicar of the Son of God. (Actually, it's not. His title is *Vicarius Christi*, Vicar of Christ). We know this is the papal title because it appears prominently on the tiara of the popes; the letters are formed out of hundreds of jewels. *Vicarius Filii Dei* tallies to 666, which means the papacy is the beast. End of proof.

The editors of *Pasugo* must count on the magazine's readers being inattentive. They print as part of the article a line drawing of the tiara with the words *Vicarius Filii Dei* lettered in, just so you know where they appear. Then—and this shows real chutzpah—they print a photograph of Pope Paul VI, the last pope to wear the tiara. Of course, in the photograph there's no hint of any lettering on the tiara. The photograph contradicts both the text and the line drawing, but no one seemed aware of that until I pointed it out during the debate.

Ventilacion did the only proper thing. He ignored my point and changed the subject. He had a wonderful way of doing this. My favorite example concerns the translation of scriptural passages which supposedly include the name of his sect. This is a major issue with Iglesia members. They believe the Bible mentions their church by name. They desperately want to find the phrase "Church of Christ" in the sacred text.

Their argument is facile: "What is the name of Christ's church, as given in the Bible? It is the 'Church of Christ.' Our church is called the 'Church of Christ.' Therefore, ours is the church Christ founded." Not many people will be impressed with such an argument—when it was first presented to me during a question-and-answer period some years ago, I had trouble not laughing aloud—but the folks at the debate thought it made a lot of sense. The problem was that the verse Ventilacion was citing didn't contain the phrase "Church of Christ." I noted that the Greek means "Church of God," not "Church of Christ." He didn't seem to care.

Of all the debates I've been in, this was at once the most frightening and the most frustrating. It was the most frightening because Iglesia ni Cristo is a true cult, not a mere sect, and it was easy to see why bodyguards were *de rigueur*, even if their muscle wasn't needed this night. And the debate was the most frustrating because my opponent wouldn't adhere to elementary norms of civility and because the audience, at least the Iglesia portion of it, seemed impervious to even the simplest argument against its position. But judge for yourself, as you read the transcript.

Debate Transcript
Karl Keating vs. Jose Ventilacion

MODERATOR: Tonight we will discuss, in a debate, two subjects: one is that the holy, catholic, apostolic, and Roman Church is the only true Church, according to the Bible. That's the first proposition. The second proposition will be that the Church of Christ which appeared in the Philippines in 1914 is the only true Church, according to the Bible.

I'd like to emphasized certain rules in this debate. I'm sure that you are all very eager to hear the speakers and that you have your favorite. We do not allow booing, yelling, shouting, stomping your feet, or heckling. In case there is any violence—we don't expect that tonight—arrests will be made. There are policemen here. So I hope that's clear. And now we will start with the debate, and I'd like to bring in Mr. Keating as the first speaker.

KEATING: Thank you, Mr. Moderator. I want to thank Jose Ventilacion for agreeing to this debate. I want to thank all of you for coming.

What is the true Church? That's the question for tonight. I'm not going to leave you in suspense. I'll give you the answer right up front. The true Church, established by Jesus Christ, is the Catholic Church. It is the only one entitled to call itself the Church of Christ.

Let's look at some of the credentials of the Catholic Church. First, historical continuity. It is the only church that can trace itself all the way back to apostolic times. The Eastern Orthodox churches broke off from Rome in 1054. The Protestant churches broke off at the time of the Reformation in the sixteenth century. Iglesia ni Cristo was established in 1914. It has no historical continuity. Only the Catholic Church goes all the way back, and even Iglesia ni Cristo admits that. It acknowledges that in the first century the Catholic Church already was existing.

Another point: apostolic succession. The Catholic Church maintains full apostolic authority. What does that mean? It means today's Catholic bishops are in a direct line from the apostles who received their authority from Jesus Christ himself. In the New Testament, we see our Lord saying to the apostles and consequently to their successors, "Who hears you hears me." No other church can claim this. We see the apostles passing on their authority by laying on of hands, ordaining bishops and priests. In the Book of Acts, we see the first occasion of this when a replacement was obtained for Judas by the laying on of hands. Iglesia ni Cristo entirely lacks this continuity.

Then there is Christ's own promises. Look what he said about the continuity of his Church. Matthew 16:18: "Thou art Peter and upon this rock I will build my Church, and the gates of hell will not prevail against it." Will not prevail against it. Matthew 28:20: "I am with you always, even until the end of the world." Always. John 14:16: "I will pray to the Father and he will give you another comforter who will abide with you forever." Christ promised that nothing would prevail against his Church, that he would be with it always, and that the Holy Spirit, the comforter, the Third Person of the Trinity, would be with it always.

Was Jesus Christ a liar? I suppose Iglesia ni Cristo must say yes because it says Jesus Christ was not with the Church always. The Holy Spirit was not with the Church always. They abandoned the Church in the first century, and it fell into complete apostasy. That's what not being with the true Church implies. If you do say that Jesus Christ is not a liar—and I believe that's what you say—then you must admit that you are not accepting everything that Scripture teaches. The Catholic Church is the only one that maintains the fullness of scriptural doctrine.

We can talk about any number of points. Let me bring out one. Look at

John 6. Do you know what happened in John 6? Jesus had just finished miraculously producing natural food for his followers, from loaves and fishes. Then he said he will give them spiritual food that also will come miraculously. He said, "If there is to be spiritual life within you, you must eat my flesh and drink my blood." What did the Jews who were listening think? They said, "How can this man give us his flesh to eat?" They took him literally. And what did Jesus *not* do? He did not correct them. He did not say, "No, no, you misunderstood me." Remember, whenever he was talking and the crowds didn't get the message, he at least took the apostles aside and said, "Okay, you guys, this is what I mean." He didn't do that this time because nobody misunderstood him when they took him literally. They understood him correctly.

He repeated himself, "Eat my flesh, drink my blood." Then what happened? Some of his disciples, those who had accepted everything up to this point, said, "This is a hard saying. Who can accept it? And they walked with him no more." This is the only place in the New Testament where anybody left Jesus for a doctrinal reason. And you know who also left at that time, did not walk away from him but left him in his heart? Look in verse 64. It was Judas. Judas fell away here because he would not accept the Real Presence of Jesus in the Eucharist. Think about that doctrine. It is a doctrine which the Iglesia ni Cristo refuses to accept. It is one that the Catholic Church always has taught.

Iglesia ni Cristo is known more for its anti-Catholicism than for anything else. Do you read its magazine, *Pasugo*? I've gone through a number of issues. There are many articles in each issue against the Catholic Church but few that are pro-Iglesia ni Cristo. Why this emphasis on the Catholic Church? Because Iglesia ni Cristo agrees with Mormonism. You know in what? In this: Mormons will tell you, if you ask them, that if their church is not the true church, the only other possibility is the Catholic Church. By implication, Iglesia ni Cristo is saying the same thing. If it's not us, it must be you. Only the Catholic Church is the focus of all these barbs.

Have you ever noticed how the attacks on the Catholic Church verge on the fantastic, on the incredible? No serious scholar of any camp could accept them. No serious lay reader could accept them unless he has closed his mind. I'll give you one example that may be brought up later, the nonsensical charge that the pope is the beast of Revelation, whose number is 666. This is one of Iglesia ni Cristo's favorite comments. It appears in its magazine as often as every four issues, but it is nonsense. It has no scriptural warrant, no historical warrant. But why this constant attack against the Catholic Church? Because Iglesia ni Cristo's own doctrines are so weak they could not stand up if given in isolation. There must be a bogeyman out there to go after. The Nazis had the Jews; Iglesia ni Cristo has the Catholic Church.

Let me summarize. The Catholic Church is the only church with complete historical credentials. Iglesia ni Cristo has none. The Catholic Church is the only church that has preserved all the original Christian doctrines. Iglesia ni Cristo ignores or contradicts many of them. The Catholic Church is the only church based solidly on the whole of Scripture, omitting nothing. Iglesia ni Cristo is famous for misapplying Scripture. Iglesia ni Cristo claims to be the Christian Church of the New Testament, but it is not. Iglesia ni Cristo claims to get its distinctive doctrines straight from Scripture, but it does not. Iglesia ni Cristo claims that Felix Manalo was a messenger sent from God, but he was not. Iglesia ni Cristo claims to be the Church of Christ, but it is not. It is only the Catholic Church that has a solid foundation in history, in Scripture, and in reason. Iglesia ni Cristo is neither historical, nor scriptural, nor reasonable as, I am confident, Mr. Ventilacion will now proceed to demonstrate.

VENTILACION: Let me ask you on your basic doctrines, Mr. Keating. You mentioned Matthew 16:18, right.

KEATING: Right.

VENTILACION: Okay. You mentioned about the rock on which a church was built, right?

KEATING: That's right. Peter is the rock.

VENTILACION: Peter is the rock. Thank you. You believe that Peter is the foundation stone of your Church?

KEATING: He is the earthly head of the Church, appointed by Jesus Christ, who himself is the cornerstone of the Church.

VENTILACION: I'm asking you the question: is he the foundation stone of your church? Yes or no, Mr. Keating.

KEATING: I've just answered the question, Mr. Ventilacion.

VENTILACION: Is he a foundation stone?

KEATING: He is a foundation stone because Jesus Christ says so.

VENTILACION: Don't you also teach in your doctrines that Jesus Christ is also a foundation stone?

KEATING: Of course.

VENTILACION: Therefore, in the Catholic Church, you are teaching two kinds of foundation stones.

KEATING: Of course.

VENTILACION: You have two foundation stones?

KEATING: An earthly foundation established by Jesus Christ, and Jesus Christ himself, the ultimate foundation.

VENTILACION: Whether it is an earthly or heavenly foundation, you are teaching two foundation stones, right?

KEATING: Of different qualities and different kinds.

VENTILACION: Thank you. Now, in 1 Corinthians 3:11 of the Good News Bible, which is the Catholic study edition, it says that, "For God has already placed Jesus Christ as the one and only foundation". Do you agree with that?

KEATING: He is the one and only ultimate foundation, of course.

VENTILACION: I am not saying ultimate. The Bible is saying, "For God has already placed Jesus Christ as the one and only foundation." Do you agree with that? That Christ is the only—

KEATING: I've answered that already.

VENTILACION: So you agree?

KEATING: Of course I agree. I agree with the entire Bible. And I noticed you have not said anything about what is the rock in Matthew 16:18. Are you going to ask me about that?

VENTILACION: I'm asking you, please, on what I am presenting so please answer, Mr. Keating.

KEATING: Go right ahead.

VENTILACION: "For God has already placed Jesus Christ as the one and only foundation." Do you agree that Christ is the one and only foundation? Yes or no.

KEATING: That's the third time you've asked the question. Did anybody else miss my answer? I said, three times now, yes, Jesus Christ is the foundation of the Church.

VENTILACION: Now, it says here the one and only foundation. Do you agree with that?

KEATING: I agree with that, if you take it correctly.

VENTILACION: Now, this is the follow-up question.

KEATING: Go ahead.

VENTILACION: The verse also says, Mr. Keating, "And no other foundation can be laid." Do you agree with that?

KEATING: I agree with the whole Bible.

VENTILACION: Okay, now. If Jesus Christ is the one and only foundation, how could you place Peter as another foundation?

KEATING: I can because Jesus Christ said that on Peter he would build his Church.

VENTILACION: If Jesus Christ is the one and only foundation and the Bible says "no other foundation can be laid"—do you accept that?

KEATING: Of course.

VENTILACION: Okay, thank you. So, you believe now that you have laid the apostle Peter as another foundation.

KEATING: I haven't laid Peter as anything. Jesus Christ did.

VENTILACION: Jesus Christ laid the apostle Peter as the foundation stone?

KEATING: Matthew 16:18: "Thou art Peter and upon this rock I will build my Church." The word "rock" refers to Peter.

VENTILACION: Does the word "Peter" means stone or foundation stone?

KEATING: It means foundation stone. Large massive stone. Rock.

VENTILACION: I'm not asking you if he is a rock. I'm asking you if Peter means stone or foundation stone.

KEATING: The new name given to the apostle Simon means large, massive rock as used in a foundation.

VENTILACION: I'm not asking you as if it is a large, massive rock. I'm asking you the meaning of the word. Is Peter the foundation stone or simply a stone?

KEATING: Neither one. Rock. Don't you know the Greek?

VENTILACION: That is not your time to ask questions, Mr. Keating. You will have time to ask questions. You said that Peter is the foundation stone, right? Where could you find a verse in the Bible that says Peter is a foundation stone?

KEATING: I said Peter is the rock.

VENTILACION: Just a stone, not a foundation stone.

KEATING: I said the rock on which the Church would be built. Now—

VENTILACION: Well, that's your own opinion. I'm asking you—

KEATING: That's what Jesus Christ says in Matthew 16:18. It's not my opinion. It's what the verse says.

VENTILACION: That is your opinion. I'm asking you now where does it say in the Bible that Peter is the foundation stone? What verse?

KEATING: Matthew 16:18 says Peter is the rock—

VENTILACION: It doesn't say there that—

MODERATOR: Time is up. We will now hear the negative side of the proposition. Brother Ventilacion.

VENTILACION: We are here not personally against Mr. Keating. We are not against the Catholics. We are not against anybody here. We are not against any Catholic member here. We are against the false teachings of the Roman Catholic Church because the system, or the teachings, that they are presenting to you are not in the Bible.

I went to the basic doctrine of the Catholic Church because the basis of their teaching that theirs is the true Church is because the apostle Peter is the foundation stone upon which Christ built the Church. And because the apostle Peter was the foundation stone, the apostle Peter has successors, the popes, so it means then that because there are popes until this time, so the Catholic Church can trace back its origin from the apostle Peter, who was the first pope. But is that true? Once we have proven today that Peter was not the foundation stone of the Church, built by our Lord Jesus Christ, then the reasoning of Mr. Keating that theirs is the true Church will crumble.

According to Matthew 16:18, who is the rock or the foundation stone upon which the Church was built? Let us examine chapter 16:18. It says here, "And so I tell you, Peter, you are a rock and on this rock foundation I will build my Church. And that evil will never be able to overcome it." Christ is the one speaking. He did not say to Peter. "You are a rock foundation." He said here, "And I tell you, you are rock, and on this rock foundation, I will build my Church." That's why I asked him, "Is Peter the foundation stone?" He said, "Yes." In the Catholic Bible, which is the Douay-Rheims version, they also state that Jesus Christ is the chief foundation stone. What I am holding now is the Douay-Rheims version, which is the Catholic version. It says here in the footnote, "Christ himself, the chief foundation stone." Now, if Peter is the foundation stone and Christ is also the foundation stone, then it means then that they have two foundation stones.

According to 1 Corinthians 3:11, could you put another foundation? That's what the Catholic Church did. In 1 Corinthians 3:11, it says here, "For God has already placed Jesus Christ as the one and only foundation, and no other foundation can be laid." When they place the apostle Peter as another foundation, they are violating the Scriptures. The Bible says, "No other foundation can be laid." That's why I asked him, if Jesus Christ is the one and only foundation, could Peter be a foundation? He said, "Yes."

That answer, Mr. Keating, is going against the teaching of the Bible that you could not lay or place any other foundation aside from what God has placed. And you could not read, from the Bible, that God placed the apostle Peter as the foundation of the Church. What you can read, Mr. Keating, is that God has already placed Jesus Christ as the one and only foundation. So what happens now to the claims of the Catholic Church, that theirs is the true Church because Christ built his Church upon Peter? That claim is not in the Bible. It is a misunderstanding of the meaning of Christ's statement in Matthew 16:18.

Let us ask the apostle Peter, according to the apostle Peter, who is the stone which was rejected, which became the cornerstone? Did he introduce himself as the foundation stone? Let us ask the apostle Peter in Acts 4:10–11: "Be it known to you all and to all the people of Israel that by the name of our Lord Jesus Christ of Nazareth, this is the stone which was rejected by you the builders which has become the head of the corner." What did the apostle Peter say? He did not say, "I am the stone." He said, "This is the stone," referring to our Lord Jesus Christ. I would like Mr. Karl Keating to show us proof, from the Bible, that the apostle Peter teaches himself as the foundation stone. Even in his letter, in the letter of the apostle Peter to the Christians, whom did he preach or teach as the foundation stone?

He said this in 1 Peter 2:5–6: "Be you also as the living stones built up, a spiritual house, a holy priesthood to offer up spiritual sacrifices acceptable to

God by Jesus Christ." What did the Bible say? The apostle Peter himself said even in his letter—he was pointing to our Lord Jesus Christ as the foundation of the Church. Remember that this letter was addressed to the Church. He said to them, "You are also living stones built up as spiritual house." They know that spiritual house is the Church. And the apostle Peter is teaching them that the stone in which the spiritual house was built is Christ Jesus.

That's why I challenge Mr. Keating to show a verse in the Bible that Peter said, "I am the foundation stone." Nobody could read that. What you can read from the Bible is that the apostle Peter mentioned that Christ is the foundation stone. Well there could be a secondary stone, that's what they are saying, because Christ is the chief foundation stone and Peter is the secondary stone. But, again, let me rephrase—let me, again, mention 1 Corinthians 3:11: "No other foundation can be laid."

What did the apostle Peter say concerning the stone that was placed by God? What would other people do with the stone? I'll read again the statement of the apostle Peter here in Acts 4:10–11: "Be it known to ye all and to all the people of Israel that by the name of our Lord Jesus Christ of Nazareth, this is the stone which was rejected by you the builders, which is to become the head of the corner." What did the apostle Peter say the people shall do concerning the stone, the foundation stone of the Church? He said, "They will reject it." That's why the Catholic Church replaced Jesus Christ. They said when Jesus Christ went up to heaven, he was replaced by the apostle Peter. It's like Jesus Christ, according to them, is the invisible head of the Church, and the apostle Peter is the head of the Church.

Now, let's continue. In Ephesians 2:20, here is another apostle. What did the apostle Paul say about the foundation of the Church? Did he say, "Well, my fellow apostle Peter is the foundation stone"? What did he say? He said, "Build upon the foundation of the apostles and prophets, Jesus Christ himself being the chief cornerstone in whom all the building being framed together groweth up into a holy temple in the Lord." According to the apostle Paul, who is the foundation stone? He said, "Jesus Christ himself." He said, "Built upon the foundation of the apostles and the prophets." Because the apostles and the prophets were in the Church, they too were built upon Christ. Is the apostle Peter an apostle? Yes. Is he built upon Christ? Yes.

If Peter is a foundation stone and he is built upon Jesus Christ, what shall appear, my beloved friends? Then it appears that the foundation stone is built upon another foundation stone. And that is not in the Bible. The Bible never mentioned a foundation stone that is built upon another foundation stone. But that is what is appearing if we shall follow the line of reasoning of the Roman Catholic Church. Now, Mr. Keating, instead of resorting to proving that their church is the true Church from the Bible, I was watching him. If he was opening the Bible, he did not. He was just merely quoting the Bible.

The resolution states, "Resolved, that the Catholic Church is the only true Church, according to the Bible." Where did he go? Apostolicity, and he mentioned other things. Why don't you read the Bible to show that the Catholic Church is indeed the true Church, why don't you read the Bible? You could not read from the Bible the words "Catholic Church." Why? Because that name was only invented by St. Ignatius of Antioch. That's why we should not be surprised, my beloved friends, that Mr. Keating is not even opening the Bible to prove his contention that the Catholic Church is indeed the true Church.

Now, why don't we examine their teachings? I believe that there are a lot of Catholic friends here who give honor to Mary. The Catholic Church claims that they are united, not only in government but even in doctrines or teachings. That's what they claim. That's why the four marks for the Catholic Church, they said, are one, holy, catholic, and apostolic. Let us go to the so-called unity. Are they united in their doctrines?

MODERATOR: Thank you Brother Ventilacion. We will have a seven-minute rebuttal from Mr. Keating.

VENTILACION: He will first question me for five minutes.

MODERATOR: Oh is that what it is?

KEATING: I'd like to point out to you that the debate is not being conducted on the terms that Mr. Ventilacion and I agreed to in writing. You'll notice, it's three against one. It's unbalanced.

VENTILACION: Don't mislead the audience. You said a while ago, "It's okay Jose that you have the two seconds. Why are you trying to point this out to the audience?

KEATING: When I came up to him before the debate and complained about him having helpers, he said, "If you don't agree to this we'll cancel the debate." I know many of you drove a long way. I'm not going to do that to you. So, let me ask a question now. Let's get—

VENTILACION: Why don't we ask the moderator here, because he knows what transpired before this debate.

KEATING: No, that is when you and I talked privately. He was not here yet.

VENTILACION: Why don't you ask the moderator, and ask him if you agreed that I have two seconds here during this debate. Did you agree or not?

KEATING: After you threatened to quit, yes. What was I going to do, disappoint everybody?

VENTILACION: I said, I'm not quitting. I said we will not do this debate if you will not agree that I have these two people here. Did I say I quit?

KEATING: If you say, "If you don't give me your money, I'll shoot you," of course I'll give you my money. Now to my question. Let's get back to Matthew 16:18. You were skirting around it. Jesus says to Peter, "You are Peter and upon this rock I will build my Church." Who is the rock?

VENTILACION: The rock is Christ.

KEATING: What makes you say the rock is Christ?

VENTILACION: Matthew 16:18, Catholic version, mentions that Christ himself is the true foundation stone.

KEATING: You are avoiding my question.

VENTILACION: I'm not avoiding your question.

KEATING: In Matthew 16:18, let's get to the meaning of the word. What language did Jesus speak?

VENTILACION: He spoke in Aramaic. That's what you were telling the people?

KEATING: That's correct. He was speaking in Aramaic.

VENTILACION: It was translated to Greek.

KEATING: That's right. Now, what name in Aramaic did Peter get? What is "Peter" in Aramaic?

VENTILACION: *Kepha.* That is what you said in your book.

KEATING: *Kepha.* That's right. You read my book.

VENTILACION: *Kepha,* which means a stone. Not a foundation stone.

KEATING: You said you read my book. You should know better. [Speaking to one of Mr. Ventilacion's seconds.] Why don't you get him my book and bring it up? The word "*Kepha*" in Aramaic means exactly the same as the Greek word "*Petra,*" large rock.

VENTILACION: This is my answer Mr. Keating. My answer is this. The apostle Peter was the direct audience of our Lord Jesus Christ. When he said that Christ is the stone, upon which the Church was built, I agree with the apostle Peter. Don't you agree with him?

KEATING: Again, I am asking the questions.

VENTILACION: Okay.

KEATING: You still didn't answer my question. Apparently, you admit that Peter's name, in Aramaic, is *Kepha*?

VENTILACION: Yes, we do not deny that, Mr. Keating.

KEATING: And you admit that the word "*Kepha*" means either a stone or rock? Which one?

VENTILACION: Yes, I agree with that. But it is not Peter who is the foundation stone.

KEATING: Which one? Is it stone or rock? They're different things.

VENTILACION: It's the same, Mr. Keating.

KEATING: Greek has different words for it. English has different words for it. Aramaic has different words. In Aramaic, the word for stone is "*ephna*."

VENTILACION: What is your question, now?

KEATING: I want you to answer the same one. Are you saying that in Aramaic the word "*kepha*" means a mere stone?

VENTILACION: In John 1, the apostle Peter was named. This is from John

1:42. Jesus looked at him and said, "Your name is Simon, son of John, but you will be called Cephas." This is the same as Peter and means a rock.

KEATING: That's right. Thank you. It means rock. So, "Thou art Peter—Rock—and upon this rock." That's what I was driving at. Now I have a different question. You said, as a conclusive argument against the Catholic Church, the name "Catholic Church" does not appear in Scripture. True. Where does the name "Church of Christ" or "Iglesia ni Cristo" appear?

VENTILACION: I'm going to read for Mr. Keating. Acts 20:28.

KEATING: Acts 20:28? That's what I was waiting for.

VENTILACION: Aramaic, the language of Jesus, Mr. Keating. From the Aramaic, "Take ye therefore to yourselves and to all the flock over which the Holy Spirit has appointed you overseers to feed the church of Christ." Translated from the Aramaic—translated from the Aramaic, the language of Jesus. Thank you.

KEATING: That was the Lamsa version, I presume?

VENTILACION: This is the Lamsa version, translated from the Aramaic, the language of Jesus. You follow that Aramaic.

KEATING: The version that we all accept, the official version, is in Greek. The word in Greek, there in that passage, Acts 20:28, is "churches," not singular "church."

[Talking over one another.]

VENTILACION: Your question is could you find the Church of Christ in the Bible. I read it. So what? What's next?

MODERATOR: It's getting more interesting, isn't it? Now we will have a seven-minute rebuttal from Mr. Keating.

KEATING: Now that I have the floor to myself, I want to point out something: in Greek, it is not "church of Christ," it is "churches of Christ." The phrase "Church of Christ" as such, the phrase "Catholic Church" as such—neither one appears in the New Testament. Saying that the word or phrase doesn't appear means nothing. I don't argue against the Iglesia ni Cristo because its name isn't in the Bible. That's a dumb way to argue, and I don't think Mr. Ventilacion ought to argue against the Catholic Church because its formal name is not there either. That proves nothing.

Let's go to another issue. One of the constant teachings of the Catholic Church is the divinity of Jesus Christ. This is a doctrine that Iglesia ni Cristo opposes. It says that Jesus Christ is not God but a creature, maybe the highest creature but still a creature. The ancient name for that heresy was Arianism.

Let's look at what the Bible says. John 1:1. Open your Bibles if you have them. "In the beginning was the Word and the Word was with God, and the Word was God." Now, who was the Word? We find the answer in John 1:14: "And the Word was made flesh and dwelt among us." Was it God the Father who was made flesh? No. Jesus Christ was made flesh and dwelt among us. The Son of God. Therefore, he is the Word, and in John 1:1, the Word is called divine. He's called God. Iglesia ni Cristo takes the Jehovah Witnesses' position here.

In 1 Timothy 6:15, God is also called "the blessed and only potentate, the King of Kings and Lord of Lords." What about Jesus Christ? He's called the same thing. Revelation 17:14: "They shall make war with the lamb"—the lamb is Jesus Christ—"and the lamb shall overcome them, for he is Lord of Lords and King of Kings." Jesus Christ, then, is God.

Look at Revelation 19:16, which is referring to the word of God: "On his thigh a name is written, King of Kings, Lord of Lords"—the same titles that define God the Father define Jesus Christ. God the Father is called the first and the last. Isaiah 44:6: "I am the first, and I am the last." Jesus is also the first and the last. Revelation 22:13: "I am the Alpha and the Omega, the beginning and the end, the first and the last." And Revelation 1:17: "I am the first and the last, I am he that liveth and was dead who rose from the dead." Who is that? Jesus Christ, the first and the last. The Father did not die and rise again. Jesus gives himself the same proper name that God the Father has. God calls himself "I Am" in Exodus 3:14. "Thus thou shalt say unto the children of Israel, I Am has sent me unto you." And Jesus says in John 8:58, "Before Abraham was, I Am"—not "I was" but "I Am."

Look at some other verses. In Colossians 2:9, Paul tells us, "In Christ the fullness of deity dwells bodily." Isaiah 45:23 says, "To God every knee shall bow." In Philippians 2:10 Paul says that to Christ "every knee shall bow." Christ gets the same worship as God the Father. Remember, if you read *Pasugo*, that Iglesia ni Cristo says, "If you bow down to something or somebody, you are worshiping it or him, and you only worship God." The Bible says you should bow down to Jesus. So, the Bible says you're to worship him, which means he must be God.

Lastly, let's look at John 21:28: "And Thomas answered and said unto him, 'My Lord and my God.'" What does Iglesia ni Cristo say? "Oh, Thomas was just mistaken." But Jesus does not correct Thomas. He accepts his acknowledgement of his lordship, his divinity.

MODERATOR: Thank you, Mr. Keating. We now have a three-minute cross question by Brother Ventilacion.

VENTILACION: Mr. Keating, I have the book which is entitled *Religion: Doctrine and Practice,* which is written by your priest. It says here that Jesus Christ established the Church. Yes, from all history books, secular and profane, as well as from the Bible, considered as a human document, we learn that Jesus Christ established the Church, which from the earliest times is being called after him, the Christian Church or the Church of Christ. Do you agree with this?

KEATING: The Church that Jesus Christ established, obviously, has been called the Church of Christ.

VENTILACION: Your priest said it's from the Bible. What verse is that in the Bible that Christ—

KEATING: I don't know who you are quoting.

VENTILACION: This is Francis Cassilly.

KEATING: I have no idea who he is.

VENTILACION: You don't know who he is?

KEATING: No. And the book looks about 60 years old.

VENTILACION: He is from Creighton University in Omaha, Nebraska. This is from the Society of Jesus. This is an imprimatur of George Cardinal Mundelein. My question is: do you agree with Mr. Cassilly that the Church was called the Church of Christ since the earliest of times?

KEATING: That's correct, but it's not in the Bible.

VENTILACION: Do you also agree that the Bible says that it is the Church of Christ?

KEATING: It does not use the phrase "Church of Christ." That does not mean it is not the Church of Christ. It is the Church of Christ but that phrase happens not to be used.

VENTILACION: Is this here, as it's been called after him, the Christian Church or the Church of Christ? It was called the Church of Christ. It's from the Bible. What Bible does it say that the Church of Christ is the church established by Christ?

KEATING: I don't understand that question. Try it again.

VENTILACION: Okay. I repeat. Your priest said that Christ established the Church of Christ, quoting the Bible. What verse says that Christ established the Church of Christ?

KEATING: It says that he would establish his own Church in Matthew 16:18. We can take him at his word that he established it.

VENTILACION: I'm asking about the words "Church of Christ." Where did you find that in the Bible?

KEATING: I explained earlier that it's not in the Bible.

VENTILACION: It's not in the Bible?

KEATING: Not the singular, no.

VENTILACION: But your priest said it is from the Bible.

KEATING: Does he give a citation?

VENTILACION: Okay, never mind. Next question. Peter is the first pope, right?

KEATING: That's right.

VENTILACION: During the Council of Jerusalem—which you call the Council of Jerusalem; I call it the meeting of the apostles—during that time, in the Council of Jerusalem, Peter was pope, already?

KEATING: That's right.

VENTILACION: Okay. Now, during the time that they should have a decision, concerning the Gentiles who were turning to God, who made the judgment or decision? Was it the apostle Peter or the apostle James?

KEATING: Although James spoke last, he agreed with Peter's decision which was spoken earlier.

VENTILACION: I'm asking you who made the decision? Is it Peter or James?

KEATING: Peter.

VENTILACION: Peter? What verse, in the same chapter, do you find that the apostle Peter said, "This is my decision." What verse in chapter 15?

KEATING: He didn't use those words, and neither did James.

VENTILACION: If I could read from the Bible that the apostle James said, "This is my judgment or decision," would you accept then that apostle James is the leader of the Church during the apostolic times?

KEATING: Of course not.

VENTILACION: You will not? Okay. Therefore, I will read.

MODERATOR: Sorry, gentlemen. We now go to a 7-minute rebuttal by Brother Ventilacion.

VENTILACION: Mr. Keating could not prove that his church is the true Church, so he went to proving that Christ is God. Well we could have a debate concerning Christ or the Trinity if he would like, but that's not the point of our debate here, Mr. Keating. The point of our debate is to prove which church is the true Church. If you could not prove that your church is the true Church, how much then could you prove that Christ is God? I'll be waiting if you would like to challenge this.

I'm going to read again from this book. Mr. Keating is not familiar with this book. It is by Francis Cassilly, a member of the Society of Jesus, one of the learned priests, according to their standard. He said that Christ established the Church since the earliest times. Where did the priest learn that Christ established the Church since the earliest times? He said from history as well as from the Bible. What was the name of the Church that was established by Christ? The priest also said that it was called after Christ, the Church of Christ—of course, because it was Christ who built the Church. He could not call it the Catholic Church. It was not Catholic who established the church. That name, "Catholic," came from St. Ignatius of Antioch, and it is outside of the Bible.

Now, let's continue. I will not go to whether Jesus Christ is God or not. We will go to the basic doctrines of the Catholic Church. They said that the apostle Peter was the first pope during the Council of Jerusalem. Now, let's find out if that is true. Who made the decision that they should no longer trouble the Gentiles? He said the apostle Peter made the decision. I asked him, what if I could read that it was apostle James who made the decision? Now, let's find out. What did the apostle Peter say?

This is in Acts 15:7: "After much discussion, Peter took the floor and said to them, 'Brothers, you know well that from the early days God selected me from your number to be one from whose lips the Gentiles would hear the message of the gospel and believe. God, who reads the hearts of men, showed his approval by granting the Holy Spirit to them, just as he did to us. He made no distinction between them and us that purify their hearts by means of faith also. Why, then, do you put God to the test by trying to place on the shoulders of this convert a yoke which neither we nor our fathers were able to bear?'"

He never said "This is my decision." He never said "This is my judgment." Who else spoke after the apostle Peter that the whole assembly fell silent? They listened to Barnabas and Paul. When they had concluded the presentation, James spoke up. "Brothers," he said, "listen to me." He told the apostles, "Listen to me," including the apostle Peter. He said, "It is my judgment, therefore, that we ought not to cause God's Gentile converts any difficulties." Well, what I am reading is the Holy Bible, the New American Bible, the new Catholic translation.

Now, if the apostle Peter was the first pope, would it not be, Mr. Keating, a usurpation of the authority of the apostle Peter? Look at that, a pope in person at a council and somebody subordinate would make a decision for him? That's why the apostle Peter is not the first pope. Therefore, their foundation is crumbling again. It is crumbling again. It was not the apostle Peter who made a decision. That's in the Bible. I challenge him again. Show a verse in the Bible that says the apostle Peter said, at the Council of Jerusalem, "This is my judgment" or "This is my decision." Mr. Keating could read a whole chapter of Acts, but he could not find a verse where the apostle Peter would say, "This is my judgment." Rather, it was apostle James who made the decision.

What is the proof, then, that the apostle Peter recognized the authority of the apostle James? When the apostle Peter was released from prison, whom did he tell the members of the Church to tell concerning his release from prison? He motioned to them to be quiet and explained how the Lord had brought him out of prison. Report this to James and the brothers, he told the members of the Church. Report it to James. If Peter was a pope, why then would he tell the members to report it to James? This is the proof that he is not the leader of the Church. In Acts 8:14, it says, "When the apostles in Jerusalem heard that Samaria had accepted the word of God, they sent Peter and John to them." The apostles in Jerusalem sent Peter. How could he be a pope or a leader of the Church when he was sent? Who is greatest, the one that is sent or the one that is sending?

MODERATOR: We now have a three-minute cross-question from Mr. Keating.

KEATING: Mr. Ventilacion, can we tell which is the true Church by its teachings?

VENTILACION: Exactly. That is my position.

KEATING: All right. If Iglesia ni Cristo teaches a false doctrine, would that imply that Iglesia ni Cristo is not the true Church?

VENTILACION: If it is teaching a false doctrine—

KEATING: Yes or no, please.

VENTILACION: I'm answering you.

KEATING: Yes or no.

VENTILACION: If you could find a false doctrine of the Church of Christ, then, this is not the true Church, but I guarantee you, you could not find one.

KEATING: If the Catholic Church, though, teaches true doctrine, you would admit it would have to be the true Church?

VENTILACION: Well, I just presented in my first presentation that you are contradicting yourself concerning your doctrine about the Virgin Mary.

KEATING: Okay. So far you've admitted that the church that teaches truly is true. The one that teaches falsely is false.

VENTILACION: It is. As long as it is the doctrine in the Bible, that is a true doctrine.

KEATING: If Christ really is divine, then Iglesia ni Cristo must not be the true Church. Right?

VENTILACION: Do we believe—

KEATING: I'm not asking you if you believe it. I know what your position is.

VENTILACION: Why don't we have another debate, Mr. Karl Keating, on the deity of Jesus Christ?

KEATING: Because the true Church is identified by its teachings.

VENTILACION: That is not the topic of our debate here.

KEATING: It's exactly the topic. It's exactly the topic of our debate. What I want to get out of you is this: is Jesus Christ—

VENTILACION: Jesus Christ is divine but not God, because even the Christians are partakers of the divine nature. Are we God too?

KEATING: Let me ask you a question maybe you'll answer. In the House of Representatives when the Speaker and the majority leader and the minority leader and the whips are sent by the members of the House to go see the President in the White House, they are sent by the members of the House. Does that imply that the members of the House are above their superiors?

VENTILACION: What you are talking about is not in the Bible.

KEATING: I am asking you a question. You will do anything, won't you, to avoid answering a simple question?

VENTILACION: No, I'm not avoiding.

KEATING: Your point about Peter being sent is that therefore he must be inferior. I've asked you what about the case of the House of Representatives? You're not willing to answer that because you know what the answer would imply.

MODERATOR: Thank you very much, gentlemen. And I'd like to thank the audience, too, for their fine and very peaceful, I would say, demeanor. Now, we're going to end the first portion of the debate.

VENTILACION: When the Church apostatized, then there was a need for Christ to re-establish his Church because the Church is necessary for salvation. Now, according to Dr. Henry Halley, one of the famous biblical authors, he mentioned that the Church had changed its nature, had entered its great apostasy, had become a political organization in the spirit and pattern of Imperial Rome. The proof that there was an apostasy is the Catholic Church itself. We are going to present to you today from the Bible that after the first century the Church was apostatized.

Christ mentioned or prophesied about the re-establishment of his Church. What is the proof, my beloved friends? I'm going to read from John 10:16. Christ mentioned, "Other sheep I have which are not of this fold. They also I must bring, and they will hear my voice, and there will be one flock and one shepherd." In this verse that I am reading, Christ is prophesying about the re-establishment of his Church. Why? Because he said, "I have other sheep, which are not of this fold." What did Christ say that he will do to these other sheep? He said, "I will also bring them, they will hear my voice, and there will be one flock."

What is the meaning of the word "flock"? The flock, according to Acts 20:28, in the Lamsa version of the Bible, which I read a while ago but I have to repeat again: "Take ye therefore to yourselves and to all the flock, over which the Holy Spirit has appointed you overseers, to feed the church of Christ." So, the flock is the Church of Christ. Christ mentioned his other sheep, which will become one flock or one Church of Christ. And this is in the future, because Christ said, "There will be one flock."

So, aside from the flock, during the times of Christ and the apostles, there will still be another flock. Christ said, "My other sheep, they are not of this fold." Why? Where are the other sheep of Christ? Why, suddenly, do they not belong to the first century Church of Christ? Because in Acts 2:39 it says, "For the promises onto you and to your children and to all who are afar off, as many as the Lord our God will call." Why is it that they do not belong to the flock, or to the first century Church? Because God shall call them. They are not yet called to the Church. That is why it is the future. There will be a re-establishment of one Church. Christ said, "My other sheep will become one flock of the Church of Christ." Now, who were called? The apostle Peter said, "They shall be called, or God will call them." Who were called, already, during the time of Christ and the apostles? These are the members of the first-century Church of Christ. Romans 9:24 says, "Even us whom he called, not of the Jews only, but also of the Gentiles." So now, Acts 2:39, when the apostle Peter said, "for the promises to you," he was talking to the Jews, "and to your children" was referring to the Gentiles and to all who are afar off.

These are not Jews or Gentiles. They are the other sheep of Christ. "But God will call them, or God shall bring them." From where? The Bible says, "from afar off." Where is this afar off? Where will the other sheep come from? God himself will answer that question. In Isaiah 43:5 this is what is recorded: "From the far east will I bring your offspring, and from the far west I will gather you." So, what is this far off, where the other sheep of Christ, the third group of people that will constitute the one true church of Christ, will come from? God himself said in the prophecy, "From the far east will I bring your offspring." What country is the fulfillment of this? The Philippines. Why?

The Philippines, no one could deny it, is in the Far East. It is not only in the Far East, a priest by the name of Horacio de la Costa wrote a book entitled *Asia and the Philippines*. On page 169 he said, "It cannot be without significance that the country which stands almost at the geographical center of the Far East, the Philippines, should also be that in which Christianity has taken the deepest root." So, the Philippines is not only in the Far East, it is lying almost at the geographical center of the Far East. So, when Christ said, "I have other sheep," this is the Church of Christ that appeared in the Far East. The country is the Philippines.

According to the same prophecy, when shall God bring this Church of Christ from the Philippines? I read Isaiah 43:5-6 in the King James version: "Fear not for I am with thee. I will bring thy seed from the East and gather thee from the West. I will say to the North and to the South, keep not back. Bring my sons from far and my daughters from the ends of the Earth." Our question is when shall God bring these people from the Far East? God said, "Bring my sons from far and my daughters from the ends of the Earth." That is the time element involved in the prophecy. When you say the ends of the Earth, that is not the same as the end of the Earth or the end of the world. We have to first find out when is the end of the world or end of the Earth.

Matthew 24:3: "And as he sat upon the Mount of Olives, the disciples came unto him privately saying, Tell us when shall these things be? What shall be the sign of thy coming and of the end of the world?" The apostles were asking our Lord Jesus Christ, "When is the end of the world?" They were asking him, "What shall be the sign of thy coming and of the end of the world? When shall these things be?"

The end of the world refers to the Second Coming of Christ. But it is not the time that the Church of Christ will be re-established in the Far East or in the Philippines. God said, in the prophecy, "And the ends of the Earth." When is this? Here is the statement of Christ in Matthew 24:33: "So, likewise, you, when you shall see all these things, know that it is near, even at the doors." What is the first sign, given by Christ? In the same chapter, in Matthew 24:6, he said, "And you shall hear of wars and rumors of wars. See that you be not troubled for all these things must come to pass, but the end is not yet." So, what was the first sign given by our Lord Jesus Christ? He said, "You shall hear of wars and rumors of wars." What war is the fulfillment of this prophecy of our Lord Jesus Christ?

What I am going to read is an excerpt from a book entitled *The Story of the Great War*: "The first campaign of the southeastern battlegrounds of the Great War began on July 27, 1914, when the Austrian troops undertook their first invasion of Serbia." This was a book that was copyrighted 1916, two years after the start of the Great War. They called it the Great War, but historians later called it the First World War. Another book that says the First World War started on July 27, 1914, is *The Nations at War* by Willis J. Abbott. Austria, backed by Germany, declared war upon Serbia on July 27, so the First World War started on July 27, 1914. That is the war mentioned by Christ in Matthew 24:6, "That you shall hear the rumors of wars."

At the same time that we could see the war, we could see the Church of Christ reappeared or re-established in the Philippines. What I have here is a copy of the incorporation record. "This is to certify a copy of the articles of incorporation of Iglesia ni Cristo, dated July 24, 1914, registered on July 27, 1914." The Church of Christ appeared at the same time that the First World War erupted in Europe. Why? Probably our friend here would say, "That is just a matter of coincidence." We do not call it a matter of coincidence because it is a divine mandate. It is in the Bible. God used the phrase "ends of the Earth." The war started on July 27, 1914, at the same time that the Church was registered with the Philippine government as a religious organization.

So, I have proven my point here, my beloved friends, that this Church is, indeed, the Church established by Christ. They would say it is the church established by Manalo. We do not have that kind of doctrine. Ask the members of the Church of Christ that are here now. Ask them, "Who established your church?" If they would say Manalo, then that is wrong. Probably you are asking a Catholic, not an Iglesia ni Cristo. If you will be asking an Iglesia ni Cristo, he would tell you, "It is Jesus Christ, based upon his prophecy in John 10:16 about his other sheep."

Did you hear Mr. Keating say that they deny the deity of Jesus Christ? Why? Because Jesus Christ is not the Father. And our mission here, the mission of the whole Church of Christ now, is to proclaim to the people of the world that there is only one God and that is the Father. He said, three Persons in one God. He could not read. He could not read it from the Bible that God said "I am three Persons." He could not read from the Bible that Christ would say "I am God" or "I am a true God." I guarantee you that. Mr. Keating could not read from the Bible that Jesus Christ himself said, "I am God."

MODERATOR: We now have a five-minute cross-question from the negative side. Mr. Keating.

KEATING: Tell me, where does the Bible use the word "Philippines"?

VENTILACION: Mr. Keating, the word "Philippines" came long after the Bible was written.

KEATING: That's right. It's not in the Bible. Second question.

VENTILACION: The proper word is Far East.

KEATING: Second question. The words "far" and "east" do not appear in the Hebrew in the same sentence.

VENTILACION: It doesn't appear in the same sentence?

KEATING: No. The phrase does not, but I'm going to allow "Far East" for the purposes of argument. Why do you say that Far East must apply to the Philippines, when the Far East includes China, Korea, Japan, Taiwan, Hong Kong, and Indochina?

VENTILACION: Okay. This is it. The whole Far East is not only the Philippines, but the Far East, in Isaiah 43:5, is the Philippines because the Church appeared in the Philippines.

KEATING: You quoted somebody who said that the geographical center of the Far East was the Philippines.

VENTILACION: Center of the Far East.

KEATING: That's right. Has anybody here ever looked at a map of the Far East? Has anybody here ever looked at a world map? If you look at a map of the Far East, the Philippines is in the southeast corner. Please explain how the southeast corner can be the geographic center.

VENTILACION: It's the priest himself.

KEATING: What the priest said doesn't mean anything. The priest is incorrect. You're relying on a priest who happens to know no geography.

VENTILACION: The priest doesn't mean anything, Mr. Keating?

KEATING: His comment means nothing because he happens to be geographically wrong. Is it your opinion that the Philippines is the geographic center of the Far East? I'm asking you, Mr. Ventilacion, if you would dare to say such a foolish thing to a geography teacher?

VENTILACION: Well I'm not, but I'm teaching you—

KEATING: Let me go on to one of your verses. Let's go to Isaiah 43, where it says, "The sons came from far and the daughters from the ends of the Earth." What you did not mention is what the Hebrew original actually says. The Hebrew means "the end" in the sense of space, not of time. It does not use the sense of time.

VENTILACION: That is your opinion.

KEATING: It is not my opinion, it's Hebrew. It's the Hebrew language.

VENTILACION: That's your Hebrew opinion.

KEATING: The Old Testament was written in Hebrew. Do you think it was written in English?

VENTILACION: What I'm talking about is your Hebrew opinion.

KEATING: You are refusing to look at the Hebrew?

VENTILACION: Yes.

KEATING: Yes? Why do you refuse to look at the Hebrew original? Why, because it's against what you believe, right?

VENTILACION: Is it the original Hebrew? Is it not that the original Hebrew was destroyed?

KEATING: We have the Old Testament in Hebrew, do we not? Is it in Hebrew or is it in English?

VENTILACION: You are mentioning Isaiah 43:5, right?

KEATING: Yes. You quoted it in the English. You said the word "ends" refers to time. It does not refer to time. It refers only to space.

MODERATOR: Thank you gentlemen. We now go to a 15-minute talk by the negative side, Mr. Keating.

KEATING: Let me not put too fine a point on it. Iglesia ni Cristo relies for its credentials on a fraudulent history. It claims that the Church that Jesus Christ established entirely apostatized—that is, ceased to exist—in the first century. In my first remarks, I quoted from Matthew 16 where Jesus said he never would abandon the Church. But if the Church ceased to exist because it had no members, that's exactly what he allowed to happen, and so he must have been a liar.

Mr. Ventilacion says, "Oh, the church was restored in 1914." Where have we heard that before? I'll tell you where we've heard it before, and I'll tell you where Felix Manalo got it. In 1830 God supposedly told Joseph Smith to restore the true Church, the Mormon Church. In 1879, God supposedly told Charles Taze Russell, who frequently is cited in *Pasugo* as an authority, to re-establish the true Church. Members of his church are known as Jehovah's Witnesses. In 1879 God supposedly told Mary Baker Eddy to organize the true Church. Hers is known as the Christian Science Church. In 1931 God supposedly told Herbert W. Armstrong that he would be the new messenger who would rise up to found the new Church. He called his church he Worldwide Church of God. In 1936 God supposedly told Sun Yung Moon that he would be the new messenger. This messenger, Moon said, would rise out of the Far East, which is not the Philippines but Korea. Moon's one true Church is called the Unification Church. His followers often are called "Moonies."

Like all these other churches, Iglesia ni Cristo claims that its founder, Felix Manalo, is the true messenger. This is nonsense. Look at the man's background. Although he was baptized a Catholic, he left the Catholic Church as a young teenager. He became a Protestant. He went through five Protestant denominations, including the Seventh-day Adventist Church. Finally, he decided to start his own church, which he did in 1914, but he did not begin with all of today's Iglesia ni Cristo doctrines in place. Maybe you are not told that. In 1919 Manalo went to America because he wanted to learn more about religion. Where did he go? He went to study with Protestants, who, later on, the Iglesia people would say are apostates just like Catholics.

Why, five years after being called by God as the new messenger, did Manalo go to the U.S. to learn from apostates? The fact is that he didn't use the new messenger doctrine in 1914. He didn't use it even in 1919. He didn't use it until 1922. Why? Because there was a schism in Iglesia ni Cristo. Manalo wanted to accumulate as much power as possible, so he raised himself in the eyes of his followers by claiming to be the new messenger. This is balderdash. If he had been the new messenger when called by God in 1914, why didn't he tell anybody until 1922? The answer is because he didn't even know about it until 1922. And he didn't know about it until he learned from the American Seventh-day Adventists and learned from the American Jehovah's Witnesses. He borrowed the distinctive doctrines for his church from American sectarian groups. The lack of divinity for Christ, the lack of the Trinity? That's from the Jehovah's Witnesses. The apostasy of the early Church? That's from the Mormons. You need to find out where your beliefs really come from.

What about World War I and 1914 being the year? Is it just a coincidence that Manalo filed the articles of incorporation for his church, registered it in the Philippines, in 1914? Mr. Ventilacion would have you think, no. He would have you think it was a divine act. He would have you think that World War I was foretold in Isaiah 34:2. Have you ever read Isaiah 34:2 carefully? Read what it says. It says, "All nations and their armies will be involved in the war." That quotation I take from *Pasugo*. That's its understanding of Isaiah 34:2. "All nations of the world."

Did World War I involve all nations, even though it was called a world war? It didn't involve any nations, except for the U.S. and a couple of token troops from elsewhere, from the Western hemisphere. Except for countries like Tanganyika, it didn't include any nations in Africa. Aside from Palestine and Turkey, it didn't include any nations in Asia. It didn't include Australia. It didn't even include all the nations of Europe. Most of the nations of the world did not participate at all in World War I. Don't let yourself be fooled that just because it's called a world war that therefore all the world was involved. That's not the case. If you know any international history, you know that's not the case. So, World War I was not the war that Isaiah 34 was talking about, which means you cannot use Isaiah 34:2 to identify 1914 as the year for anything.

Do you see how Iglesia ni Cristo must bend facts of history? What does it say? "Oh we don't look at history. We look at the Bible." But then it goes and argues history. It goes so far as to argue that in Isaiah there are references to army tanks and airplanes. Give me a break. That's not in there at all. On what biblical basis is authority in the Iglesia ni Cristo passed along? On no biblical basis. Why did Eraño Manalo become the successor of Felix Manalo? Because he was his son, that's why, not because he had any authority. Was there an election of some sort? No. It was a family concern. That's all.

I mentioned, in my opening remarks, Iglesia ni Cristo is fond of claiming that the pope is the beast of Revelation. We know that the beast of Revelation has the number 666, right? Now here is the argument. Follow this carefully. The popes have what is known as a tiara, a triple crown. The beast can be identified as a man whose name adds up to 666 or a man whose title adds up to 666. Iglesia ni Cristo says two things: first, that the title of the pope, in Latin, is "*Vicarius Filii Dei*," and second, that that title appears on the three bands of the tiara. I have in front of me a photocopy of the September 1976 issue of *Pasugo*. Here is a drawing made by the staff showing the tiara, with those words on it. This is just a pen drawing.

Does the title *Vicarius Filii Dei* add up to 666? Yes, it does. But, is it a title of the popes? Have they ever used it? No. Do you know what *Vicarius Filii Dei* means? It means "Vicar of the Son of God." Pope have never used that title. No pope ever. The official title of the pope is Vicar of Christ, not Vicar of the Son of God. We Catholics claim he is the representative on Earth of the God-man, the Messiah, not of the Second Person of the Trinity as such. The title "Vicar of Christ," in Latin, is *Vicarius Christi.* The letters don't add up to 666. So, this is the first thing that Iglesia ni Cristo has done—and it repeats this story every four issues or so in its magazine.

I showed you the picture where someone penciled in the words "*Vicarius Filii Dei*" on the tiara. Have you ever seen a good photograph of the tiara? Iglesia ni Cristo says these words are written in jewels on the tiara and that the word "*Dei*," which means "of God," is written in a hundred diamonds. Is that the case? All we have to do is turn to that September 1976 issue of *Pasugo*, to the beginning of that article, where there is a picture of Pope Paul VI, who was the last pope to wear the tiara. The picture shows that there are no words at all on the tiara.

The writers in *Pasugo* have lied again to you. Worse, they are insulting you because on one page they show you that there are no words on the tiara, and elsewhere they make a line drawing and add in the words, and they think you are too stupid to see it.

I was warned by some well-intentioned people that I shouldn't come here tonight and talk tough about the fraudulence of Iglesia ni Cristo. They said, "The Iglesia people will shout you down," but you haven't shouted me down. They said, "They will interrupt you," and you have interrupted, but not too often. They said, "They are closed-minded," and maybe some of you are. Of course, you find closed-minded people in every church, don't you? You also find open-minded people. Many of you who are members of Iglesia ni Cristo were brought up as Catholics. You probably learned next to nothing about the Catholic faith. I must conclude that because you are swallowing this nonsense that Iglesia puts out about the Catholic Church. Forget, for the moment, Iglesia's own credibility. Look at what it says against the competition. Why does it feel it must lie regularly about the Catholic Church, such as with this thing with the pope's tiara and 666?

Iglesia ni Cristo doesn't want you to know things. It doesn't want you to know the truth about the Catholic faith, about the Bible, or about your own religion. You've got to ask yourself, if that's the case, how can this possibly be of God? How can a church that has borrowed its principles from nineteenth-century Protestants and sectarians possibly be God's real Church? Thank you.

MODERATOR: We will now hear a five-minute cross-question period from the affirmative side. Brother Ventilacion.

VENTILACION: Mr. Karl Keating, I would like to ask you, in John 10:16, did not Christ say that, "I have other sheep"?

KEATING: Yes, he did, and he meant the Gentiles.

VENTILACION: Okay. Christ said that there shall be one shepherd and one flock. Who is the one shepherd?

KEATING: We all know who that is. It's Jesus Christ.

VENTILACION: It's Jesus Christ? Why did Christ say, "And there will be a flock and one shepherd"? Isn't it that Jesus Christ was already a shepherd?

KEATING: He was already the shepherd.

VENTILACION: Right. So, when he said there will be one shepherd, is he still the one shepherd, then?

KEATING: He founded his Church. He's the shepherd of it.

VENTILACION: Let me ask you another question.

KEATING: Of course, at the end of John's Gospel he also names Peter as a shepherd: "Feed my lambs, feed my sheep, feed my sheep."

VENTILACION: So, in John 10:16, is this the apostle Peter?

KEATING: No. At the end of John's Gospel. "Feed my lambs, feed my sheep, feed my sheep." That's where he gives the position of shepherd, in some sense, to Peter.

VENTILACION: That answers my question. Now, in John 13:20 Christ said, "Whosoever accepts the one that I sent, receives me." Do you believe that?

KEATING: I believe everything the Bible says.

VENTILACION: So, you believe that Christ could send another messenger, then?

KEATING: Not one from the Philippines named Manalo. No.

VENTILACION: But you believe that Christ could send a messenger?

KEATING: The messengers he sent out, two by two, were his own disciples.

VENTILACION: We believe that Brother Felix Manalo was a messenger.

KEATING: Fine. You can believe it, but it has no scriptural basis.

VENTILACION: This is the question. When he taught us that the Father is the only true God, is that a wrong teaching?

KEATING: Of course it's wrong. Jesus is God, the Holy Spirit is God, the Father is not the only God. There is one God who is three divine Persons, Father, Son, Holy Spirit.

VENTILACION: This is the question, because Father Felix Manalo taught us about the one God.

KEATING: I don't care what Manalo taught.

VENTILACION: In John 17:3, Christ is the one speaking, right?

KEATING: Read it to us.

VENTILACION: Okay. These were the words. "And this is eternal life that they may know you, the only true God." To whom did Christ address that word?

KEATING: To his Father.

VENTILACION: To the Father. Hold on. I'm not yet through.

KEATING: I'm not through answering either. I was interrupted by the audience. Will you let me finish my answer?

VENTILACION: If the Father—

KEATING: Will you let me finish my answer?

VENTILACION: Go ahead.

KEATING: What you fail to do is make a distinction between the Trinity and tritheism, three gods. We believe in one God who is in three Persons, not in three gods. Your arguments are all against three gods.

VENTILACION: I repeat, again, my question. Christ said, "The Father is the only true God." Is that wrong or right?

KEATING: There is only one God. The Father is the only true God, Jesus Christ is the only true God, the Holy Spirit is the only true God.

VENTILACION: Where in the Bible does it says that the Holy Spirit is the only true God?

KEATING: What do you think the Holy Spirit is, some force?

VENTILACION: Don't ask me, I am asking you. Where does it say in the Bible that the Holy Spirit is the only true God? What verse?

KEATING: You want those exact words?

VENTILACION: Yes.

KEATING: Just like I wanted the exact words of where the Philippines are mentioned?

VENTILACION: I'm asking you about those words, what you said. Where does it say that the Holy Spirit is the only true God? What verse?

KEATING: Those exact words are not used.

VENTILACION: Then why did you say that if that is not in the Bible?

KEATING: I didn't say that is not in the Bible. What I said is that the Bible teaches—

VENTILACION: It is in the Bible, then?

KEATING: The Bible teaches—

VENTILACION: It is in the Bible, then?

KEATING: The Bible teaches that the Father is God, that the Son is God, that the Holy Spirit is God.

VENTILACION: That is not my question. My question, Mr. Keating, is this. You said that the Holy Spirit is the only true God. If the Holy Spirit, granting—but not conceding, granting—that the Holy Spirit is the only true God, how many only true Gods do you have?

KEATING: One!

VENTILACION: One? The Father is the only true God? How do you understand the word "only"? Is there another one aside from him?

KEATING: The word "only" comes from the word "one."

VENTILACION: My question is, when Christ said that the Father is the only true God, what did he mean by the word "only"? Is there another God aside from him?

KEATING: Jesus was not saying that he was not God, or that the Holy Spirit was not God.

VENTILACION: He was teaching that the Father is the only true God, right?

KEATING: In my opening remarks I gave you all kinds of quotations proving that Jesus Christ is divine. You have not talked about any of them.

VENTILACION: You cannot answer the question.

MODERATOR: Thank you very much, gentlemen. We now go to a seven-minute rebuttal from the affirmative side. Brother Ventilacion.

VENTILACION: You know, Mr. Keating did not prove his church is, indeed, the true Church. So, during his presentation, he attacked on the concept of Jesus Christ as God or not. That is not in our discussion today in the debate. But he went into that, so I just followed him. When I asked him that when Brother Felix Manalo taught us that the Father is the only true God and is that a wrong doctrine, he said yes. He said that the Son is the only true God, and the Holy Spirit is the only true God. He admitted, also, that the Father is the only true God. So what does it mean? What Brother Felix Manalo taught to us, that the Father is the only true God, is also admitted by Mr. Karl Keating. Right, Mr. Keating?

Why is it then that the debate went to this? It is to prove which church is the true Church. I told him we can debate another time concerning if Christ is God or not or the Holy Spirit is God or not, but he forced me to do this. So I have been asking him, basing from the teachings of Christ, what did Christ say? Christ said, "The Father is the only true God." I repeat that word again. "And this is eternal life, that they may know you, the only true God." I asked him what he means by that word "only." Is there another God? He said, the Son is also the true God. The Holy Spirit is also the true God. What does he mean by the word "only"? When Christ said that the Father is the only true God, that is not placing Christ as God.

In John 17:3 Christ proclaimed, "The Father is the only true God." But after that, what did Christ mention about himself? This Brother Felix Manalo taught us, too. "And Jesus Christ, whom you have sent." Whose words are these? These are the words of Christ. Did he say that "I am also a true God?" Mr. Keating said Christ is also an only true God, but Christ did not present himself as the only true God. I challenged him again, if he could prove, from the Bible: where did Christ say that he is the only true God? Mr. Keating, I hope you hear that challenge.

Where did Christ say that "I am the only true God"? Where in the Bible did it mention that the Holy Spirit is the only true God? That's what you believe, so I ask you: how many only true Gods do you believe in? He has the Father as the only true God. He has the Son as the only true God. He has the Holy Spirit as the only true God. You have three only true Gods. I thought you believed in only one God. Now, it happens there are three only true Gods. I hope Mr. Keating can find that in the Bible.

Most of our members here were Catholics before. Brother Felix Manalo taught us that the Father is the only true God, and that is from the Bible. We accepted that Brother Felix Manalo was, indeed, a messenger of God. But the truth remains. The truth remains. The basic doctrine concerning God was already taught to us by Brother Felix Manalo. What about the apostles? When the apostles were preaching, whom did the apostles teach as the only true God? This Brother Felix Manalo also taught us.

The apostles teach that the one God is composed of three? In 1 Corinthians 8:6 I read, "Yet there is for us only one God, the Father." What did the apostles say? The apostles said, "Yet for us there is only one God." The apostles are in the true Church. Mr. Keating is teaching that the only one God is not only the Father but the Son and the Holy Spirit. It is a combination of three Gods. But the apostles said, "For us, there is only one God, and that is the Father." The apostles did not say the Father, the Son, and the Holy Spirit.

Did not Brother Felix Manalo teach us this, my beloved brethren? Yes. Therefore, the spirit of Christ and the spirit of the apostles is the same spirit that guided Brother Felix Manalo. That's why we, most of us, who were Catholics before—why did we leave the Roman Catholic Church? Because just on the basics they are already wrong. How much more on the other doctrines of the Catholic Church? That is why we could not accept that the Catholic Church is the true Church. They are the fulfillment of the apostatized church. We believe that when Christ said "I shall have other sheep" there shall be one flock, that's one Church, there shall be one shepherd. That shepherd is Brother Felix Manalo, not Jesus Christ, because Christ said, "There will be." That is in the future. Now, no matter how he will attack the personality of Brother Felix Manalo, we remain in believing that he is a messenger of God because of the teachings.

On April 18, 1915, in the *Sunday Visitor*, which was published in Huntington, Indiana, it mentions that the pope's title is *Vicarius Filii Dei*. This is according to the book *The Beast of Revelation*.

KEATING: Are you saying that's true? Are you saying that the pope's tiara has *Vicarius Filii Dei* written on it? Are you saying that?

VENTILACION: *Vicarius Filii Dei* means Vicar of God.

KEATING: I know what it means. It means Vicar of the Son of God. Is that on the pope's tiara?

VENTILACION: According to the—

KEATING: According to your knowledge, is it on there or is it not?

VENTILACION: According to what I have learned from the book *The Beast of Revelation*, in our *Sunday Visitor* they published that in—

KEATING: What you have done is you accepted, uncritically, an anti-Catholic work. You mentioned the book—

VENTILACION: It's your problem to debate with the Adventists, not with me.

KEATING: You use their argument. You admit it's wrong. Now you say, "Don't complain to me, argue with them."

VENTILACION: Question: in your book, does it say 616 or 666?

KEATING: In the ancient manuscript it has both but 666 is obviously the proper one.

VENTILACION: Which Catholic book could you show me that it is 616?

KEATING: Ancient manuscripts. Do you have any books—

VENTILACION: I'm asking you a Catholic book. Right now.

KEATING: Okay. I will give you one.

VENTILACION: The Catholic book?

KEATING: Look at Nestle's New Testament which gives the Greek. It gives a reference, in the footnote, to both numbers.

VENTILACION: I will not also believe you because you cannot show me.

MODERATOR: We will have a seven-minute rebuttal from the negative side, Mr. Keating.

KEATING: I hope you are all paying close attention to what he is doing. He refuses to answer questions straight. He admits that *Pasugo* publishes lies. He says it's not our fault because we took it from another publication. He won't go back to the original sources. I'm continually amazed at Mr. Ventilacion's apparent ignorance of what the doctrine of the Trinity means. I have never come across somebody who talks in public about the Trinity and doesn't even know its definition. He claims to have read my book and apparently other Catholic books. How come he doesn't know what the doctrine of the Trinity is? He keeps saying it means three Gods. It doesn't. Every Protestant book that talks about it, every Catholic book that talks about it, every Eastern Orthodox book that talks about it makes the distinction clearly. What's the problem with Iglesia ni Cristo? You see Iglesia's position will fall apart if it admits that the Trinity is about one God, not three Gods.

He asked me for any proof, any proof at all, that the Holy Spirit is divine. Let me cite a verse for you. Look at Acts 5. There is the story, at the beginning, of Ananias and Sapphira. Remember what they did? They sold their property and gave part of it to the common fund, but they kept back some, and they lied about it. They committed fraud. They said, "We are giving all of our property, all of the proceeds, to the Church," but they were lying. And what happened? Both of them were struck dead by God, right? Verse 5:3 says, "They defrauded the Holy Spirit." The very next verse says. "It is God, not man, that you have defrauded." Verse 3 says, you defrauded the Holy Spirit. The next verse says, it is God that you have defrauded. Therefore, the Holy

Spirit is God. All the early Christians knew that. They didn't have a problem with it.

Felix Manalo came to the U.S. and got it in his head that he would borrow from off-shoots from Protestantism such as the Jehovah's Witnesses and the Mormons. He borrowed the idea that the Holy Spirit isn't God, that Jesus isn't God. Why? Because he could go back to the Philippines preaching a new gospel, different from the one taught by the Catholic Church. Doing that, he could get a following. He wasn't out for truth. Remember the line "even if an angel should preach to you a new gospel"? Manalo claimed to be that angel from the Philippines. He used the term "angel" to describe himself as messenger. That's the false gospel, but it's not original with Manalo. He wasn't bright enough to make it up on his own. He borrowed it from others. Let me repeat verses I mentioned earlier. God the Father is called Lord of Lord and King of Kings. So is Jesus, in Revelation 17:4. God the Father is called the Alpha and the Omega. That is the designation for God. So is Jesus the Alpha and the Omega, in Revelation 1:8. Jesus uses the Father's own proper name for himself: "I Am."

What did the Jews start to do when he said that? Do you remember what follows, after John 8:58? They took up stones to kill him. Why? Because they thought he committed the ultimate blasphemy, which is to say that he was God. They wouldn't have taken up stones if he said, "Oh, I'm the image of God only, or I'm related to God, or God is my Father, the same way he's your Father." They were going to kill him, because he claimed to be God, and they knew what he was saying when he said those sacred words: "I Am."

Hebrew 1:8 addresses Christ. It says, "Thy throne, O God, is forever." That's talking to Christ, calling him God. Colossians 2:9: "In Christ the fullness of deity dwells." Complete deity in Christ. Isaiah 45:23 says, "To God the Father every knee must bend." Mr. Ventilacion pointedly ignored Philippians 2:10, which says that "to Jesus Christ every knee must bend." *Pasugo* repeatedly brings up the fact, according to it, that if you bow to something, then you worship it as God. So if you bow to Jesus, you must worship him as God, according to Iglesia's own principle.

But Mr. Ventilacion didn't bring that up, and he didn't mention what the apostle Thomas said when he put his hand into the risen Christ's side and then believed that he had risen from the dead. Thomas said, "My Lord and my God," and Jesus did not rebuke him. Jesus praised him. He said, "You're right, better, though, those that do not see and yet believe." But it's still good to believe when you see. Jesus did not say, "Oh, no, you're mistaken." Do you remember when, later on, someone came up to Peter and knelt before him on the ground, as though to worship him? Peter said, "Get up. I am just a man." That's right. Did Jesus tell that to Thomas? "I'm just a man"? No, he did not, because he's not just a man, he is God.

MODERATOR: We now go to a three-minute cross-question from the affirmative side. Brother Ventilacion.

VENTILACION: Well, your presentation was concerning Christ, so I have to go there. You said Manalo's teachings, right? You mentioned about Manalo's teachings?

KEATING: I mentioned quite a bit about Manalo.

VENTILACION: If Felix Manalo taught us from the Bible that Jesus Christ is a man, is that wrong?

KEATING: Jesus Christ is both man and God.

VENTILACION: That's not my question. My question is—

KEATING: I don't know what Manalo taught from the Bible. I know what he claims.

VENTILACION: That's what I'm saying—

KEATING: I know what Manalo claims, but that's not teaching from the Bible.

VENTILACION: You said you quoted Revelation 8:1 which, you said, says that Christ is God. Does it say in Revelation 8:1 that Christ is God?

KEATING: I said Revelation 1:8.

VENTILACION: Okay. Did Christ say "I am God" in Revelation 1:8?

KEATING: He says, "I am the alpha and the omega, the beginning and the end, sayeth the Lord, which is, which was, and which is to come, the almighty."

VENTILACION: Therefore, that is—

KEATING: Jesus is calling himself the Almighty.

VENTILACION: That is only your opinion.

KEATING: I'm reading from the text. What do you mean it's my opinion? You mean when I bring up a point up that contradicts you, you say that's my opinion, even though it's straight from the Bible?

VENTILACION: My question is this. Did Christ say in Revelation 1:8, "I am God." Answer yes or no.

KEATING: That's the meaning of it.

VENTILACION: In John 8:58 did Christ say, "I am God" or "I Am"?

KEATING: He used the proper name for God, which is I Am.

VENTILACION: Mr. Keating, I have to repeat my question, please. My question is this—

KEATING: Jesus said, "Before Abraham was, I Am."

VENTILACION: Did he say, "I am God?"

KEATING: He didn't need to because that's the name of God, I Am. That's what Moses was told. Look at Exodus 3:14. Moses was given the name of God. God said, "My name is I Am." God's name is not "I am God" but "I Am."

VENTILACION: Let's get to Thomas now. You said Thomas said to Jesus, "My Lord and my God," right?

KEATING: That's right.

VENTILACION: So you believe Thomas?

KEATING: I believe the Bible.

VENTILACION: That's not my question. My question is, do you believe Thomas when he said, "Jesus is my God?"

KEATING: I believe Thomas and Jesus, who approved of what he said.

VENTILACION: In John 20:17 did not Christ tell the Christians who is the God that they should believe? Before Thomas said, "My Lord and my God" to Christ, did not Christ tell them who is the God of the Christians?

KEATING: He says in that verse, "I am ascending to my God."

VENTILACION: Very good. Now—

KEATING: I want to finish the answer. It's not complete.

VENTILACION: I will ask from your—

KEATING: I'm not done with my answer. Why does he say that? Because he has two natures. His human nature in which he ascends to God. In his divine nature, he's already God. Your mistake is you think that every verse in the New Testament must be taken with the same sense. Some of them refer to our Lord's divine nature, some to his human nature. You ignore that distinction.

VENTILACION: This is my question. Did not Christ say he has a God?

KEATING: His human nature was created. Obviously he had a God.

VENTILACION: So, if he has a God, who is his God?

KEATING: He said, "I ascend to the Father."

VENTILACION: Is not the God of Christ also our God?

KEATING: Why are you avoiding what Thomas was saying? I thought we were talking about Thomas.

VENTILACION: Mr. Keating, you are out of order.

KEATING: I have to be out of order to get my point across to you.

VENTILACION: I'll tell you why later. Be patient.

MODERATOR: Thank you for the audience who are still here.

VENTILACION: I don't know why Mr. Keating always goes to if Jesus Christ is God or not when the topic here is to prove if the Church of Christ which appeared in the Philippines is the true Church. He did not disprove what I read. He has never disproved. Our presentation here is that Christ mentioned other sheep who will become one flock or one Church of Christ. The re-establishment of the Church happened in the year 1914.

Inasmuch as he would like to discuss Jesus Christ, let's follow him to that. He said, in Revelation 1:8, Christ is God. What if we read it, okay? "I am alpha and omega, the beginning and the ending, sayeth the Lord, which is, and which was, and which is to come, the almighty." This is not Jesus Christ. Mr. Keating said this is Jesus Christ. This is the Almighty God. Why would we believe that this is the Almighty God and not Jesus Christ? The word "Almighty" means the source of all power. He believes that too.

Let's go to the power that is of our Lord Jesus Christ. What kind of power does our Lord Jesus Christ possess? He said in Matthew 28:18, "And Jesus came and spake unto them saying all power is given unto me in heaven and in Earth." Who is the source of the power of our Lord Jesus Christ? He said, "all power is given unto me." There is a source of his power. He is not the Almighty. The Almighty does not derive his power from somebody else. Christ said, "all power is given to unto me." Where did he receive that power? In Matthew 11:27 Christ said, "All things are delivered unto me of my Father."

Now, Mr. Keating, I would like you to take note of what shall happen when the day of judgment shall come. Will you please explain your doctrine concerning equality here? They say, "The Father, the Son, and the Holy Spirit are equal." Here is what shall happen on the day of judgment. Read 1 Corinthians 15:27-28: "God put all things under his feet." Under the feet of Christ. It is clear, of course, that the words "all things" do not include God himself who puts all things under Christ. But when all things have been placed under Christ's rule, then he himself, the Son, will place himself under God.

Mr. Keating believes that the Father, the Son, and the Holy Spirit are equal. In this verse it says the Son, on the day of judgment, will place himself under God. Where is the equality doctrine now? Now, he said, why didn't you believe Thomas? Because Thomas was wrong. Why? Because when Christ told them about God, Thomas was not there. Everybody knows that Thomas is also called "the doubting apostle," right? He did not believe that Christ was resurrected. Before John 20:28, when Thomas said to Jesus "My Lord and my God," he did not hear the message of Christ.

What was Christ's message to them that Thomas was not able to know? Christ told them, "Touch me not, for I am not yet ascended to my Father. But go to my brethren and say unto them, I ascend unto my Father and your Father and to my God and your God." Very clear. It is so clear, Mr. Keating, that Christ is not the one true God. The Almighty God is the one who placed all things under Christ, and that is where Christ will go. He told the apostles, he told Mary Magdalene, "Tell the brethren that I go to my God. But he is not only my God, he's also your God." But Thomas was not able to know this. Why? Thomas, one of the Twelve, was not with them when Jesus came. He did not know. He never heard about this message. Because if he knew that Christ said, "Tell them," including Thomas, "I'm going to my God," then Thomas would not say, "My Lord and my God."

So, though Mr. Keating could not answer my question, I ask him, "Which one do you believe—Christ, who said "I'll go to my God, which is also your God," or Thomas, who said, "Jesus is my God"? Which one do you believe, Mr. Keating? Do you believe Thomas who was absent, doubting Thomas, or should you believe the Savior himself saying, "I have my God"?

Let's go back to Brother Felix Manalo. Mr. Keating criticized Brother Felix Manalo for teaching that Christ is not God. Brother Felix Manalo taught us the same teachings taught by the apostles. Why is it so hard for him to accept that Brother Felix Manalo is a messenger of God when the teachings that he taught us are all in the Bible? The apostles told us the same thing, that the Father is the only true God. That's why I am always challenging him. Show me a verse in the Bible that says Christ is the only true God. Show me in the Bible where it says the Holy Spirit is the only true God. He could not show to you any verse in the Bible where Christ said, "I am God." He could not show any verse in the Bible that says the Holy Spirit is the only true God. Therefore, the conclusion is this: this church preached by Brother Felix Manalo is the true Church from the Bible.

MODERATOR: We now have a three minute cross-question from Mr. Keating.

KEATING: You just said that it is hard for me to accept that Felix Manalo was a messenger. Apparently, it was hard for Felix Manalo to accept that he was a messenger, because he didn't preach that doctrine until 1922. My question for you is: if he was a messenger from 1914, how come he didn't know about it until 1922?

VENTILACION: How did you know that?

KEATING: Very simply. No Iglesia publication published before 1922 makes the claim. I refer to the book on the Iglesia ni Cristo by Leonard Tuggy, who's not a Catholic.

VENTILACION: Ah, Leonard Tuggy. You know Mr. Leonard Tuggy is a Baptist minister, who wrote a book against the Iglesia ni Cristo. Your foundation came from a person who wrote against the Iglesia ni Cristo.

KEATING: Do you have, in your possession tonight, any publication by Iglesia ni Cristo published before 1922 that says Manalo is a messenger?

VENTILACION: Brother Felix Manalo, since the beginning, taught this Bible. This is the Bible.

KEATING: Do you have such a publication, sir?

VENTILACION: This is the publication, if you want a publication. This is it.

KEATING: Answer the question, or have your position be condemned by all honest people in this audience.

VENTILACION: This is it. If you would like a publication, this is it, the Bible.

KEATING: Show us *Pasugo* or another magazine.

VENTILACION: *Pasugo* came out in 1939.

KEATING: I know it did.

VENTILACION: What's the problem?

KEATING: Do you have any publication, published by Iglesia ni Cristo, with you tonight, published before 1922—

VENTILACION: We do not have any *Pasugo*.

KEATING: The answer is no because there is no such publication that has that doctrine.

VENTILACION: We do not have any *Pasugo*. It came out in 1939.

KEATING: Do you have any other publication, published before 1922?

VENTILACION: There is no publication.

KEATING: Nobody published anything about Iglesia ni Cristo before 1922?

VENTILACION: Show me.

KEATING: I'm asking you. Does your church have any?

VENTILACION: That's why I told you none, because *Pasugo* came out in 1939.

KEATING: Did any Iglesia writer write anything in any publication before 1922 and say in that publication that Manalo was called as a messenger? What's your answer?

VENTILACION: We do not have any publication—

KEATING: You don't have such a thing, because there isn't one.

VENTILACION: Except the *Pasugo*. It came out in 1939.

KEATING: I said I'm not referring to *Pasugo*. I'll even accept a newspaper account from the Philippines where it says, say in 1918, that Manalo is a messenger.

MODERATOR: That ends the debate portion of our event tonight and I'd like to thank the audience for being so nice, peaceful, and quiet. I'd like to thank the two gentlemen for their being scholarly, eloquent, and sincere in presenting their sides.

So I now open the floor to questions from the audience. But when you do it, please tell who you are directing it to.

SPEAKER: My question is aimed at Mr. Ventilacion. You quoted Corinthians: "Yet there is for us only one God the Father who is the creator of all things and for whom we live, and there is only one Lord, Jesus Christ, through whom all things were created and through whom we live." Sounds to me like it's synonymous. Christ is the one through whom all things are created. God the Father is the creator of all things. So how do you explain that they are not both God when Catholics say, yes, they have those same powers?

VENTILACION: I would like you to listen to Acts 2:36, my friend. It says here, "Therefore let all the house of Israel know assuredly that God hath made the same Jesus, whom you have crucified, both Lord and Christ." There is no other person that was made Lord by God in the Christian era, except Jesus Christ.

KEATING: The questioner has a very pointed question, which, again, has been sidestepped. God the Father is called the Creator. Jesus Christ is called the one through whom all things were created. How many Creators can there be? Only one, God. There is only one God. Only God can create. A creature cannot create. A creature is created. He is not a creator. There is no way around that. "Jesus Christ, through whom all things were created." That can only mean he is the creator, and he is God. There is no other possibility, unless you are going to say that creatures can create.

SPEAKER: I would like to address this question to Mr. Keating.

SPEAKER: It is your teaching, in the Catholic Church, that the true Church was established upon the apostle Peter. Now my question is: was this same true Church ever established upon our Lord Jesus Christ? Please give me citations or verses supporting your answer.

KEATING: Mr. Ventilacion and I both gave verses regarding the establishment of the Church. My point in Matthew 16:18 was that although Jesus Christ, obviously, was the only one who could establish a church, he left behind him a visible representative on Earth who is the successor to Peter.

VENTILACION: My answer to that question is, if the Church has been built upon Peter since the beginning, then Christ, from the beginning, is not the foundation stone. You see the point? If, in Matthew 16:18, the apostle Peter became a foundation stone, then Christ did not become a foundation stone because from the start it was already the apostle Peter.

SPEAKER: I'd like to address my question to Mr. Keating. I would like him to show me a verse in the Bible where the word "Trinity" is used. And I don't want anything that tells me three in one. I want to see the word "Trinity" in the Bible.

KEATING: The word "Trinity," like the word "Philippines" and the phrase "Church of Christ," does not appear in the Bible.

SPEAKER: Tertullian, didn't he decide to use it?

KEATING: No. The first use of "Trinity" was by Theophilus of Antioch in 181. Look it up. He uses the Greek word *Trios*, which means "Trinity."

SPEAKER: But is that in the Bible? Show it to me in the Bible.

KEATING: If you are going to use that principle, then you can't say that Manalo is a messenger from the Philippines, because "Philippines" is not mentioned in the Bible.

MODERATOR: We are supposed to leave here around 10:30, so we have one more question. One more question. I'm sorry about the rest, but one more question. Thank you.

SPEAKER: First of all. I'd like to say that I am Roman Catholic, and I am very proud of my beautiful religion. I hear some laughter, but then again I hear some claps. Mr. Ventilacion, how many churches are there that call themselves the Church of Christ but are not of your same denomination and could use the same argument that they are the Church of Christ?

VENTILACION: That is probably your opinion. But this is what I can say. Not just because they use the name "Church of Christ" are they the true Church. What is to be confirmed is if their teachings are in the Bible. There is the Church of Christ here in the United States that, like the Catholics, believes in the Trinity. We don't believe that because they carry the name "Church of Christ" they are the true Church. That is not our stand, my friend. Our stand is this—

SPEAKER: Mr. Ventilacion, I believe you contradicted yourself, because earlier—

VENTILACION: You are entitled to your own opinion.

SPEAKER: No, excuse me. I'll explain why I think you contradicted yourself. Earlier you said that in Acts it talks about the Church of Christ, and you seemed to use that as proving that your church is the Church of Christ. But then you say, if other churches say they are the Church of Christ, well they can't be because—

VENTILACION: We are having a debate here.

SPEAKER: Thank you.

KEATING: This gentleman brought up a very good point. Notice Mr. Ventilacion's arguments. He says, "Ours must be the true church because it is called the Church of Christ." But when Felix Manalo came to the United States in 1919 to study, there already were churches that called themselves the Church of Christ. They came out of what is known as the Campbellite Movement from which your messenger got some of his doctrines. There are several Protestant denominations that call themselves Church of Christ and use exactly the same argument. Why aren't they the authentic church? They came before Iglesia ni Cristo. You see, Iglesia ni Cristo's argument is no good. All it is is a word game, trying to put one over on you by saying, "If this is called the Church of Christ, it must be the Church of Christ." Anybody can do that. In fact, a lot of churches have done that. Taking on a new title by itself means nothing. The man's point was well taken.

BOOK 4

Face Off with an Ex-Priest

Karl Keating vs. Bartholomew F. Brewer

Introduction

My opponent in this debate was Bartholomew F. ("Bart") Brewer, a former Discalced Carmelite priest and, at the time we squared off, the head of Mission to Catholics International. The topic for the evening was "Is the Roman Catholic Church Christian?" His answer would be a firm "No." The venue was Calvary Baptist Church in National City, the town immediately to the south of San Diego. Calvary Baptist had the reputation of being the most ardently anti-Catholic church in the county, perhaps because Brewer's organization was headquartered on the church's property. His pastor served as moderator at the debate.

The crowd was not evenly-split. Of the 350 spectators, no more than 50 were Catholics. The remainder were Fundamentalists, and they seemed to come in two flavors: those predisposed, naturally enough, to favor my opponent, and those who already were zealous members of his (quite vocal) fan club.

There would have been more Catholics in attendance, no doubt, if the diocesan paper had advertised the debate in its upcoming events column, the way the main secular daily did, and if more parishes had published notices in their Sunday bulletins. All had press releases in ample time. But there long had been, in official Catholic circles, almost a denial that Fundamentalism was wooing Catholics away from the church of their upbringing, and even clerics who admitted such a problem existed tended to prefer a policy of benign neglect or were skittish about anything deemed controversial—and what's more controversial than a controversy?

The lack of publicity by Catholics may not have made much difference, since the venue surely scared off partisans of Rome. A priest I knew planned to attend but got cold feet—all the more understandable for Catholic laymen, few of whom might feel comfortable entering what they perceive to be hostile territory. From my point of view, though, it was more important to have an abundance of Fundamentalists in the audience. It was their minds that I hoped to change. Besides, I wasn't sure Brewer would debate anywhere except on his home ground. You take what you can get.

Another wrinkle: Brewer preferred not to have a true debate format, with multiple back-and-forths. We originally agreed to speak for 30 minutes each and then take questions, the whole show to be done in two hours. A couple of weeks before the debate he called and said he preferred to have us talk for 45 minutes each. A bit long, I replied, but all right. Did I have a preference in speaking order? he asked. Not really, I said, my suspicions not being aroused. Good, said Brewer. He wanted to go second, and so it was agreed. The debate would begin at 7:30 p.m., and we could still get people out by 10:00 p.m., allowing an hour for questions.

After an introduction by the pastor-moderator, I gave my remarks, emphasizing some of Fundamentalism's weak points, encouraging the audience to exercise skepticism when listening to anti-Catholics, and citing a few egregious bloopers by those who made their living attacking the Church. The audience was politely attentive, chuckling at the throwaway lines, leaning forward as I made my main points. It seemed some of my ideas were getting through. In retrospect, I can't say whether most listeners were thinking about what I was saying or just marveling that a Catholic had no fangs. Few of the Fundamentalists had ever heard a Catholic speak before. I had a sense of being on display. After the debate, many people came up to me, thanking me just for showing up, something they half-expected me not to do, I guess. After all, when they walked in, they probably thought "What could a Catholic possibly have to say?" They found out soon enough.

I hadn't timed my talk well. I took 50 minutes instead of the agreed-upon 45, yet the moderator hadn't admonished me. I felt both sheepish and grateful. My talk done, I sat in the front row, where Brewer had been waiting.

He ascended the pulpit, piled half a dozen books on one side and his Bible on the other. Adjusting the microphone, he started to preach. It took me a few minutes to understand what he was doing since I had expected a different kind of presentation. I should have known better.

Brewer started out louder than my loudest and then turned up the volume. In a few moments someone behind me called out, "Amen, brother!" He was echoed by others. Soon there were two or three dozen voices crying out. Brewer began more deliberately to play to the crowd. As though giving a political speech, he would make a pointed remark and then pause, giving his backers time to throw in some "amens" and an occasional "hallelujah."

I had heard him speak in a Baptist church before—that was before he knew me by sight, so he didn't know a Catholic was present—and I had seen him on a television talk show, listened to him on radio, and read his writings. Often enough I had been annoyed at his sharp phrasing but accepted it as his shtick, yet I admit to being surprised at the level of invective this night. He was on a roll. And he kept on rolling. 45 minutes, 50 minutes, an hour. He said he would talk on several main points, and he had at least one to go when, an hour-and-a-half into his presentation, he was interrupted by Catholics who had had enough. The moderator, who seemed to have forgotten that he was wearing a watch, got up and pulled Brewer from the pulpit.

I insisted on a few minutes' rebuttal. A little steamed (though not because of the logorrhea, which worked to my benefit by giving me the crowd's sympathy), I commented on Brewer's more bizarre charges, the worst of which—made while he was discoursing on the supposed non-existence of the priesthood—was that Pope Pius IX (reigned 1846–1878) "had three girlfriends" while pope. It was a canard, I remarked, noting that one could read about such slanders against Pio Nono in *No Popery*, written by Fr. Herbert Thurston, S.J., in 1930. This citing of a specific reference work seemed to take care of that issue, and I felt lucky to have stumbled across the book some months earlier. (You never know when obscure sources will come in handy.)

Then came questions. The moderator whispered to me that maybe the question period should be kept to a few minutes so people could get home, but I insisted questions be taken until no one had anything more to ask—a rash move on my part, since I ended up staying until 2:30 a.m. The crowd didn't have to stay quite that long; the formal question period ended around 11:30 p.m. (most people, bless 'em, were still present). About two-thirds of the questions were directed to me.

Many former Catholics came up to me and said they wish someone had told them about the Church while they were still in it. A Catholic whom I hadn't seen for years confided that she had been tempted to "unpope" but that the debate broke the spell. Several Fundamentalists said they were surprised that any case at all could be made for the Catholic religion; they seemed inclined to do some research on their own. One woman, who identified herself as a member of Calvary Baptist Church, said, "I'm not going to fellowship here any longer"—but that was less a reflection on my talk, I think, than on what she perceived as a setup.

Bart Brewer had been raised in Philadelphia. As a young man he thought he had a vocation to the priesthood, and he ended up being ordained for the Discalced Carmelite order. After a while his superiors sent him to the Philippines. The assignment did not last long, Brewer admitting in a tract that he got into some trouble there. Back in the U.S., he underwent a change of religious allegiance. First he became a Seventh-day Adventist because his mother had become one. Later he became a Baptist. At some indeterminate point he concluded that his calling was to undermine the Church he once had been part of. Perhaps it simply was that he wasn't trained for anything other than religious work and didn't see any other avenue open to him. He founded Mission to Catholics International and headed the organization for many years. ("International" was a bit misleading, since Brewer's touring and speaking seemed to be confined to the U.S.)

Although Brewer had received standard seminary training, he seemed to know little about Catholicism, other than that now he opposed it. In opposing it he adopted the tones of anti-Catholic Protestants of the nineteenth and earlier centuries, warning his listeners about dark "Papist" conspiracies as he showed them hosts (presumably unconsecrated) in a ciborium. He affected a Southern drawl, in emulation perhaps of television preachers he admired. It was as though such an accent were expected of one in his position, even someone who had grown up in the City of Brotherly Love. Along with the drawl came an unctuousness that brought to my mind Dickens' Uriah Heep.

Despite all that, I had a soft spot for Brewer, frustrating though I found him. Yes, he was an apostate priest who spoke cavalierly and inaccurately about his former faith, but he seemed to me a self-broken man. I couldn't help thinking that, deep down, he was disappointed with the hand he had been dealt—or that he had dealt to himself. This turned out to be the only debate he ever had with a Catholic, though he and I occasionally spoke about a rematch.

Debate Transcript
Karl Keating vs. Bartholomew F. Brewer

MODERATOR: A couple of people have asked me, is there going to be a fight? We don't plan on having one. Seriously though, this is something that we have worked on for several months, myself and Bart Brewer and Karl Keating. We met together several months ago and determined the date to have this meeting. And we, I think, consider each other our friends, and we are here for a legitimate debate and, through mutual consent, Mr. Keating is going to be our first speaker. And he will be given 45 minutes for his time. When he is finished, Mr. Brewer will come, and he will have 45 minutes. Then we will have a question-and-answer time.

KEATING: First, my thanks to Bart Brewer for agreeing to this public discussion. Then to our host for so kindly agreeing to let us use the church and for taking on the responsibility of moderator. He tells me that I might well be the first Catholic to speak from this pulpit. Depending on how things go, I might very well be the last. Apparently, some people hope so.

A few days ago, my office received an anonymous phone call. The man said that tonight's debate is the work of the Devil. It's actually quite the opposite. The one thing the Father of Lies doesn't want is for people to come together in a friendly discussion to search for the truth because he fears we might find it. If that caller isn't pleased that I'm here, perhaps it might please him to find that I'm at a considerable disadvantage tonight. After all, it's easier to attack the Catholic religion than to defend it. An attack can be phrased in just a few words. A defense might take paragraphs or pages. Normally an attack has three elements. One is that there is something completely true in it. Second, there's something true but so abruptly stated that it's misleading and so its implication is incorrect. The third element is simply false. The Catholic apologist must try to untangle the web in far too short a time.

Mr. Brewer and I have not compared notes. We don't know what each other will be speaking about tonight. I don't know the specific charges he'll make, but in the last few years I've read his materials, and I know that he's made dozens. Obviously, I'm unable to anticipate them all. If, after his talk, I could keep you here until this time tomorrow, I could answer every objection he brings up, but my lungs and your posteriors won't last that long. Maybe we can touch on a few of the points in the question session.

My goal tonight isn't to prove to you the truth of the Catholic religion. There isn't time for that. I'd be satisfied to suggest to you that what you've heard about the Catholic religion from anti-Catholics you ought to take not just with a grain of salt but with the whole salt shaker. You haven't been told the whole story.

To Catholics who are in the audience I say, "Have confidence in your religion." In the last few years I've been asked hundreds of questions regarding the Catholic religion. I by no means have had all the answers on the tip of my tongue. As you'll see, I won't have them on the tip of my tongue tonight. But when I say to an inquirer, "Let me look it up and I'll get back to you tomorrow," in each case I've been able to find an answer that satisfies not just me as a believing Catholic but also the person who put the question to me. He may not agree with the answer, but at least he sees what the Catholic position is.

To Fundamentalists I say, "Reserve judgment until you have a chance to see what knowledgeable Catholics say about their religion. Be cautious in swallowing charges that might be unflattering. Do some homework on your own. Stop and wonder why, if even a portion of the charges you've heard are true, the Catholic Church, and the Catholic religion, didn't collapse in a paroxysm of laughter centuries ago."

Let me take a look at things from the view point of the common Catholic. If you're a Catholic you certainly have been through it. It's the middle of the afternoon on a Saturday, and there is a knock at the door. You open it to find a man with a wide smile, a Bible in his hand, and a question on his lips. "Have you been saved, friend?" You tell him that you're a Catholic, in hopes that it will scare him away, which it does not. He leans over and takes out of his valise several Catholic versions of the Bible. "Which do you think we should use?" he says, "New American Bible, Jerusalem Bible, maybe the old Douay-Rheims?" You engage him in conversation for a while, and you end up merely frustrated. He goes away with an air of triumph, and you go away with a sore throat.

Or the altercation—somehow it always seems to end up being an altercation—might happen after Mass. You exit church to find people passing out tracts excoriating the Eucharist. If you so much as look one of them in the eye, he comes toward you. The crowd of Mass-goers is so large that you can't wiggle your way through fast enough. You can't escape. When the man reaches you, he says, "Here, read this. It will tell you about the idolatry of the Mass." "No thanks," you say, "not interested." So he proceeds to tell you, word for word, just what you would have read. As he does that, he backs you toward the curb. You listen to him or you step into whizzing traffic.

Or, it might happen in a social setting, say, after your pro-life group has concluded its business meeting. Everybody sits back for a little conviviality and a spot of tea, and a born-again sidles up to you and says, "Wouldn't you like an assurance of salvation?" You begin to answer by saying, "Yes, but . . ." She waves you to be quiet, and she flips through a heavily underlined New Testament to look for the objection to the comment you never got a chance to make. From there it is all downhill.

These discussions, whether with the man at the door, or the people outside of church, or the woman at the social setting, seem to go nowhere. You know things are being taken out of context but you can't remember what the context is. There are snappy rejoinders coming to mind, but they never quite manifest themselves. Later, you kick yourself for not having said the right thing. If you put Catholic beliefs into your own unconsidered words, you find out all you've done is put your feet in your mouth. You've confirmed your adversary's worst suspicions, and the worst thing is that for some questions you don't have the vaguest hint of an answer. You begin to think that, God forbid, the Fundamentalist might be on to something.

On the other hand, if you're a Fundamentalist, you have a different perspective. You may have been brought up in Fundamentalism. Maybe you're a convert from some other religion, maybe even from Catholicism. Regardless, your view of the Catholic religion is largely negative. It strikes you as a strange amalgamation of some things that are true and, mostly, things that are untrue. You have the impression that it's at once Western and Eastern, that it has something to do with the capitals of the West, such as Paris and London, and something to do with the exotic capitals of the East, such as Baghdad, Cairo, and New York.

The Catholics you meet are pretty much like other people. Some are smart; some are not. You've heard that there are more than a billion of them in the world, and you suspect they can't all be stupid, but sometimes you wonder what it is they see in their religion. You don't worry about it particularly because you've been told that their priests and their bishops hoodwink them and that the people swallow everything they hear from the pulpit. You've been told a lot of other things about the Catholic religion. Some are true, many are not, but you don't know which are which. You accept them all because you don't know why you shouldn't.

You have been told, for example, that the Catholic religion didn't start until the reign of the Emperor Constantine, in the early fourth century. Or maybe that it didn't start until the reign of Pope Gregory the Great at the turn of the seventh century. Now that happens to be historical nonsense, but you've never looked it up in a history book to see for yourself. You just accept it as being true. You've heard that Catholics pay to get their sins forgiven in confession. You never have come up to a Catholic and asked if that's so. If you did, he'd laugh at you the same way you'd laugh at him if he said, "Is it true that in Fundamentalist services you just sit around all morning thumping Bibles?" You've heard that between New Testament times and the Reformation there were lots of churches that weren't connected with Rome, that opposed what many people called the Roman system, that were basically the same as today's Fundamentalism, but you've never been told names and dates for the very good reason that there were no such groups.

I want to take representative examples of these charges or impressions and look at them at some length. Let's begin with a historical question: was Peter ever in Rome? It's not a major point. The world doesn't turn on it, but you always find anti-Catholics bringing it up. I think it's probably best stated by Loraine Boettner in his book *Roman Catholicism*. Boettner, as many of you know, was the dean of American anti-Catholics. Every major anti-Catholic organization, and probably all the minor ones, relied heavily on his work. He says, "The remarkable thing about Peter's alleged bishopric in Rome is that the New Testament has not one word to say about it. The word 'Rome' occurs only nine times in the Bible and never is Peter mentioned in connection with it. There is no allusion to Rome in either of his epistles. Paul's journey to the city is recorded in great detail. There is, in fact, no New Testament evidence, nor any historical proof of any kind, that Peter was ever in Rome. All rests on legend."

Well, what about it? Admittedly, the scriptural evidence for Peter being in Rome is thin. Nowhere does the Bible say unequivocally that he was there. On the other hand, it doesn't say he wasn't. But Boettner is wrong when he says that there is no allusion to Rome in Peter's epistles. There is, in the greeting at the end of the first epistle where he says, "The Church, here in Babylon, united with you by God's election, sends you her greeting, and so does my son Mark." "Babylon" was a code word for Rome. It's used that way five times in the Book of Revelation. In extra-biblical works such as the Sibylline Oracles and the Apocalypse of Baruch and the Fourth Book of Esdras, which were all written about the same time, it's again used that way, quite clearly, to mean Rome. Boettner says, "But there is no good reason for saying that Babylon means Rome. Why didn't he [Peter] just say Rome?" Well, the good reason is called "persecution."

Peter was known to the authorities as a leader of the Christian Church, and the Church, under Roman law, was organized atheism. The worship of any gods other than the Roman was considered atheism. Peter would do himself no favor, nor would he do a favor to those connected with him, by advertising his presence in the capital, which he might very well have done by sending letters out saying, "Here I am in Rome." Peter was a wanted man. All Christians were, so he had a good reason to hide his location.

In any event, let's be generous. Let's say that an opponent of Catholicism, in good faith, can say that Peter wasn't in Rome, if he looks only at the Bible. But he shouldn't put on historical blinders. He should look at historical works of roughly the same period to see what they say. Clement of Rome, who later would be the fourth pope, or the third successor to Peter, wrote his letter to the Corinthians and made reference to Peter ending his life where Paul ended his. We all know Paul died at Rome. Ignatius of Antioch, in the year 110, in his letter to the Romans remarked that he wasn't in a position to command the Romans the way Peter and Paul had been. This indicates that Peter, like Paul, had been in Rome. Irenaeus, writing later in the second century, said that Matthew wrote his Gospel while Peter and Paul were evangelizing in Rome and laying the foundation of the Church there.

There are other ancient writings that could be cited, and they all speak to the same. There is no ancient writing that claims that Peter ended up in a city other than Rome and died there. No other city ever laid claim to him. Boettner, like many other Fundamentalist apologists, said "exhaustive research by archaeologists has been made, down through the centuries, to find some inscription in the catacombs and other ruins of ancient places that would indicate Peter, at least, visited Rome. But the only things found to give any promise were a few uncertain bones."

Boettner saw his book through the presses in 1962. Some years later Pope Paul VI was able to issue a report on the archeological excavations that took place under the high altar in Peter's Basilica, excavations that began after World War II. They demonstrated conclusively that Peter's bones and his grave were there. For example, most of the graves next to where his grave was located say something like "Peter is here." They can be dated to the first century.

I've discussed Peter's presence in Rome at some length, but I don't want you to think this is the only historical point on which Boettner and other anti-Catholics are in error. It's fair to say that in Boettner's book of 460 pages there is, on average, one major blunder per page. The most obvious weaknesses of the anti-Catholic position relate to history. This is where the faults of anti-Catholic pundits are most glaring. Many charges against the Church rely on imaginary and sometimes falsified history. Take away that history and the charges collapse. I will not resist giving you a few juicy examples.

Some Fundamentalists argue against papal infallibility, which was defined formally at the First Vatican Council in 1870, by quoting a speech supposedly given by Bishop Joseph Strossmayer of Croatia. The gist of the supposed speech is that Strossmayer just finished reading the New Testament through and now he comes before the Fathers of the Council and says, "Gentlemen, I've read the New Testament, and there is no evidence of a papacy in its pages." Well, the problem is that the speech attributed to Strossmayer is a well-known forgery. You can check the *Catholic Encyclopedia*, which will tell you that. If you don't like the *Catholic Encyclopedia*, go to the books it cites, some by non-Catholics. Every Protestant scholar who's written a book about Vatican I will have the same story. They all, Catholic and Protestant, agree the speech is phony.

I correspond with a Fundamentalist, a young fellow who used to be a Catholic. He said, finally, after we went back and forth on this, "Okay, I admit the Strossmayer speech a forgery, but I'm going to keep distributing the speech anyway because its theology is true." Well, what can you say about that attitude?

When it comes to Transubstantiation, which is the technical name for turning bread and wine into the body and blood of Christ during the Mass, Fundamentalists say, "That didn't come into being until the year 1215 at the Fourth Lateran Council." But all you have to do is pick up Ignatius of Antioch, writing in 110. He condemned people who did not confess that the Eucharist is the flesh of our Savior, Jesus Christ. So you can't very well say that 1,105 years later the doctrine was made up. Similarly, Boettner said it wasn't until the eleventh century that the Mass was declared a sacrifice, but in the second century Irenaeus wrote a book where he specifically said that it was.

Many anti-Catholics say confession to a priest didn't arise until the Middle Ages, but in the third century Origen wrote that for absolution a distinct accusation or admission of the sins—a listing of them—would be required, and confession had to be made privately to a priest.

In many matters anti-Catholic commentators leave listeners with the wrong notion of what happened. It said that in 1572 Pope Gregory XIII was so pleased that the Huguenots—that is, French Protestants—were massacred on Bartholomew's Day that he ordered hymns of praise to be sung and a medal to be struck in celebration. These commentators don't tell you the real facts. They don't tell you that the Queen Mother of France, Catherine de' Medici, was the real power behind the throne of her weakling son, Charles IX. She organized the plot against the Huguenots. The problem, in her mind, was that the king's chief minister happened to be a Protestant. She didn't want him to have influence over her son, so what better way to get rid of him than to claim that there was an uprising by Protestants? He and many others were done away with.

Fundamentalists commentators who bring up the story also don't tell you that Catherine arranged to have the French ambassador go to the papal court and tell the pope, "Your Holiness, it was a coup attempt. The Protestants tried to kill the king." The pope had no reason to doubt the report and therefore had hymns of praise sung, and he had a medal struck. But when he found out the truth, he roundly condemned the king and the king's mother.

You've heard people talk against relics. The most common argument is that, if you take all the relics of the True Cross and you put them together you've got enough wood to build a ship. What anti-Catholics don't tell you, because they probably don't know, is that in the nineteenth century a Frenchman named Charles Rohault de Fleury cataloged and measured all known relics of the True Cross. He computed that their total volume wouldn't make up more than one-third of a cross. So, there is a scandal concerning the Cross, but the scandal isn't that there are so many pieces floating around that you could build a ship. The scandal is: what happened to the rest of the True Cross?

Some Fundamentalists—and I'm thinking here for example of the author of a book called *The Mystery of Babylon Revealed*—say that under the Inquisition as many as 95 million people were killed in Europe. Keep in mind that the Inquisition didn't operate throughout Europe. It was restricted to southern France, Spain, Italy, and the southern part of Germany. It never was in England, never in Scandinavia, and never in Eastern Europe. The present-day population of the areas where it operated doesn't approach 95 million. The population was only a fraction of that when the Inquisition existed. Scholars, both Catholic and Protestant, say that number of deaths is exaggerated between 10,000 and 50,000 times. The figure of 95 million isn't a typographical error. It's an example of bad faith in writing against a Church that one opposes.

Consider Ralph Woodrow. Some of you have read his book *Babylon Mystery Religion*, which is not to be confused with *The Mystery of Babylon Revealed*. Woodrow's thesis is that Catholicism arose out of Babylonian sun worship. He tries to prove this by using photographs of the interior of St. Peter's Basilica in Rome. You've all seen pictures of that interior. You've seen Bernini's twisted columns and the great baldachin over the high altar. On one such photo Woodrow superimposes an arrow pointing to the back wall, at what appears to be a sunburst. He says, "See, that sunburst proves that Catholics worship the sun." Unfortunately for Woodrow, he didn't have a clear photograph of the interior of St. Peter's. If he had, he would have seen that what his arrow pointed at was not a representation of the sun but a representation of the Holy Spirit in the form of a dove exuding rays of light.

Frank Sheed was well known as a Catholic street corner preacher, an author, and a publisher. He said that you can't stop people from drawing true inferences from true facts. If the fact is that Jesus rose from the dead, certain things follow. You don't stop there, even if that would be all that the Bible said on the incident. If Jesus said "This is my body" at the Last Supper, certain things follow from that. You can't prevent people from trying to find out rationally what those things might be. This is doctrinal development, drawing true conclusions from true facts. Fundamentalists have their own brand of doctrinal development. They too believe things that are not found on the face of Scripture—for example, the Trinity. The word "Trinity" cannot be found in the Bible. Its first use is by

Theophilus of Antioch in 181. A Fundamentalist will say, "The word may not be in the Bible, but the doctrine is there." That's what Catholics say when Fundamentalists say, "Hey, the word 'Transubstantiation' is not in the Bible." That's true. It's a term of art just as "Trinity" is a term of art. But the doctrine is there.

There are other things that Fundamentalists say don't find warrant in Scripture. Some of them believe that drinking, dancing, and gambling are immoral without exception, yet you won't find in the Bible across-the-board condemnations of those activities. You'll find only condemnations of their abuse. When it comes to wine, some Fundamentalists go so far as to say that Christ didn't drink any. That's hard to believe when in his first miracle he turned jugs of water into wine. The host of the wedding had plenty of wine, he thought, but the guests consumed it all. Jesus made, miraculously, a large amount of additional wine. In a sense he was inviting the people to drink further, an indication that he approved of drinking wine.

Consider next salvation and justification. For Catholics, salvation depends on the state of the soul at death. Christ has already redeemed us; he's unlocked the gates of heaven, so to speak. He did his part, and now we have to cooperate. He will not save us without our cooperation. You won't get to heaven unless you follow his instructions. If we're to pass through the gates into heaven, we have to be spiritually alive. If a soul is in a purely natural state, suffering from the penalties of original sin, it's without sanctifying grace and is spiritually dead.

For Fundamentalists sanctifying grace is just a figment of Catholics' imagination. What matters is accepting Christ as your Lord and Savior. When you do that, Christ covers your sinfulness. He turns a blind eye to it. It's as though he hides your soul under a cloak. Any soul hidden under the cloak is admitted to heaven, no matter how putrescent the soul beneath the cloak. No one without the cloak, no matter how pristine, will be admitted to heaven.

The Reformers saw justification as a legal act by which God declares the sinner to be meriting heaven, even though his soul remains objectively sinful and unjust. It's not a real eradication of sin but a covering or non-imputation. It's not a real renewal or a real sanctification, only an external application of

Christ's justice. The soul doesn't actually become holy.

The Catholic Church understands it differently. Justification is a true eradication of sin, a true sanctification of the inner man. The soul becomes objectively pleasing to God, objectively good, and so it merits heaven. It merits heaven because it is good now. Scripture conceives of forgiveness of sins as a complete removal of them. In the Psalms the terms used are "blot out" and "clears away." Isaiah also uses "blots out." John says "takes away." When the Bible mentions "covering," in almost all those cases it refers not to God forgiving sins but to us ignoring one another's sins.

On the positive side, the Bible shows that justification is a re-birth. In John and Titus we learn that it's a generation of a supernatural life in a former sinner. It involves, as Paul says in Ephesians, an inner renewal and, in First Corinthians, a real sanctification. The soul itself becomes beautiful and holy. It's not an ugly soul hidden under a cloak. Because it's beautiful and holy, it can be admitted to heaven where, the Bible says, "nothing unclean shall enter." An ugly soul hidden under a cloak is still unclean and does not get admitted to heaven.

Now an allied topic, the assurance of salvation. There are verses in the Bible that call this notion into doubt. "I buffet my own body and make it my slave, for I, who have preached to others, may myself be rejected," says Paul in I Corinthians. He also says, "Beloved, you have always shown yourselves obedient, and now that I am at a distance, you must work to earn your salvation in anxious fear." Some translations say "in fear and trembling." That's not the language of self-confident assurance. Paul also tells us, "All of us have a scrutiny to undergo before Christ's judgment seat, for each to reap what his mortal life has earned, good or ill according to his deeds. God will award to every man what his acts have deserved." But if the only act of consequence is being saved, a one-time event, what difference do all the other acts make, as far as your salvation goes?

These verses demonstrate that we'll be judged by what we do, not just by the one act of whether we accept Jesus as our Savior. But it's not to be thought that being a do-gooder is sufficient. The Bible is quite clear that we're saved by faith. The Reformers were right to say that. To that extent they merely repeated ancient doctrine. Where they erred was in saying that we are saved by faith alone. Luther admitted, when he translated the Bible into German, that he foisted in the word "alone." It is not there in the Greek. He admitted that. He also admitted that he wanted to get rid of the Epistle of James and throw it out of the Bible. He called it "an epistle of straw" because it specifically says that we are not saved by faith alone. But Luther didn't have the gumption to do that.

Consider Romans 5:2: "We are confident in the hope of attaining glory as the sons of God." The saints in heaven do not have the virtue of hope. They don't have the virtue of faith. They don't need faith because they see God. They don't need hope because they've already achieved what they hoped for on Earth. They have only the third theological virtue, charity. But Paul says that we, Christians on Earth, have hope. "Our salvation is founded on the hope of something. Hope would not be hope at all if its object were in view." That doesn't mesh with the notion of an assurance of salvation. "Are you saved?" inquires the Fundamentalist. "I'm redeemed," says the Catholic, "and, like the apostle Paul, I'm working out my salvation in fear and trembling, with hopeful confidence but not with a false assurance. And I do this as the Church has taught through all the centuries."

The Reformers rejected the papacy and they rejected, therefore, the teaching authority of the Church. They looked elsewhere for it and they thought they found the rule of faith in the Bible. They really didn't have anywhere else to look. But reason and experience tell us the Bible can't be each man's private guide to the truth. If individual guidance were a reality, we'd see every Christian believing the same thing. It does no good to say that we believe the same on the major points. You would have to believe the minor points identically also because, if the Holy Spirit enlightens you, he's not going to distinguish between major and minor points. He would enlighten you completely. He would not teach you error.

It has to be acknowledged that the Bible nowhere says it's the sole rule of faith. It never phrases it that way. It even denies it. At the end of John's Gospel the evangelist says that not everything concerning Christ's life is recorded in the Gospels. Presumably, that includes some of his teachings. Paul says in

Second Timothy, "Much Christian teaching is to be found in the tradition which is handed down, by word of mouth." In Second Thessalonians he says, "Stand fast and hold the traditions which you have learned, whether by word or by our epistle."

The early Christians knew the fullness of the faith was handed down orally. They were the people who, as Acts puts it, "occupy themselves continually with the apostles' teaching." That was long before any of the New Testament was written. Fundamentalists make noises about Christ condemning traditions. "Why is it that you, yourselves, violate the commandments of God with your traditions?" he says to the Pharisees. Paul warned, "Take care not to let anyone cheat you with philosophizing, with empty fantasies drawn from human tradition." But these, obviously, refer to erroneous human traditions, mainly those that were handed down by the Jews and were supplementary to the original Mosaic Law.

Let me just say something addressed more to Catholics than to Fundamentalists. Whatever forces might drive a man to Fundamentalism—and it has to be granted that emotional factors play a part—he remains a Fundamentalist for doctrinal reasons. He might have left his previous church, whatever it was, because he didn't like the priest or minister or because people in the congregation were rude to him, but that's not why he sticks with Fundamentalism. Those emotional pushes and pulls are short-lived. He could have found a minister as eloquent, or congregants as friendly, at the mainline Protestant church down the street. No, the reason he stays in the Fundamentalist church is doctrine. His conversion had to do with doctrine. Many Catholics think Fundamentalism isn't so much a matter of theology but of pathology. They think Fundamentalists lack roots, they're at odds with their culture, they feel lost and lonely—that's why they're Fundamentalists.

One well-known Catholic scholar, Fr. Eugene LaVerdiere, wrote a tract called "Fundamentalism a Pastoral Concern." He said that the only genuinely Christian response to Fundamentalism is the life and work of Jesus. He said the answer is not a biblical argument but the strength of faith and the power of love. Putting it crudely, he said the only way to conquer Fundamentalism is to love it to death. Although it's true that people switch religions partly for emotional reasons, Catholics who once were Fundamentalists and have come back to the Church deny that loneliness and the like were the things that kept them Fundamentalists. Whatever emotional reasons they may have had for leaving the Church of Rome, they decided its teachings were untrue.

People who come back to the Catholic Church from Fundamentalism come back for the same reason. They come back for doctrinal reasons. They admire the truth that is in Fundamentalism—and there is much truth there—but they see that Fundamentalism is only a partial truth and that the fullness of truth can only be found in Rome. The committed Fundamentalist is convinced the Catholic Church is wrong, and he thinks he can prove it from the Bible. Glad-handing isn't going to suffice to get him a better picture of the Church. He's not going to change his mind just by smiling at him. He wants Catholics to explain the Bible and points of history. Unless Catholics do that, he won't be satisfied, and he shouldn't be satisfied. It's been on the level of doctrine that Fundamentalism has achieved its considerable power in this country. This power lies not in the objective truth of the Fundamentalist position, since Fundamentalism is a mixture of truth and error, but in the fact that Fundamentalists say God's truth matters and that we must act upon it, whatever its consequences. Who says A, must say B. That's the attraction, and it's a powerful attraction.

If Catholics expect to answer the Fundamentalist challenge to the Church, they are going to have to answer not just with the heart but also with the head. After all, it's the truth that sets us free. I think, at least on that point, we can all agree. Thanks for your kind attention.

MODERATOR: Just as Mr. Keating is the founder and leader of Catholic Answers, Mr. Brewer is the founder and leader of Mission to Catholics. It's interesting that both groups have the same status as far as the government is concerned. They are both incorporated as non-profit corporations, and I'm sure the speakers can attest to that—no profit. Mr. Brewer is a former Catholic priest, now an ordained Baptist minister. He'll come now and make his presentation.

BREWER: I want to thank the moderator for allowing my friend Karl Keating and me to use this beautiful auditorium. I want to thank you people for being here. I know many of my preacher friends are here tonight, from all over. And many of my relatives are here. I want to thank you lovely people for coming here tonight. I know you've come from near and far. That's very gracious. And, please, remember as I offer my presentation tonight, indeed my aim is to speak the truth in love.

My presentation tonight is not a scientific, historical, or philosophical defense of biblical Christianity but instead a declaration of God's Word, for his Word is above his name. Truth is not something you dialogue. Truth is not something you debate. Truth is something you declare. Truth is something you proclaim. And so tonight, beloved, please pay close attention to biblical content which will expose as false, as non-Christian, four major areas of Roman Catholic teaching: the Roman Catholic priesthood; the Roman Catholic sacrifice for the Mass, which would include Transubstantiation; the Roman Catholic concept of biblical authority; and the Roman Catholic concept of soteriology or salvation.

As a youngster growing up in Philadelphia, my home parish was the cathedral of Sts. Peter and Paul, where the rector, Hubert Cartwright, later Bishop Cartwright, often said that the Brewer family was more Roman Catholic than Rome. There was the daily Mass, weekly confession, the daily recitation of the rosary in the utmost respect, I mean the utmost respect for every Catholic priest, every Catholic nun. There was a God consciousness. I mean there was a Christ reverence, beloved. We were serious about God. We were serious about the Church of Rome. I know I wanted God's holy will in my life. I wanted to please God. I sincerely thought that God was calling me to be a Roman Catholic priest, so I chose the Discalced Carmelite order, perhaps one of the more strict, one of the more ancient of the religious orders in the Church of Rome.

Never did I question, nor did anyone else, my vocation, my calling to the Catholic priesthood, during those twelve years of formal religious, academic training or formation. Nor did I entertain, for a moment, any contrary teaching, any practice, because for us, for me, the voice of the Church was the voice of God. We made no formal distinction between the two.

On ordination day I heard the all seminarian choir sing, "Thou art a priest forever, according to the order of Melchizedek." When I heard that sung, at the Shrine of the Immaculate Conception of Mary in Washington, D.C., I was ecstatic with joy. Through the invocation of the Holy Spirit, and the laying on of hands, according to the gospel of Rome, when the bishop invoked the Holy Spirit and placed his hands upon my head, I was ordained to the priesthood of Jesus Christ. According to Romanism, I was ordained a priest forever. But, thank God, it was not to be forever. "When the veil of the temple was rent in twain from the top to the bottom" (Mark 15:38). That did away with the Old Testament priesthood. The letter to the Hebrews which, by the way, the Church of Rome is not too excited about, makes it very clear that the sacerdotal, sacrificial system of the Jews is consummated and superseded in Jesus Christ, the risen Savior.

There is no organized, special, sacrificing, mediating, hierarchical priesthood this side of Calvary. And by the way, we're not dealing with biblical interpretation tonight, really. I would hope and pray that we're dealing with the plain facts of God's word, the Bible.

Hebrews 7 makes it clear that the priesthood of Jesus Christ belongs to him and no one else. It may not be shared in. Please remember that. His priesthood is unchangeable. His priesthood is untransmissible. His priesthood is non-transferable. There is no priesthood today except the priesthood of all believers, according to Peter and John. There is one God and one mediator between God and men, the man Christ Jesus, who gave himself a ransom for all.

The theory of a mediating, sacrificing, official priesthood mainly started with an individual by the name of Cyprian. Cyprian was a great theological authority, in the West, until the time of Augustine and later was endorsed by Roman Catholicism. You find nothing in the New Testament about a sacrificing, mediating priesthood. Absolutely nothing, either explicitly or implicitly, in the pure wheat of God's word, the Bible.

Less than 300 years after our Savior's ascension, there were all kinds of heresies. In fact, as you know, Paul told the Corinthians that heresies were necessary because they would distinguish the true believer from the make-believer. Augustine said that between the first century and the fifth century there were something like 80 heresies. In fact, only 100 years after Pentecost, much of the truth had already become so concealed that its real meaning was almost lost. One does not have to be a Church historian to see how the soil for Roman Catholicism was prepared long before that church came into existence. It was a beginning of that apostasy which furnished the soil for the Church of Rome. The Roman Catholic system is the logical result.

Had there been no Roman Catholic system, necessity would have dictated that something fill the void left by the apostasy that Paul spoke about, that Paul predicted. Romanism is simply a perversion of true Christianity. Romanism cannot claim to be the Church of the New Testament. The Roman Catholic Church, with her popes, bishops, priests, and ritual actually claims to excel, claims to excel, mind you, the Church of the New Testament.

Beloved, I believe that smacks of arrogance and pride. The Roman Catholic priesthood has no root or foundation whatsoever in God's word, in the Bible. Frequently people ask, "Bart, what does a priest do? What is he doing all day? What is his work like? What kind of routine does he follow?" His day begins with Mass. Every morning he goes to the altar and there "renews the sacrifice by which Christ wrought our redemption." The Church of Rome teaches that Christ offered the first Holy Mass. Mass is said to be identical with Calvary; it is a continuation of Calvary. In fact, Romanism, the papal system, teaches that the Mass is not a mere re-dramatization or a mere re-enactment of Calvary. Oh no, the Church of Rome teaches that it is one and the same, that it is identical with Calvary.

As a Romish, papal priest, because of my great ignorance of the Word of God, I offered or celebrated or said over 4,000 Masses during my ten years as a Roman Catholic priest. I was taught that Jesus Christ, offering the sacrifice of the Cross, offers a Holy Mass as our High Priest, and the invisible head of the Church, using the priests of his Church as instruments. That's what I was taught. I knew that Golgotha was unique. I knew that. I knew it happened once in history. I knew it was enough to atone for the sins of man, but, mark you, I was also told that in the Mass, in the sacrifice of the Mass, both for the living and for the dead, this atonement is supplied to the souls of men, women, and children. In other words, through the Roman Catholic Mass, the body and blood of Jesus Christ are constantly being mystically sacrificed and presented to the Father in heaven. It is an everlasting extension of a redemption. There is no end. That's why there are four Masses beginning every second of the day, in some part of the world.

One of the oldest, most superficial arguments, perpetrated by Rome, is from Malachi 1:11: "For from the rising of the sun even unto the going down of the same, my name shall be great among the Gentiles, and in every place incense shall be offered unto my name in a pure offering. My name shall be great among the heathen, said the Lord of Hosts." Romanism says that "the sacrifice of the Cross cannot be meant, as this was offered at one place only. Prophecy is fulfilled in the Holy Sacrifice of the Mass, which is offered in all parts of the world."

But wait a minute, beloved, listen; we are not to be naïve. We're not to be simplistic, are we? You mean to tell me we are to succumb to a lot of pious religious rhetoric? The Bible tells us not to twist the word of God, and I charge the Church of Rome tonight for butchering what is plain and clear and explicit in God's word, the Bible. Now if you will, Peter warned about those who will twist the writings of Paul. And even the apostle Paul warned the Corinthians about those who will corrupt or change or chop or butcher or vandalize or twist the Holy Word of God, the Bible. And so we are to be scrupulous, beloved. We're not to be ignorant. We are told to study the word of God, amen? And then we are to rightly divide the word of truth. We are to cut it straight. You and I have that serious responsibility, do we not? I say that because a close look at the meaning of this text, and I'm referring to Malachi 1:11, indicates not a literal, external offering but a spiritual, internal offering.

By the way, it's very interesting, when a Roman Catholic apologist refers to the Church Fathers, he will not tell you that there are three categories of Church Fathers: genuine, dubious, and spurious. That's why when we go to the so-called Church Fathers, we better do our homework, because it's conceivable that one may quote a spurious or dubious Church Father.

You know, folks, to a great extent the so-called Church Fathers in the post-apostolic era were biblically, theologically unsound. May I say that again? I hope it doesn't sound like heresy. I believe many of the Church Fathers were biblically, theologically unsound. Yet, in many ways, they were clearly opposed to the Church of Rome. I mean to what later on became Roman Catholic teaching and practice. Let me give you an example from John Chrysostom. Okay, this is what he said in reference to the Christian sacrifice. He said, "And through him we offer a sacrifice to God." What sacrifice does he mean? He himself has explained, saying, "The fruit of the lips which confess his name: prayers, hymns, thanksgiving. These are the fruit of the lips. They offered sheep and calves, given to the priest, but we offer none of these things but thanksgiving and the imitation of Christ in all things as far as it is possible. May our lips thus blossom forth. Be not forgetful while doing a liberality, for with such sacrifices God is well pleased. Let us give to him such a sacrifice that he may offer it to the Father." And here's another statement by John Chrysostom, who lived in the fourth century: "But who taketh away the sins of the world? As if he were always doing it. For he did not only take then when he suffered, but from that time to the present he takes away sins. He is not always crucified, for he offered one sacrifice for sins, but he always purifies by that one sacrifice."

Recently, a Roman Catholic professor back East tried to show me from the Old Testament, from the Bible, that there is a root or a foundation for the Roman Catholic sacrifice of the Mass. Where do you think he went? You have any notion? Genesis 14:18, where it says that Melchizedek brought bread and wine because he was a priest of the Most High God. In this context, Melchizedek offered no sacrifice because the author of the letter to the Hebrews, describing the character and conduct of Melchizedek, says nothing of sacrifice. Now, beloved, if it's there, love me enough to show me. But it simply is not there, in the Bible, not your Catholic Bible, not my translation. If Melchizedek did offer bread and wine, he did so as a type of Christ's offering on the Cross, for Melchizedek was a type of Christ. I had no power to consecrate, or convert, or transubstantiate elements like bread and wine into the literal body and blood, soul and divinity, bone and marrow, of the Lord Jesus Christ. That is nothing more than sorcery. That's what it is. That is sorcery.

Show me, from God's word, the Bible. There is no word about it, yet, on ordination day, the bishop said, "Receive thou power to offer sacrifice and to celebrate Masses, both for the living and for the dead." What heresy. That hurts the heart of God. Folks, that kind of teaching stinks. That kind of teaching has no support whatsoever in God's word, the Bible. I'll tell you why. The Bible tells us why: because the apostles were commanded to preach the Gospel, not to offer sacrifice. The theory of a sacrificing priesthood with an earthly sanctuary is absolutely contrary to Holy Scripture.

As early as the last part of the second century, or maybe the third century, the heathens were calling the early Christians—and by the way they were not Roman Catholic—the heathens were calling the early Christians atheists because they had no altar, no priesthood, no sacrifice. That's right. Athanagoras, in response to those who were antagonistic to the early Christians, declared, "Those who charge us with atheism have not the faintest conception of what God is. Foolish and utterly unacquainted with natural and divine things, they measure piety by the rule of sacrifices. As to our not sacrificing, the Framer and Father of this universe does not need blood nor the odor of burnt offerings nor the fragrance, needing nothing, either within or without. The noblest sacrifice is to know who stretched out the heavens, who adorned the sky with stars and made the earth to bring forth seed of every kind, who made animals and fashioned man. We lift up holy hands to him. What need has he further of the Hecatomb? Yet, it does behoove us to offer a bloodless sacrifice and the sacrifice of our reason."

And then the great [Anglican] Bishop [Joseph] Lightfoot has gone through the Christian writings of the second century and shown how far they are from the sacerdotal priesthood of Roman Catholicism. I notice my friend, Mr. Keating, mentioned Clement of Rome, but again, beloved, we've got to be scrupulous with historical facts. As I said before, there are three categories of Church Fathers according to Roman Catholic authorities. You had the genuine Church Fathers, and then you had the dubious, and then you had the spurious. In the epistles of Clement of Rome, Polycarp, and Barnabas and in the *Shepherd of Hermes*, even in the epistles of Ignatius, there is no trace of a priesthood with daily sacrifice. Justin Martyr admits that Christianity had its priests and sacrifices, but the priests are the Christian people, and the sacrifices are spiritual.

Isn't that something? Does that grab you, or not? Listen to what he said, so you don't think that I'm misrepresenting anyone. "We are the true high priestly race of God. Even as God himself bears witness, saying that in every place, among the Gentiles, sacrifices are presented to him, well pleasing and pure. God does not receive sacrifices from anyone except through his priests. I mean those offered by the Christians, in every region of the Earth, with the thanksgiving of the bread and of the cup, bearing witness that they are well pleasing to him."

Do you find Paul telling Timothy and Titus to offer sacrifice as part of their ministerial duties? They are exhorted to give themselves to reading, to exhortation, to doctrine (1 Tim. 4:13). They are told how to conduct themselves in the house of God (1 Tim. 3:15). They are told how to govern their families. They are told to preach the Word, be it in season, out of season. "Reprove, rebuke, exhort with all long suffering, and doctrine" (1 Tim. 4:2). However, there is not one word about offering sacrifice.

In the Book of Acts, churches are founded, sinners saved—and that's a beautiful word, "saved." Nothing wrong with it. I know Romanists and apostate Protestants, they make fun of that word, but that's a good Bible word. In the early Church, in the Book of Acts, for example, which covers maybe about forty years or so—that's inspired Church history, and that's where we need to go—not to what is known as ecclesiastical history. But in the Book of Acts, churches are founded, sinners saved, miracles performed, but nowhere do we find anything resembling the so-called sacrifice of the Mass both for the living—and mind you, for the dead. Paul, Silas, Peter, and John never offered Mass in Jerusalem or Antioch. Roman Catholicism is not the system which the apostles preached, for we read nowhere in their inspired record of such a service as the Romish Mass. Roman Catholic priests not only usurp an office that belongs to Jesus Christ, and him alone, but they are without authority, from the Scripture, to offer sacrifice today because the word of God absolutely disproves the existence of a literal sacrifice. The Bible is dogmatic about the fact that there is but one sacrifice.

Arthur W. Pink was correct when he said that Hebrews is the death knell of Roman Catholicism. Chapters 7-10 make it clear that there is one Calvary and not many Masses. Romanism is very clever, being the religious harlot she is. She says there is one Calvary, yes, but many Masses. No, that conflicts with God's word, the Bible. You see, the word "once," or "once for all," is found in those great, classical chapters about nine or ten times. And that word once, once for all, speaks to the finality, the sufficiency of what Jesus did on Calvary's tree. He offered himself a recompense for you and me. He offered up his life to God on behalf of sinners. This offering was absolutely perfect and complete. In other words, nothing can be added to it. This is why the Roman Catholic Mass is useless. It's futile, unnecessary, unscriptural, and un-Christian. Not only is the Mass idolatrist. (By the way, you may think I enjoy saying some of these things tonight, I do not, but they must be said.) Not only is the Mass idolatrist; the Mass is pagan. And if you don't think so, you don't know your Bible. The Bible says that Christ by one offering perfected, forever, them that are sanctified. There is now no more offering for sin.

Christ's offering of himself was a work so perfect, so complete, so sufficient, so efficacious that it needed not to be repeated. It cannot be repeated because in order to be efficacious, Christ must suffer. He has declared that without shedding of blood there is no remission and, hence, that if the offering of Christ had to be repeated, Christ must need have suffered often. Holy Writ makes it clear that to the true Christians, that there is but one sacrifice.

The Church of the popes asserts that the sacrifice of the Mass was instituted at the Last Supper and that whenever this was observed, Christ was offered in a true, proper, and propitiatory sacrifice. Now, to accept this notion is to say that Christ must had been offered thousands of times, between the institution of the ordinance or sacrament and the publication of the epistle to the Hebrews. Now, think about that, really. This false idea is destroyed by the following text: "This he did once when he offered up himself" (Heb. 7:27). I believe this great truth is repeated by the apostle as to warn of a future Romish, papal rite known as the Mass. "Just as man once dies, so Christ was once offered"—such language is irreconcilable with the theory of Christ's continued sacrifice in the Roman Catholic Mass.

The very repetition of the Jewish sacrifices is evidence their insufficiency. The Roman Catholic Masses are constantly repeated. If the Roman Catholic Mass had been true, Christ had then been offered thousands of times. Catholicism teaches that Christ is unbloodily offered in the Mass. If so, there can be no remission of sin connected with that sacrifice because the Bible says, "Without shedding of blood is no remission" (Heb. 9:22). Yes, the Mass is a diabolical invention, an insult to the all-sufficient work of my Savior on Calvary's tree. To accept the Romish Mass is to impugn, to question, to attack, to deny, to confound the holy character of Jesus who declared, "It is finished" (John 19:30).

There can be no Mass because there is no dogma of Transubstantiation. Supposedly, the priest, by virtue of ordination, is given the power to change or convert bread and wine into Jesus Christ. He has the power to produce divinity, to make God out of mere matter. Isn't that something? It makes me shudder, beloved.

Have you heard of Jean Vianney, a very well-known Roman Catholic saint from France? This is what he said: "Without the priest, the death and passion of our Lord would be of no avail to us." Isn't that something? See the power of the priest! By one word from his lips, he changes a piece of bread into God—a greater feat than the creation of the world. Folks, that is heresy, that is blasphemy, and that hurts the heart of God. So serious is Romanism about this idea that there are curses for those who deny that the priest can convert or change bread and wine into the real body and blood, soul and divinity, bone and marrow of the Lord Jesus Christ. She, Rome, has a curse for him who denies the miraculous conversion of bread and wine into Jesus Christ. Even if the consecrated bread be severed into a thousand parts or into a million crumbs, each part or crumb is the entire Christ. If the wine be divided into drops, too many to number, each drop is the entire Christ. She, Rome, has a curse for him who denies this pagan, superstitious, medieval belief that has no root in God's word, the Bible.

But this is not all. The Church of Rome says that the host or wafer—they call it the host; some of us call it the "wafer God"; some call it the "dough God"—Rome says that the wafer, once it is consecrated, is to be worshipped with the worship of *latria*. I don't know what that is. That's Greek or Latin. I guess I should know, but anyway, it's not English. But it means that the wafer is to receive divine worship. Isn't that something? And Canon VI of the Council Trent says there's a curse for those who deny that particular teaching. How sad to think that our Roman Catholic friends worship a god of flour and water!

Some of Rome's most illustrious theologians hold that Transubstantiation is not found in the New Testament. I find this very interesting. I never knew that, during my twelve years of study for the priesthood. In fact, I've spoken with Roman Catholic priests who deny the dogma of Transubstantiation. One belongs to a very well-known cathedral, in this part of the country, in this state. I suppose he's taking stipends or donations for offering the Mass. But he told me, at least, "Bart, I don't accept Transubstantiation." And there are thousands, perhaps millions of Catholic people who reject that superstitious belief, and yet they profess to be Roman Catholic. I find that very hypocritical and unethical. But—and this should make us grieve—tonight, there are millions of Catholic people who really believe that the priest has that kind of power, to change bread and wine into the Lord Jesus Christ.

You see, beloved, one of the most superficial arguments used by the Church of Rome to promote what is known as the Holy Eucharist is from John 6:53–56. This passage has no connection whatsoever with the Lord's Supper. This discourse was given at least thirteen months before the institution of the Lord's Supper. This is evident from the fact that two Passovers elapsed between the delivery of these words and the institution of the ordinance, which by the way is not a sacrifice. And you can compare John 6:4 with John 12:1. Our Lord uses the present tense, "Except ye eat." It was their responsibility to partake of that spiritual food, even at the time when he delivered the discourse. Therefore the words cannot refer to the sacrament. I don't like that word "sacrament" anyway. It doesn't refer to the ordinance, which was not then instituted. Common sense dictates that this passage be taken figuratively. It refers to the one way of salvation, by faith.

I believe verse 53 is the key to the proper, correct interpretation of this chapter or the proper understanding of this chapter. It says, "He that cometh to me shall never hunger, and he that believeth on me shall never thirst." How are we to feed on Christ? By coming to him. How are we to drink His blood? By believing on him. And then verse 63: "It is the spirit that quickeneth. The flesh profiteth nothing. The words that I speak unto you, they are spirit, and they are life." Christ constantly employed figurative language in order to enforce the truth.

The apostles understood our Lord correctly. They didn't twist the word of God. They were accustomed to figurative language, in which the Savior always spoke. They understood that the words "this Passover" did not mean the literal Passover. And likewise, the words "This is my body" did not mean the literal body but the commemoration of it. They did not believe that Christ, whom they saw, and with whom they spoke, took his own body in his own hands and broke it into twelve parts, each part being a whole body, and gave his flesh and blood to them to eat or consume. It was contrary to God's law to drink blood. And much more, human blood. The words "Do this in remembrance of me" and the apostolic declaration "For as often as ye eat this bread and drink this cup, ye do show the Lord's death till He comes" prove that this ordinance commemorates the Savior who is bodily absent. You get that? How could it be done in remembrance of him if he were present in body, soul, blood, and deity? How could it be said that we show the Lord's death till he come, if he were already come, literally, upon the Romish altar?

Paul calls the elements the bread and the cup. "For as often as ye eat this bread and drink this cup" and "so let him eat of that bread and drink of that cup" (1 Cor. 11:26-28). Note that the Church of Rome does not receive this passage in a literal sense but in a non-natural sense. "After the same manner, also he took the cup when he had supped saying, 'This cup is the New Testament in my blood. This do ye as oft as ye drink it in remembrance of me. For as often as you eat this bread and drink this cup, ye do show the Lord's death till he come" (1 Cor. 11:23–26). Christ said, "This cup is the New Testament." Was the cup literally changed into the New Testament? He did not say or mean that the cup was literally the New Testament. Therefore, he did not mean that the bread was literally his body. To insist upon a hyper-interpretation, to insist upon a literal interpretation, is contrary to common sense and to the practice of Roman Catholicism in other respects.

A well-known Catholic theologian of yesteryear, Karl Adam, in his book *The Spirit of Catholicism,* writes, "We Catholics acknowledge, readily, without any shame, nay with pride, that Catholicism cannot be identified simply and wholly with primitive Christianity, nor even the Gospel of Christ." I'm quoting a Roman Catholic author. He is right. Romanism is a subtle departure from historic, biblical, fundamental, evangelical Christianity. The study of Roman Catholicism, superficially, may lead one to think that the Roman Catholic Church is Christian. Perhaps it was founded by Jesus Christ. After all, she believes that Jesus Christ is the Incarnate Son of God. His Virgin Birth, his miracles, his substitutionary work on the Cross, his Resurrection, Ascension, and Second Coming. These are official Roman Catholic teachings. However, these truths, which she has, have been distorted, nullified by her poisonous doctrines.

The sixteenth-century Reformers said that Roman Catholicism is apostate, not because of a denial of truth but because of additions which become a departure from it. There is an Italian expression, and it goes like this: "*Roma veduta, fede perduta.*" Rome seen, faith lost. It should read, "When Catholic Rome is seen and studied, all faith in Romanism is lost."

Now, my friend Mr. Keating and I agree that there must be a rule by which we can know divine truth. I mean there has got to be something to go by, to test Christianity. However, the Romanist has one rule and the Christian another. The differences are not only in certain doctrines but also in what constitutes a basis of authority.

It is no secret that the Church of Rome promotes Scripture and Tradition. Dr. Charles Berry, a personal friend of mine, a former Augustinian priest and professor, was told in the seminary that placing authority only in the Bible is comparable to being in a row boat with one oar. You've got to have two oars, the Bible and Tradition. The Council of Trent accepted the Bible and Tradition. Cardinal Robert Bellarmine said that the Bible is useful for the Church but not necessary. How do you like that? Cardinal Stanislaus Hosius said, "It would have been a better situation for the Church if no Scripture at all had ever existed." In France the reading of the Bible was forbidden by the

Council of Toulouse in 1229. The next year its translation was forbidden at the Council of Rheims. Its translation was forbidden for the French people. The papal bull known as *Unigenitus*, in 1713, condemned the proposition that "the reading of the Holy Scripture is for all."

I realize that things are somewhat different because of Vatican II, but, again, we don't want to be naïve. I believe the changes are cosmetic, superficial, and minor. I realize that Catholicism today is promoting Bible studies or biblical studies. However, I don't believe it's genuine. As long as the Church of Rome will unite the Word of God with humanistic tradition, I believe that hurts the heart of God. I believe God hates that, that is compromise. Right away, the Roman Catholic will appeal to the Word of God to support Tradition. Isn't that something? That really fascinates me. The Roman Catholic really doesn't believe that the Bible is the final authority. And yet, the Romanist will go to the Scripture to support Tradition. And here is a classic example: I heard my friend Karl use John 20:30. "And many other signs truly did Jesus in the presence of his disciples which are not written in this book." Surely, no one here tonight will deny that much of what Jesus did is not written. But what is written is sufficient, for the next verse reads, "But these are written that ye might believe that Jesus is the Christ, the son of God, and that believing, ye might have life through his name" (John 20:31).

Of course, Rome doesn't like to think that Tradition is extra-biblical revelation. Maybe not in theory, but in practice, it is. But I heard—I think Karl mentioned tonight, 2 Thessalonians 2:15: "Stand fast and hold the traditions which ye have been taught whether by word or our epistle." It's amazing. In my day as a Catholic we would use that text, out of context, and the same old Roman Catholic recipes are still being projected, at precious people who have been seduced with another gospel.

Second Thessalonians 2:15, right here in this text, there is no distinction between oral tradition and written tradition. We will not deny that what is found in the Bible was first taught by word. You and I would not deny that. But we believe that all of what was necessary for salvation and the teaching of Christ and his apostles is committed to writing, by the inspiration of the Holy Spirit. And were the apostles alive now we would receive, with humility and obedience, their word, whether delivered orally or by writing, wouldn't we? If the Church of Rome can only prove it, why don't they prove it? No Roman Catholic priest, in all these years, has made any attempt to show this Judas priest this point, namely, that her Tradition is apostolic. If only they will prove that their traditions are apostolic, we will receive them. But this they cannot do. The Scripture alone is what the apostles taught.

When Paul wrote to Timothy to keep that which was committed to his trust, he was not advocating the Bible plus but rather the necessity of adhering to the teaching of the apostles. "Who can deny that there were many things said and done by Christ and his apostles which are not written, for the world, itself, could not contain the books that should be written" (John 21:25). But sufficient is what is recorded. "But these are written that ye might believe that Jesus is the Christ, the Son of God and that believing ye might have life though his name" (John 20:31). The burden of proof is with Rome to show that her traditions are apostolic.

Catholicism teaches that Tradition was first oral though later on written down by Church Fathers. Boy, the Church Fathers have a high place of prominence in the Church of Rome. Why, I do not know. The early Christians wrote little because they lived in a time of severe persecution. What is found in the writings of the Church Fathers in the second and third centuries has little reference to doctrines disputed between Christians and Roman Catholics today. Therefore, Tradition for hundreds of years was nothing more than mere report, and this is what Rome receives with equal reverence. Isn't that something? As the written word of God, we cannot build our faith on mere report. This makes for a very insecure foundation.

Moreover, beloved, the Church Fathers contradict each other. Some of the Church Fathers of the second century believed in the personal reign of Jesus Christ, some did not. Some believed in images, some did not. Some accepted the canonicity of the apocryphal or spurious books, and some did not. And so there was no unanimity. There was no unanimous consent among the early Christian writers. Rome can never prove that her Traditions are divine and apostolic. Not only is Rome's authority in the Scripture and in Tradition but in the Church. What really has weight is not so much the Bible and Tradition but what is known as the teaching authority or the Magisterium. For the Catholic, be he cleric or lay member, it's simple obedience to the pope, more than anything else. That's really the bottom line. You see, the Roman Catholic religion refers to herself as infallible, but the question tonight is this: where is this infallible authority? Is it only in the pope, when he speaks *ex cathedra?* Is it in Church councils or in Church councils with the pope as head? Catholics are divided on this matter.

When all is said and done, the attribute of infallibility is said to belong to the assembly of a few bishops and theological experts, with the pope at their head. Frankly, beloved, I find nothing in the Bible about a man being infallible, and there is nothing in divine revelation about an infallible church, when it comes to biblical interpretation. What infallible authority has declared that Romanism is infallible? There is none. Rome argues that without the authority of the Roman Church we cannot prove the genuineness and authenticity and inspiration of the Bible. I remember that at lunch last winter Karl used that very fallacious argument. If the authority for Scripture rests in a few pontificating clerics, then the truth of the Bible rests on a shaky, sandy foundation.

In proof of papal infallibility, the Catholic hierarchy likes to go to Matthew 16:18: "Thou art Peter and upon this rock I will build my church, and the gates of hell shall not prevail against it." And then verse 19: "I will give unto thee the keys to the kingdom of heaven." Now, I know Mr. Keating does not go along with the distinction we have in the Greek between the Greek *petros,* which means a shifting, insecure rock, and *petra,* which refers to a solid, immovable rock. I think this distinction points to the fact that Christ was actually speaking in Greek, not Aramaic. Right now I can just hear one say, "Oh, let's not quibble about the Greek. Let's not quibble about the Greek gender endings because our Lord did not speak in Greek but in Aramaic. Well, I don't believe this helps the person that takes that position. Matthew gave the account of the incident and quotes Jesus directly. Matthew could have quoted it, "Thou art *petros* and upon this *petros* I will build my Church," but he did not. He quoted it, "Thou art *petros,* and upon this *petra,* I will build my Church." Matthew could have used the same word, but he did not, beloved.

The Roman Catholic officials, in an effort to escape the force of this argument, say, "There is no use quibbling about the Greek. Our Lord did not speak in Greek." But wait a minute. Matthew reports it in Greek. Do you not believe that Matthew was inspired? Why discredit Matthew and this account? All this just in an effort to try to uphold the primacy of Peter. Friends, do you not know that Jesus promised to send the apostles the Holy Spirit? That included Matthew. He promised to lead them into all truth. That also included Matthew. Why discredit Matthew's record? Besides, if you do your homework from Roman Catholic sources, you will see that they accept Greek as one of the original biblical languages. Shame on the Church of Rome for saying that it makes no difference how Matthew wrote it. Do you not have any respect for the correctness and inspiration of Matthew's Gospel? Maybe you do. But if you say Christ didn't write in Greek, it was Aramaic, then you show that you have no regard, whatsoever, for Matthew.

Now folks, do me a favor tonight, before you leave. I know it's getting late. And, listen, I appreciate your patience very much. Tell me, what commentaries written during the first thousand years of Christianity mention the primacy or the papacy? Not one mentions the primacy of the Bishop of Rome. I was really surprised to hear Karl start off with the idea of Peter being in Rome. I was quite surprised to see that he would go that direction, but I believe there is no commentary, whatsoever, written by some well-known Roman Catholic authority on this particular verse. Such an idea and interpretation did not even exist as a heresy, namely the primacy of Peter. God obviously knew that centuries later that the Roman Catholic system would seriously distort the position of Peter the apostle. He inspired Isaiah, in Hebrew, to write this: "And you are my witnesses. Is there any god besides me? Or is there any other rock? I know of none" (Isaiah 44:8). The word "rock" is an emblem of deity. Isn't that precious? And there is no other god, and there is no other rock. If you say that there can be another rock, you would exegetically have to admit the possibility of another god.

That's right. If the apostles believed that no longer would God be perceived as the only rock, then why did not they ask how a human could be described in terms of an Old Testament emblem of deity? If they entertained the notion that Peter was the rock, to the Jewish mind it would have seemed that Peter also was God. What did it mean to the original apostles at the time this was spoken, Matthew 16:18–19? Why did they wonder how it applied to Peter? Why did they not wonder why Peter fell so hard when he denied the Lord and forsook him? Why didn't they ever, in the New Testament, ask Peter to settle any disputes? Why did the apostles wonder who was the greatest among them, if they interpreted Peter as being the rock upon which the Church was built?

Folks, in connection with papal supremacy, Peter was not a priest. He was not a pope, and I don't believe he ever got to Rome, and if he did, so what? But he was not the rock. He was not the rock. Why do we want to take that away from Jesus? The pope is not the rock, but what does this section, Matthew 16:18-19, have to do with the dogma that certain Roman Catholic clergymen in council, convened by the pope, are infallible? Is there a word in this text about pope, council, or Roman Church? There is not. Romanism was not even in existence. And it was in Antioch that the disciples were first called Christians. Isn't that right?

The theories of certain Roman Catholic theologians concerning Matthew 16:18-19 afford a remarkable example of division in a so-called infallible community. While Bonaventure and Liguori and others teach that the pope is infallible, still others deny this doctrine. Did you know that? Dr. Ignaz von Döllinger was a very famous priest, a historian from Munich, in the nineteenth century, and this is what he said: "Even the boldest champions of papal absolutism assumed that the popes could err, and that their decisions were no certain criterion."

Have you heard of Pope Pius IX? I read something interesting lately. I read that there is an effort underway to canonize him as a Roman Catholic saint. Now, he had three girlfriends. Don't be upset. What do you expect of an unregenerate? You see that's no worse than religious idolatry. That's no worse than promoting salvation by works. Pope Pius IX, during Vatican I, made the provision that in case he were to die during the Council, its decisions would take precedence over the decisions made by previous council or popes and thus correct any inconsistencies there might be. If the pope were truly the vicar of Christ, beloved, would he dare to make provisions for contradictions?

Think about it. If the doctrine of infallibility were defined by Christ, or by any apostle, why did the Roman Catholic institution wait until 1870 to make this doctrine a dogma of the Romanists, binding under pain of mortal sin? There is a curse for the Roman Catholic who rejects the infallibility of the pope when he speaks from his chair. Why did the Church of Rome wait for centuries to define it? The truth is that papal infallibility was not generally taught until 1870. If the popes are infallible only since 1870, what were they before that time? And if they were fallible before 1870, what about their doctrine?

A year after the pope was declared infallible, the *Catholic World*, a very well-known Catholic publication, stated, "We have no right to ask reasons of the Church, any more than of Almighty God, as a preliminary to our submission. We are to take with unquestioning docility whatever instruction the Church gives," August 1871, page 598. Paul said, "These were more noble than those in Thessalonica and that they received the word with all readiness of mind and search the scriptures daily, whether those things were so." The Bereans took the Bible as their guide, and Paul commended them for doing so. The Bible, not the pope, is the safe guide. The doctrine of infallibility came gradually into the Roman system, like many of her doctrines.

I heard my friend Karl Keating mention the development of doctrine. That came about with Cardinal Newman. He was an Anglican priest that later on converted to Romanism. He became a Cardinal. Now there is an effort to canonize him as a Roman Catholic saint. My, that will bring a lot of Episcopalians and Anglicans into the Church of Rome.

Did someone say, Amen? If you did, you need to repent. Now let me say this, beloved. Let me say this. Let me say this very quickly. The Bible says, "Let no man deceive you, by any means." No wonder the New Testament constantly warns, "Be not deceived." We are told, "Believe not every spirit, but try the spirits whether they are of God, because many false prophets are going out into the world. This means that the teachings of all churches must come under the test of God's word, the Holy Scripture, because there are false apostles, deceitful workers, transforming themselves into the apostles of

Christ. It is no marvel for Satan himself is transformed into an angel of light. Therefore it is no great thing if his ministers also be transformed as the ministers of righteousness whose end shall be according to their works. Now we have seen that neither Tradition nor the Roman Catholic Church is the rule of faith. I want to show that the Bible is the only objective source of divine revelation. In Old Testament times, the written law was the rule of the people. And if you don't think so, all you have to do is look at Deuteronomy 6:6-9. And then look in Deuteronomy 6—

[Interruptions from the audience, followed by consultation with the moderator.]

Folks, I believe in submission, obedience to my moderator. He said I've gone long over the time. I'd like to mention the fact that originally it was to be 30 minutes, and then Karl and I agreed to have it for 45, but I understood that we were to be flexible when it came to the presentation, so I will have to yield to the moderator at this time. Thank you so very much.

KEATING: Bart and I didn't make any arrangements for rebuttals of each other, but there are a few things that I just cannot let pass in what he said. I feel like a man who has been commanded to unravel a bowl of spaghetti, and he's been given one chopstick. There are so many incorrect things in what Bart said. Now, his Bible quotations were accurate, but don't you think that the Catholic Church, which preserved the Bible through nineteen centuries, might realize that those quotations were in it? If you think that the Catholic Church was all powerful in the Middle Ages, why wasn't it smart enough to destroy all the Bibles? Why did it preserve them in monasteries? But let me get to some of his points. I want to mention just three things, and then we'll take questions, so I for one won't go an extra 45 minutes. Let me go backwards in sequence here.

First, what is this business about Pope Pius IX in the nineteenth century having three girlfriends? There is a very interesting book called *No Popery*. It's by Fr. Herbert Thurston, S.J. About half the book is devoted to calumnies against Pius IX. When he died he left what he owned, which was the value of a few hundred dollars today, to widowed sisters of his, who had no pension or other income. Anti-Catholics transformed his sisters into women unrelated to him, and the amount left as not being his few personal possessions but the great wealth of the Church. That's ridiculous.

Second, Matthew 16:18. Bart skirted around the matter. We know that Matthew in fact was written in Aramaic because the earliest writings we have talking about the writing of that Gospel can be found in Eusebius, the first Church historian, writing around 325. He said, "Matthew wrote in the common language of the Hebrew people." That was Aramaic. That's what people spoke. On the Cross, Jesus spoke Aramaic. "*Eloi, Eloi, lama sabachthani.*" Aramaic is still spoken today in the Mass in some Eastern Catholic Churches. In Matthew 16:18, in the Aramaic, the phrase would have been, "Thou art *kepha*, and upon this *kepha*, I will build my Church."

The play on words there is obvious. In translating Matthew's Aramaic to Greek you change *kepha*, which means rock, big rock, into *petra*. Quite true. You cannot use *petra*, though, as a man's name because in Greek nouns have gender endings. *Petra* is a feminine noun. You can't use it as a man's name. You have to change the ending to a masculine ending, so you get *petros*. The only way you can translate the Aramaic into Greek would have been "Thou art *petros* and upon this *petra* I will build my Church." French translations have a parallel to the Aramaic. The word in French for rock is *pierre*. In French the Bibles read, "Thou art *pierre*, and upon this *pierre*, I will build my Church." I mean the play on words is just too obvious, but most Fundamentalists ignore that and look at just the Greek as though it proves something. It doesn't.

The third point I want to mention is another historical blunder. Someone over here gave me a few amens a few moments ago when I mentioned that the Church made no attempt to wipe out the Bible. The guy said, "Oh, yes it did." Bart had mentioned the Council of Toulouse in 1229. Toulouse is in France. He also mentioned a council at Rheims. He said those councils banned the Bible. That's true. But do you know why they banned the Bible? Let's say your son or your daughter brings home a Bible, say the King James

Version, into which somebody has pasted un-Christian lines, maybe pornographic pictures. Would you ban that Bible from your children? Of course you would. You'd say, "The only Bible, my son or daughter, that you're authorized by your parents to use is an unadulterated Bible, which I encourage you to use. But not this one with a false translation or other things added in."

In the early thirteenth century, in southern France, there was a heresy called Albigensianism, also known as Catharism. Fundamentalists often like to picture Albigensianism as a Middle Ages version of Fundamentalism. Why? Because the Albigensianism wanted the Bible not in Latin but in the vernacular, French. The Albigensians, under either Catholic or Fundamentalist standards, were no Christians at all. They were Manichees. They thought there was a war between the spirit and the body, in such a way that marriage was immoral. They recognized that people have instincts, so they approved of concubines. They let that go by, but they would not approve of marriage because the authorities would be okaying the union of a man and a woman. The Albigensians had a sacrament, somewhat like baptism. (They didn't believe in baptism.) They had something called *consolamentum.* you got it once in your life. After that, if you committed any sin, you could not go to heaven. People tried to arrange the *consolamentum* to be given on their deathbeds. Sometimes things didn't work out right. Sometimes people recovered, after getting the *consolamentum.* Then you got to undergo what was called the *endura*, endurance, which was forced suicide. You had your choice. Either you could be suffocated with a pillow by the church elders, or they would withhold food from you until you died. It was one or the other. The reason the Albigensian church was attacked by the Catholic Church was because those are immoral doctrines, and Albigensianism was disrupting society in France.

You don't have to accept my word for it. Why don't you turn to a reputable (from Fundamentalists point of view) Protestant scholar on the Middle Ages, H. C. Lea, who was an American? He was very anti-Catholic, but in his book on the Inquisition he wrote about the Albigensians. He said that, had Albigensianism prevailed in Europe, Christianity and civilization would have been extinguished. He had no misgivings about what was done to the Albigensians. He knew theirs was an evil system.

Now those are just three examples of more than three dozen mistakes (I counted them) that Bart brought out in his talk, and they were seriously mistaken. If he and I duel, armed with decibels, I can't win. He's experienced, with ten years or more as a preacher. I can't win on that basis. I can't yell to a victory. But what you can do is look behind what each of us says. You can get our literature and compare for yourself. Put yourself a step away from the present position you have, whether you're Catholic or Fundamentalist, and take an open view. One thing I ask you though is, please, don't be entirely willing to swallow every negative thing you hear. You know from your own experience, from people you meet who are Catholic, that they aren't all fools. Has it never occurred to you that there is probably more to their religion that you've been told by people who, for whatever reason—personal grudge or whatever—hate the Church?

It would have been easy for me to come here and paint Fundamentalism black. You know very well if you're a Fundamentalist that half the people in America think of you as redneck Bible thumpers. Right. By that they mean that they think you're stupid when in fact that's not the case. Yes, you're going to find stupid people in any religion. You can't deny that, but you don't like that caricature of Fundamentalism. I don't either. I've spoken against it. I've written against it for Catholic audiences. I think that you ought to expect Fundamentalist writers and pundits to do the same when it comes to the Church of Rome. You ought to demand of them a little courtesy, a little charity, a little fair play.

MODERATOR: If you have a logical, sensible question, a reasonable question you want to ask, from either side, feel free to ask it.

SPEAKER: I'd like to address Mr. Keating regarding Peter as the first pope. Do you call Paul a liar? In Galatians, he says that Peter was the apostle to the Jews and he was the apostle to the Gentiles. Why don't you make Paul the first pope because Peter's headquarters was in Jerusalem?

KEATING: At one time, all the apostles were in Jerusalem. Peter later went to Antioch, around the year 42. Later still he went to Rome. At the time of Christ, Rome had the largest Jewish population of any city in the world, more so than Jerusalem. Peter went to the Jews in Rome and evangelized them. Most Jews did not live in Palestine at the time. Thus there's no contradiction.

MODERATOR: Okay. Yes, sir.

SPEAKER: To Mr. Keating: Do you believe everything that the Catholic Church teaches and its ordinances and laws and doctrines?

KEATING: I think I'm about to be set up for something. Yes. Now what's the next part of your question?

SPEAKER: I asked this question to a Catholic nun, and I ask it to you, and I'd like a biblical answer, not a traditional answer or historical answer. In 1 Timothy 2:1, it says, "I exhort therefore, that first of all, supplications, prayers, intercessions and giving of thanks be made for all men." Then it goes on and says, "For there is one God and one mediator between God and men, the man Christ Jesus." I asked the nun why your Catholic writings say there is only one true Mediatrix and that you can get your prayers answered quicker through Mary than you can through Jesus, and I showed her the writings, and she said her only basis was Tradition. I ask you for a biblical basis for praying through Mary.

KEATING: First of all, will you pray for me for discernment on that? If I ask you, will you pray for me that I might be enlightened in that regard? Yes? Do you violate the Bible by doing that because are you acting as a mediator between me and God? You say, now wait a minute. I'm not violating the Bible. We are commanded by Jesus to pray for one another. Is that right?

SPEAKER: I pray through Jesus to God. He's my mediator.

KEATING: In this church, or wherever you might fellowship, you regularly pray for one another. I pray for my friends, my family, for Bart before I came tonight. I may even pray for him afterwards. In doing that, what am I doing? I am being a mediator. Why doesn't he just pray for himself? There is no contradiction there.

MODERATOR: Yes, sir. In the middle right here, in the blue shirt.

SPEAKER: Mr. Keating, let us assume that Peter is the rock. I don't believe that, but let's just assume it. Can you give me a biblical place in the Bible where it says that Peter had successors and that these successors were infallible?

KEATING: The successors would be logically necessary because Christ said his Church would exist throughout the ages and that the gates of hell would not prevail. Human beings die, so it makes sense that there must be a successor to whom power could be handed on. Now, is there somebody perhaps that would want to address a question to Mr. Brewer?

MODERATOR: I just told Bart, "Nobody wants to ask you anything." In the back, back there.

SPEAKER: My question I would like to address to both speakers. It's just a simple question. Jesus spoke many times of hell, and he talked about what a terrible place it is, and I don't want to go there. I would just like to ask both speakers if they could give me any kind of assurance at all that I don't have to go there?

KEATING: Whether you as an individual will go there, of course, none of us can say. We all hope not. We all have a chance of going there. We all have a chance of ruining our lives through sin and ending up there, but whether we go there or not depends upon whether we're supernaturally alive when we die. If we're supernaturally dead, which we become by turning our backs on God through sin, we will not go there because we'll be unclean and nothing unclean can enter heaven. On the other hand, if we're supernaturally alive, we will go to heaven.

BREWER: Well, contrary to what Mr. Keating said, the Bible indeed is a sufficient source of revelation from cover to cover. To say it's not sufficient is to imply it's deficient. To imply that it's deficient is to indict God's divine sovereignty and folks, that's very serious. So the Bible's the complete revelation from cover to cover. For example, I like to share this information with you. If Scripture were not sufficient for its end, informing us of the saving purposes of God, it could not stand as our sole authority. So when you have a defective view of Scripture, you do not accept the premise that the Bible is a sufficient revelation from cover to cover. Now, when one accepts the Scripture as a complete objective revelation from cover to cover, as that person gets into the Word of God, he will understand that Christ not only saves, but also he keeps. And there—you can only be born again one time. Justification by faith is a one-time act. It's really sad that Romanism promotes processed salvation. You're born again, born again, born again. That is heresy.

SPEAKER: How do you get saved?

BREWER: How does a person get saved? Well, the Bible makes it very clear, by repenting and receiving Christ as Lord and Savior. That's not a flippant, quick decision for Christ. That means standing upon the completed work of Christ. Another way to explain it would be to exchange your own righteousness for the righteousness of Jesus, and we have that example in Romans 4, the example of Abraham: "To him that worketh not, but believeth on him that justifieth the ungodly, his faith is counted for righteousness," and yet the Church of Rome places sanctifying grace in sacraments.

Now I think what is very unfortunate is that sometimes a Roman Catholic apologist either deliberately, or perhaps not so deliberately, will not give you the whole picture. I remember as a Roman Catholic priest when prospective converts came to the office we were told to speak to them about the simplicity of the faith. That meant keeping the person away from the facts. I think Mr. Keating has done that very well tonight. He has not given us an in-depth picture of Romanism.

MODERATOR: Lady in the yellow blouse. Right there.

SPEAKER: I wanted to ask Mr. Brewer: I've been a Catholic all my life, and I've never heard as much hate spewed. Why are you so anti-Catholic? We have a lot of things that aren't in the Bible that we believe by faith. We have faith in the things that we believe to be true because we want to believe them. I don't care what you believe, but I don't denigrate you. As for your faith, whatever it is you have, methinks you protest too much. You were a priest. I wonder if you weren't just sorry that you couldn't cut the mustard.

BREWER: Thank you very much. I really need to apologize because before getting started, I should have mentioned that we love the Catholic, but we cannot support the teachings.

Have you ever heard of Augustine? He said that we are to hate error and love the man, and that is my position. Paul said, "Speak the truth in love." When Paul wrote to the Galatians, he asked, "Am I your enemy because I tell you the truth?" So tonight, we're not attacking you but a system that seduces people with another gospel.

MODERATOR: All right, over here, young man.

SPEAKER: I would like to address a question to Rev. Brewer to the point about the divisions in doctrine among Protestants, people that accept Scripture alone. Some Protestants believe that once one has entered the state of grace, he can never be lost again. Other Protestants believe one can be lost after he has entered the state of grace. Some Protestants such as the Lutherans accept the doctrine of the Real Presence. Other Protestants, such as Baptists, don't. What's your thought on that?

BREWER: Well, apparently, I have said too much already, so let me mention this, that had you been truly born again the Bible way and had you really understood the Scripture, you would not had been a convert to the Church of Rome. May I just say in short that, technically speaking, we are not Protestant. I recognize the Reformation movement as a valid movement, but technically speaking, we are not Protestant. In other words, we're not out of the Reformation of the sixteenth century. We stand upon the infallible word of God, and once you really study our Lord's attitude toward the Scripture, you will see that salvation is only by faith.

MODERATOR: This lady right here.

SPEAKER: I'd like to address this to Mr. Brewer: Why did you leave the Church? Is there a particular event or reason that you could give? You noted at the beginning of your address that we could just look at the Bible and see the clear meaning of it, yet throughout your presentation I think we were given your interpretation of the Bible. As this gentlemen's question was just referring to, whose interpretation are we to take as authentic? Are we to take yours, or are we to take his, or are we to take mine? How do we discern what is the clear interpretation because obviously you don't believe what I believe about the Bible?

BREWER: As I tried to say earlier, we're not dealing with interpretation tonight, but the plain facts of God's word. And once you understand that the Bible is authoritative, then you will accept its inspiration and inerrancy as the final court of appeal.

Why did I leave the Roman Catholic priesthood? There were two teachings during my time in the chaplaincy with the Marines that I started to question. Number one: celibacy. I believe celibacy makes many a priest a professional hypocrite. Mandatory celibacy has no support from the Bible. Optional celibacy, yes. Mandatory celibacy, no. Paul in writing to Timothy and Titus gives the requirements for an individual who has a calling to preach the gospel. The second teaching I started to question—and believe me, it was with fear and trembling—was sacramental confession. If you and I will take the totality of Scripture, we see indeed that no one can forgive sin. Christ died for past, present, and future sin. I dare say that sacramental confession is one of the great sources of immorality. It is unnatural for a male or female to confess sin to a priest.

MODERATOR: Okay. This man right here in the middle. Yes, sir.

SPEAKER: I see on one side Mr. Brewer is saying that we are to rely on Scripture and Scripture alone. And on this side, you're saying, Mr. Keating, that we are to rely on the Scripture as long as it doesn't deviate from Tradition. Is that correct?

KEATING: The Catholic position is that Scripture and Tradition are the twin sources of revelation. They don't conflict, and Scripture is properly thought of as a part of the oral tradition under which Christianity was first passed down. If Scripture was never written, Christianity would still exist. The truths would still be there, but they would have been passed down orally. When you look at the Bible, you see the one thing the Bible is not is a theological treatise or catechism. In the New Testament you have four biographies, a partial history book, which is also a travelogue, and letters to individuals and to small communities. All of those presume that the people to whom they were written were already Christians. The Bible was not written for non-Christians so they could learn what the religion is about. The Bible needs to be supplemented by the full truth that Christ left to the apostles.

MODERATOR: All the way in the back, back there.

SPEAKER: Yes, I'd like to address this to both men. I believe all of us here realize that there is no way to get in to heaven if man has sin in his life. How then, biblically, is sin purged?

BREWER: We have to remember the word "substitution." That's why there's no Roman Catholic Mass. Christ took your place on the Cross. He paid the price of sin. He purged your sin and my sin on the Cross. When a person repents, that's when justification by faith takes place. That simply means that one is acquitted of the charge of sin. Christ died for the ungodly. He died for the unrighteous. He came to die for sinners, so that's how sin is forgiven.

KEATING: Actually, I have nothing to contradict what Bart said. I would just add that our Lord, as he was leaving, left us means through which we are able to make sure that, in fact, our sins are forgiven. You know it's very easy for any of us to go into our room to pray and say, "I'm sure that my contrition is adequate enough that God must have forgiven me." Sin has a social nature. Christ understands that. He instituted the sacraments, one of which was confession. Christ instituted that sacrament so that we can be sure that our sins are forgiven.

SPEAKER: I'm asking primarily what the Catholic Church teaches on purgatory.

BREWER: Is this for me or Karl? Purgatory simply is this, if you're not good enough to go to heaven, bad enough to go to hell, there's an intermediate place where you atone for sin. However, again, the Bible makes it very clear that Christ died for past, present, and future sin. There's only one propitiation for sin, and that's why in Hebrews 1:3 it says that by himself he purged our sin. You really have to examine the evolution of Roman Catholic teaching to see that this teaching absolutely has no foundation at all in the Bible. You talk about exploiting people, that's exactly what purgatory is all about.

KEATING: Two scriptural points immediately come to mind. One is that nothing unclean shall enter heaven. Most of us when we die are not going to be perfectly clean. The second is from 2 Maccabees: "It's a holy and wholesome thought to pray for the dead." Protestants don't accept 2 Maccabees and some other books in the Catholic Bible as part of Scripture, and the reason, largely, is that the Reformers threw them out precisely because they uphold some Catholic doctrines. The official teachings of the Church as to what books belong to the Bible go all the way back to the Council of

Carthage in the last decade of the fourth century. That council included Maccabees as part of the Bible. Now if you want to pick and choose what you will accept as the Bible, that's up to you. All I'm saying is that the Catholic Church looks at the whole Bible, not just the parts that it finds conducive to its preferred doctrines.

One thing that I didn't get to bring up before, and I was going to mention when Bart was answering an earlier question, was this: most people, including all Fundamentalists, think that Fundamentalists get their doctrines by reading the Bible. Incorrect. They start with pre-existing doctrines that are substantiated as well as they can be by going to the Bible and looking for things that seem to substantiate them. You may say no, no, no. But I suspect there's not a one of you who once had no feel for the Bible at all, had never seen it, had no religious position whatever, and opened the Bible and said, "Oh, I can see that all this shows the Fundamentalist position." You learned the Fundamentalist position, and through your learning of it you found certain arguments from Scripture that seem to support it.

MODERATOR: This young man is standing up already.

SPEAKER: Yeah, I'd like to address this to both of you. What does the Bible say concerning infant baptism and in the context of salvation? I realize the Catholic Church, from my upbringing, has taught that infant baptism has something to do with the salvation of that child. I am an ex-Catholic. I have found that to be totally wrong, and I would like both of your opinions on that.

BREWER: I would not want to give you my opinion. I like to mention what the Bible states with great clarity. You know what there is about infant baptism? Nothing. And baptism is for the believer. You know, I had to swallow my religious pride one day, realizing that there is no salvation in baptism. That's one of the great heresies propagated by the Church of Rome. There is nothing in the Bible about infant baptism.

KEATING: On the infant baptism question, it's not taught directly either way in Scripture. We do find that Paul baptized whole households. Presumably households include children. If you look at the earliest books written by Christians after the New Testament, such as the *Didache* and the writings of Ignatius of Antioch and others, they refer specifically to children and infants, using both words, as being properly baptized. Here's what you have to do. If you reject their understanding of early Christianity, what you have to say is this: during the time some of the apostles were still alive, such John who died at the end of the first century, the great majority of Christians dropped the faith and took up this other stuff. And if that was the case, why are there no writings of that early period which say, "Hey, look at these people! Ignatius of Antioch, Irenaeus, and others, they're contradicting the faith that we had from the apostles"? You find no writings like that in the early history. Early Christians were the most conservative people you can imagine. They had exactly one test to see if a doctrine was acceptable, and the test was this: is it an innovation from what has been handed down from our Fathers in the faith? Nobody in the early centuries disclaimed infant or child baptism.

MODERATOR: Okay, the lady in the purple dress back there.

SPEAKER: This is for Mr. Keating. You mentioned about prayers for the dead. I was wondering how long will I pray for my loved ones who are in purgatory in order for them to get out of it? Do you know?

KEATING: Nobody knows, and the Church has never said that anybody knows. There's no way to know what efficacy any of our prayers have on that issue or anything else. You may pray for the conversion of somebody or for some temporal good. We have no way to measure exactly what the effect of your prayer may be. If you happen to pray for somebody to get to heaven, and let's say the person is already there, your prayers don't go to waste. God doesn't waste your prayers. The goodness of your prayers will be applied to somebody else if necessary.

MODERATOR: Okay. Andy?

SPEAKER: So you believe that's true? If we can work our way to heaven, it's no longer grace. If it's grace, then it's no longer works. Which is which?

KEATING: It's easy, Andy, to make a caricature of anybody's position. Now Bart's made a number of caricatures tonight of the Catholic position. I explained it would be easy for me to do the same for your position. You make a false dichotomy. It's either grace or it's works. God expects us to cooperate with him if we expect to get to heaven. He won't save us in spite of ourselves. He's redeemed us, but if we insist on not going to heaven, he's not going to force us to go there. On the other hand, his grace abounds, and there is grace enough for everybody.

MODERATOR: Okay. The lady back there in the blue sweater. There's two of them. Oh, my.

SPEAKER: I was born and raised a Catholic and I went through twelve years of private school. I was raised to believe that the Bible is the Word of God, even though there was never one in the house, they were nice to have, but not necessary, and none of what I learned was based on it, but I was told that is the Word of God, and now you're saying that it is, but Tradition is important.

KEATING: I'm sorry that as a Catholic you might have received an inadequate education. After all, Bart did. He didn't learn to tell time.

SPEAKER: My inadequate education was that the Bible was the Word of God. Is that inadequate in your eyes?

KEATING: If you weren't given the Bible and didn't get to read the Bible when you were younger, I would call that inadequate. However, you might have also not been paying attention too much at Mass, if you were going to Mass at the time, because in every Mass the Bible is read. You have a reading from the Gospel, for example, and over a three-year liturgical cycle virtually all verses of the Gospels are read aloud. You also get readings from other parts of the New Testament. You get a reading from the psalms and you get a reading from the Old Testament. It's a pity, frankly, that in the last number of decades there was not a great emphasis in Catholic teaching to encourage people to read the Bible. Here I refer to the local level. The popes and the bishops were very adamant that Bible reading was necessary and good, and they encouraged it, but that often didn't trickle down as well as it ought to have. This is one place Catholics can learn something from Fundamentalists who show a real love for the Bible. I see more Catholics taking a love for the Bible, and more Catholics are reading it. That's very good. This sorry state of affairs came up because of the Reformation when a false emphasis given to the Bible by the Protestants and Catholics got scared off. It's too bad that it happened, but it's a historical fact that it did.

SPEAKER: My last question is: how can you justify the wealth of the Vatican, and can you justify the amount of time given to requests for money by the Catholic Church as opposed to what I've seen in other churches?

KEATING: Well, I don't know what you've see in other churches.

SPEAKER: I've seen no requests.

KEATING: For my part, I've seen few requests in Catholic churches, and I've been going to Catholic churches for quite a while, but you asked me to compare specifically money questions. Do you have any feel for what the annual budget of the Vatican might be? It's about the same as the budget for the Archdiocese of Chicago. Aside from subsidizing poor dioceses around the world, the Vatican funds hospitals and orphanages and pays for missionaries in areas where they cannot be supported because the people are too poor. Almost all of the wealth of the Catholic Church consists of artwork, orphanages, hospitals, and church buildings. They've been in the church for centuries. Yes, you could sell it all off, but there wouldn't be enough to run the federal government for more than a few weeks. The wealth isn't as great as you think. St. Peter's is a magnificent building with valuable artwork in it, but there's not a lot of cash flowing around.

SPEAKER: What I'd like to know for both of you is why the Catholic Church has Christ on the cross and why Fundamentalists have Christ off the cross.

BREWER: We believe that Christ is risen, so why have a bloody figure on the cross, which is a crucifix? That stems from Roman Catholic Tradition. I really believe this: once the Catholic becomes born again, the biblical way and begins to have a relationship with Christ and gets grounded in the Scripture, then some of these things gradually dissipate.

KEATING: In this country, most Catholics belong to what we call the Western or Latin rite of the Church. A small minority here, but a majority of Catholics in the Near East, belong to what we call the Eastern rites. In the Latin churches, commonly you'll see Christ crucified. In the Eastern churches, commonly you'll see Christ triumphant. He's on the cross, but he has his arms up in victory. Each one has a certain emphasis. We don't deny that he's risen and is in heaven. The reason that the crucifix with the dying Christ became popular, and particularly in the Middle Ages, was that there was a keen sense of the suffering that Christ went through for us because of our sins. In the East, there was an equally keen sense of the victory he had over death. You can have it either way, and you can have a cross without Christ if you wish, because you'll also find some of those. Each emphasizes something different, but don't make the mistake of saying, "The local Catholic church has Christ crucified, so they must think he never rose from the dead." No Catholic believes that.

MODERATOR: This man in the blue coat.

SPEAKER: Okay. If I'm not mistaken, the popes are celibate. Paul in I Corinthians 9:5 says, "Have we not power to lead about a sister, a wife, as well as other apostles and as brethren of the Lord and Cephas?" The name Cephas refers here to Peter.

KEATING: Catholics have always admitted that some of the early popes were married. We don't know whether during Jesus' ministry Peter's wife still was alive. We know that his mother-in-law was alive because Jesus cured her. So we know that Peter, at least at one time, and maybe still then, was married. Several popes after Peter were married, as were some bishops. Over the centuries, that fell out of habit. It was decided that it was wiser for bishops to be celibate, which is to say not married. That was following Paul's admonition. He said you didn't have to follow him, but, as for himself, he chose to be celibate.

MODERATOR: Okay. In the blue shirt right here.

SPEAKER: In Matthew 1:25 it says that "he kept her a virgin until she gave birth to a son, and she called him named Jesus." The word "until" means something changed.

KEATING: The word "until" in the Greek, as a translation of Hebrew or Aramaic, doesn't have the same force it does in English. It doesn't mean that the event that we might expect necessarily happened afterwards. Similarly with other words. When we say that Jesus was the firstborn, that doesn't mean that there was a second-born of Mary. Under the Mosaic Law, any firstborn child had certain duties and rights. If you had only one child, that child would still be the firstborn. Similarly with the word "until." It doesn't mean that the thing that we might think happened afterwards actually did. It doesn't imply anything about it.

SPEAKER: Okay, in some Scriptures, it's also said that he did not know her "until"—I'd like to refer that back to Genesis where it says that the man knew his wife, which defined the "knew" part.

KEATING: We know what the word "know" means, right? It's a euphemism for marital relations, but again, the key word is "until" in the reference to Joseph and Mary. It doesn't mean that what we might expect actually happened later. It just means it didn't happen up to a certain point.

MODERATOR: Okay. Let's all stand together. We were supposed to have had two 45-minute deliveries and 45 minutes of question. That's two hours and 15 minutes, and it's been four hours.

I appreciate all of you coming. As for these men, they have book tables back there, and I'm going to ask as we're being dismissed for both of them to go back there. You can talk to them, get their literature. I hope it's been beneficial for you to be here tonight.

Thank You!

I hope you found this little book useful or entertaining—preferably both! If you did, please consider leaving an honest review at Amazon. It is through reviews that writers find most of their new readers.

If you have feedback about the book, I'd like to have it. You can write to me at Karl@KarlKeating.com.

The Books in This Series

The Debating Catholicism Series consists of four short books and an omnibus volume. They are:

Book 1: *The Bible Battle* (Karl Keating vs. Peter S. Ruckman)

Book 2: *High Desert Showdown* (Karl Keating vs. Jim Blackburn)

Book 3: *Tracking Down the True Church* (Karl Keating vs. Jose Ventilacion)

Book 4: *Face Off with an Ex-Priest* (Karl Keating vs. Bartholomew F. Brewer)

Omnibus Volume: *Debating Catholicism* (includes all four books above)

Other Books by Karl Keating

Apologetics the English Way

Can a reasonable case be made for Catholicism? Maybe even a compelling case? Or does the Catholic argument falter? Does it wilt before critiques from top-notch opponents? Judge for yourself. You don't have to be Catholic or even religious to relish the intellectual sparring that goes on in these pages.

Here is high-level controversial writing, culled from Karl Keating's favorite books. Each selection is a forceful exposition of Catholic truth. Most are from the 1930s, all come from English Catholics, and all are aimed at a single antagonist, with the public invited to look over the writer's shoulder. The reader can view the weaknesses and occasional mistakes even of his own champion.

These pages are filled with vivid personalities. These were men who knew the Catholic faith and could explain it to others. The individuals against whom they wrote may not have been converted—one or two were, in the long run—but any number of readers of these little-known masterpieces must have found their faith bolstered and their doubts assuaged. The issues covered in these exchanges are still discussed today—but probably nowhere in as glorious a style as here.

The New Geocentrists

Were Copernicus, Galileo, and Kepler wrong? Does Earth orbit the Sun, or does the Sun orbit Earth? For centuries, everyone thought the science was settled, but today the accepted cosmology is being challenged by writers, speakers, and movie producers who insist that science took a wrong turn in the seventeenth century. These new geocentrists claim not only that Earth is the center of our planetary system but that Earth is motionless at the very center of the universe.

They insist they have the science to back up their claims, which they buttress with evidence from the Bible and Church documents. But do they have a case? How solid is their reasoning, and how trustworthy are they as interpreters of science and theology?

The New Geocentrists examines the backgrounds, personalities, and arguments of the people involved in what they believe is a revolutionary movement, one that will overthrow the existing cosmological order and, as a consequence, change everyone's perception of the status of mankind.

No Apology

Karl Keating has been a Catholic apologist for nearly four decades. In these pages he shares some of his own experiences and some stories from times past. He writes about how to do apologetics and how not to. He defends the very idea of apologetics against a theologian who thinks apologetics is passé. He looks at how the faith is promoted through beauty and through suffering. He takes you from his own backyard to such distant times and places as fifth-century Jerusalem and sixteenth-century Japan.

Anti-Catholic Junk Food

You are what you eat. That is as true of the mind as of the body. Eat enough greasy food, and your silhouette will betray your culinary preferences. Give credence to enough greasy ideas, and your mind will be as flabby as your waistline. This book looks at eight examples of religious junk food, things that have come across Karl Keating's desk during his career as a Catholic apologist. You likely will find these morsels unconvincing and unpalatable, as you should. The problem is that plenty of people—including people on your block—consider such stuff to be intellectual high cuisine.

Jeremiah's Lament

For many, the best way to reach an understanding of the Catholic Church is to see how other people misunderstand it. This book is full of misunderstandings.

The people quoted in these pages came to their confusions in various ways. Sometimes it was by reading the wrong books or by failing to read the right books. Sometimes it was a matter of heredity, with prejudices passed down from father to son and from mother to daughter. At other times errors were imbibed at the foot of the pulpit, in the university lecture hall, or from door-to-door missionaries.

Whatever their origin, misunderstandings are misunderstandings. They should be recognized for what they are and set aside, even if that means a break from personal habit or family tradition. More than a century ago, Pope Leo XIII noted that there is nothing so salutary as to understand the world as it really is. That is true particularly of the Church that Christ established because to misunderstand her is to misunderstand him.

How to Fail at Hiking Mt. Whitney

Often, the best way to succeed at something is to learn how to fail at it—and then to avoid the things that lead to failure. There are books that tell you how to succeed at hiking Mt. Whitney. This book helps you *not* to fail by showing you what *not* to do, from the moment you start planning your trip to the moment you reach the summit.

You learn what gear not to buy and not to take, how to maximize your chances of getting a hiking permit (don't apply for the wrong days of the week!), how to prepare yourself physically without over-preparing, how to avoid being laid low by altitude or weather problems, how not to take too much food or water—or too little. You even discover how to shave a mile off the trip by using little-known shortcuts that can make the difference between reaching the summit and reaching exhaustion.

Most people who depart the Mt. Whitney trailhead fail to reach the top. Some fail because of things entirely beyond their control, but many fail because of insufficient preparation, false expectations, and basic errors of judgment. Their mistakes can come at the beginning (such as failing to get a hiking permit), during the preparation stage (such as being induced to buy "bombproof" gear), or during the hike (such as not heeding bodily warning signs).

Through engaging stories of his own and others' failures, Karl Keating shows you how to fail—and therefore how to succeed—at hiking the tallest peak in the 48 contiguous states.

About Karl Keating

Karl Keating holds advanced degrees in theology and law (University of San Diego) plus an honorary doctor of laws degree (Ave Maria University). He founded Catholic Answers, the English-speaking world's largest lay-run Catholic apologetics organization. His best-known books are *Catholicism and Fundamentalism* (nearly a quarter-million paperback copies sold) and *What Catholics Really Believe* (about half that many sold). His avocations include hiking, studying languages, and playing the baroque mandolino. He lives in San Diego. You can follow him at his author website and on Facebook:

KarlKeating.com

Facebook.com/KarlKeatingBooks